# Measuring Democracy

DEMOCRATIC TRANSITION AND CONSOLIDATION
Jorge I. Domínguez and Anthony Jones, *Series Editors*

# Measuring Democracy

*A Bridge between Scholarship and Politics*

GERARDO L. MUNCK

The Johns Hopkins University Press

*Baltimore*

© 2009 The Johns Hopkins University Press
All rights reserved. Published 2009
Printed in the United States of America on acid-free paper
9  8  7  6  5  4  3  2  1

The Johns Hopkins University Press
2715 North Charles Street
Baltimore, Maryland 21218-4363
www.press.jhu.edu

Library of Congress Cataloging-in-Publication Data

Munck, Gerardo L. (Gerardo Luis), 1958–
Measuring democracy : a bridge between scholarship and politics / Gerardo L. Munck.
   p.   cm.
Includes bibliographical references and index.
ISBN-13: 978-0-8018-9092-5 (hardcover : alk. paper)
ISBN-10: 0-8018-9092-6 (hardcover : alk. paper)
ISBN-13: 978-0-8018-9093-2 (pbk. : alk. paper)
ISBN-10: 0-8018-9093-4 (pbk. : alk. paper)
1. Democracy — Measurement.   2. Democratization — Measurement.   I. Title.
JC423.M788 2008
321.8 — dc22      2008032108

A catalog record for this book is available from the British Library.

*Special discounts are available for bulk purchases of this book. For more information, please contact Special Sales at 410-516-6936 or specialsales@press.jhu.edu.*

The Johns Hopkins University Press uses environmentally friendly book materials, including recycled text paper that is composed of at least 30 percent post-consumer waste, whenever possible. All of our book papers are acid-free, and our jackets and covers are printed on paper with recycled content.

*To Claudia*

# Contents

........................................................................................................................

## Figures and Tables

........................................................................................................................

### Figures

### Tables

*Preface*

...............................................................................................................................

The measurement of political concepts, and of democracy in particular, has emerged as a key issue in academic and political circles. Political scientists, responding to the process of democratization that transformed global politics in the late twentieth century, started to address the need for systematic information to analyze this political trend in earnest in the 1990s. Increasingly, this search for data led many researchers to address the methodological issues involved in measuring concepts such as democracy. Thus, a rich literature on measurement methodology developed in tandem with the rapid multiplication of data generation initiatives. This interest among political scientists in measurement has been broad-based and has not shown signs of waning. Indeed, we are in the midst of the most significant collective drive to produce political data in a methodologically self-conscious manner since the efforts launched by Karl Deutsch and Stein Rokkan in the early 1960s.

Beyond academia, the promotion of democracy has became a concern of a broad spectrum of actors since the end of the cold war, and, as an inextricable part of democracy promotion programs, concerted efforts have been made to monitor democracy in countries around the world. Intergovernmental organizations, including the European Union, the Organization of Security and Cooperation in Europe, and the Organization of American States (OAS), and nongovernmental organizations, such as the National Democratic Institute for International Affairs, and the Carter Center, evaluate whether elections are free and fair. The U.S. government uses various datasets on democracy and politics to determine which countries shall be allocated development assistance funds in a new and innovative program, the Millennium Challenge Account. And many other public and private institutions routinely collect data on aspects of politics, such as the funding of political parties and political campaigns, the health of political parties, the working of parliaments and the judiciary, corruption of public officials, public access to information and media freedom, and the capacity of states to implement public policies. In short, the design of instruments to measure democracy and other related concepts, and the generation of data on these concepts, have become a priority in the worlds of scholarship and politics.

This book brings together a series of writings that contribute to this measurement revolution in political science and the political world. It offers a discussion of the methodology of measurement that systematizes what current thinking has to offer to the specific problems that pertain to the measurement of political concepts. It focuses on the design of instruments to measure democracy, deriving specific lessons from a thorough and comprehensive assessment of existing methodologies. It presents two new measurement instruments prepared by the author for the United Nations Development Programme (UNDP) and the OAS, unique testaments of the new role of quantitative data about politics in the political process itself. The book also outlines an agenda for future research geared at developing measures of democracy that extend beyond its electoral aspect as well as of other closely related political concepts. Taken as a whole, this book offers a methodologically rigorous and grounded discussion about how to measure democracy, a rare look at an experience in which a bridge was tended between the worlds of scholarship and politics, and a discussion of steps that can be taken to maintain the momentum of the current measurement revolution.

This book is divided into seven chapters. Chapter 1 calls attention to the stakes of measures of democracy. It offers an overview of the rise of democracy promotion and shows how data, understood as quantitative or numerical representations of reality, have been used for a variety of purposes in the context of democracy promotion activities. Thus, it makes the case that measuring democracy is not solely an academic matter. Furthermore, because some common and blatant misuses of data raise questions about the legitimacy of using data in democracy promotion, it shows there is a need for engaged scholarship — that is, for academics eager to contribute to the collective effort to bring knowledge to bear on politics.

Chapters 2 and 3 offer a discussion of central methodological issues in the measurement of democracy. Chapter 2 presents a comprehensive and integrated framework for research on measurement and employs the proposed framework to assess a variety of democracy indices. The framework, which constitutes a point of reference in subsequent chapters, distinguishes three challenges involved in the production of data — conceptualization, measurement, and aggregation — and identifies both the specific tasks analysts confront in tackling each of these challenges and the standards of assessment that pertain to each task. The evaluation focuses on nine indices of democracy, which include the datasets on democracy most frequently used in quantitative research, and serves to ground the discussion of measurement methodology and derive specific lessons about how to measure democracy.

Chapter 3 is motivated by a desire to shed light on an issue that has been discussed mainly in the qualitative literature: the need to develop measures of democracy that not only make distinctions across cases but, more demandingly, can be used to identify countries that deserve to be characterized as democracies. Although pure cases of democracy and authoritarianism are self-evident, many countries around the world that have begun to hold elections seem to be located in an intermediary zone between these polar opposites. From a methodological perspective, distinguishing such countries is quite complex, requiring a particularly careful consideration of measurement scales and the choice of aggregation rule. Yet, as shown, by using Robert Dahl's conceptualization of political regime in terms of the attributes of participation and contestation as an example, it is possible to develop adequate measures of intermediary regime categories by following some methodological guidelines and by drawing on insights from an established theoretical literature on democracy and political parties.

Chapters 4 and 5 turn from a discussion of existing measures of democracy and challenges in the measurement of democracy to the presentation of two new measuring instruments and new data developed specifically for international organizations. Chapter 4 discusses the electoral democracy index (EDI), a new index created for the UNDP and introduced in the UNDP's report *Democracy in Latin America*. After the methodology used to produce the EDI is explicated, the chapter presents two analyses that validate the index: a self-referential internal analysis addresses the theoretical basis for the key choices that go into the making of the EDI, and an external analysis focuses on the impact of distinct features of the methodology by means of a comparison of the EDI to other democracy indices. An appendix presents the new dataset with disaggregate and aggregate scores of the EDI for Latin America during 1960, 1977, 1985, and 1990–2005.

Chapter 5 introduces a measuring instrument prepared for OAS election observation missions. Although the methodology, designed to evaluate the quality of elections, draws on the EDI, it also differs from the methodology used to generate the EDI. The methodology to evaluate the quality of elections measures a narrower concept than the EDI, because it focuses only on the electoral process, but it is conceptually deeper, in that it relies on more elements to assess the electoral process than the EDI. Moreover, because the purpose of this methodology is to distinguish democratic from nondemocratic elections, it is more precise. The values of the EDI are best understood as ranging between two polar opposites — pure cases of electoral democracy and of authoritarianism — with movement along this continuum tracking advances toward and moves away from electoral democracy. In contrast, the methodology to assess elections grapples with the issues discussed in chapter 3 and seeks to introduce a threshold along the index's continuum distinguishing democratic from nondemocratic elections.

Finally, chapters 6 and 7 motivate, outline, and orient a research agenda — that is, address the why, what, and how of an agenda — geared to developing measures of aspects of democracy that exceed the electoral process and the electoral connection between voters and their representatives (the focus of the methodologies presented in chapters 4 and 5). These methodologies produce, in the terminology used in chapter 2, minimalist measures of democracy, which do not encompass all the meanings of the concept of democracy. Such measures are valuable to the researcher for various reasons. First, it is hard to make a case that democracy, broadly understood, can be measured, if we lack a sufficiently well-developed and tested methodology to measure the concepts of electoral democracy and democratic elections. Second, the minimalist measures of democracy produced with these methodologies are useful in studying democracy, given that minimalist conceptions of democracy focus on necessary conditions of any broader conception of democracy and thus identify as nondemocracies countries that would also be nondemocracies under a broader conception. (The problem with minimalist measures of democracy that are presented as measures of democracy *tout court* as opposed to electoral democracy or democratic elections, as done in chapters 4 and 5, is that they might categorize as democracies countries that are not democratic.) Third, the experience of developing minimalist measures of democracy yields some important general methodological lessons, and the minimalist measures themselves serve as a building block in developing broader measures. Nonetheless, as chapter 6 argues, it is imperative to tackle the task of measuring democracy, broadly understood, and also to develop measures of other political concepts that are imbued with a strong normative content.

Chapter 6 addresses the key conceptual issue that any attempt at measurement of democracy must confront head on: what is democracy? To address this question, the chapter relies on Dahl's work on democracy and an analysis of the relationship between democracy and two proximate concepts: rule of law and human development. As shown, current theorizing on democracy offers considerable guidance concerning how to define democracy or, at least, a strong basis for making progress toward a shared definition that escapes the limitations of a minimalist conception. But the exploration of the content and boundaries of the concept of democracy also suggests another, unsettling point: that democracy is a relative value, that is, one value among others regarding politics. By implication, the normative justification for promoting democracy cannot be based solely on the status of democracy as a good thing; rather, it also hinges on the results of an empirical analysis of the potential trade-offs among multiple political values. Furthermore, as a result, the challenge of developing measures must be broadened to include non-minimalist measures of democracy but also measures of other normatively salient political concepts.

Chapter 7 seeks to lay the groundwork for a response to this measurement challenge. It highlights the value of considering the research strategy used to produce and validate data in a deliberate manner, and makes a case that the strategy exemplified by this book is likely to lead to sustained progress in the production of good political data. It identifies various literatures that contain insights relevant to the challenge of developing measures of a wide range of political concepts and argues that scholars should draw on this important resource. And it extracts lessons from previous work on measurement in the form of some pitfalls that are common, especially in efforts at measurement in the world of politics, and that future measurement efforts should avoid. In short, it introduces some key considerations that should figure prominently in an agenda that aims at the development of measures of a wide range of political concepts.

My thinking on the measurement of democracy has evolved since my initial research on the topic, published by *Comparative Political Studies* in 2002. Regarding methodological issues, I would highlight two points. First, in that 2002 article I argued that the problem with maximalist definitions is that they tend to lack empirical referents and to resolve empirical questions by definitional fiat. Now I consider the view that maximalist definitions fail on account of their broadness to be mistaken. I think that the domain of a concept extends to all units that have the potential of possessing a certain attribute and that, as long as disaggregate data are provided, empirical inquiry is not precluded simply because a concept is broadly defined. The problem with maximalist definitions is that they fail to adequately establish the boundaries of the concept under consideration and include too many conceptual attributes, that is, attributes that exceed the meaning of the concept.

Second, the 2002 *Comparative Political Studies* article argued that aggregation should be justified by showing that the lower levels of aggregation tap into a unidimensional empirical phenomenon. That argument, however, overlooks the distinction between "cause" and "effect" indicators, or formative and reflective indicators — that is, indicators that are seen as influencing the concept being measured and indicators that are seen as driven or generated by the concept being measured. Although the dimensionality of the disaggregate data is relevant to "effect" or reflective indicators, a test of scalability is not relevant to "cause" or formative indicators.

The most important change in my thinking brought about by the work on the measurement of democracy presented in this book, however, has been the way I look at academia. My experience in a political environment — where the consequences of data are not "merely academic" — has forced me to see academia from the outside and made me reexamine the way academics go about debating issues of theory and methodology. These reflections have both deepened my appreciation for the potential contributions of scholarly research and increased my impatience with the internal politics of academia.

Political scientists feel comfortable with certain styles of thinking and tend to divide into camps that frequently are cast as representing opposing approaches to the study of politics. One division is that between theorists, who tend to engage in abstract debates that end up making competing arguments appear to hinge on matters of first principles that elude adjudicability, and empiricists, who seek to sort through disputes via data analysis and tend to forget that inquiry that is not connected to theory is meaningless. Another division is that between quantitative researchers, who rely on numbers and statistics, and qualitative researchers, who use words and stories. All too frequently, scholars who emphasize theory or empirics, numbers or words, are unable to communicate with each other even when they are interested in the same subject matter.

My view is that these divisions, though rooted in the distinct talents of different scholars, tend to become ossified and that the compartmentalization of academic endeavors has an overwhelmingly negative effect. Most critically, it prevents political scientists from focusing on the real challenge: the need to bridge the worlds of scholarship and politics. Scholars make a claim on the resources of the societies in which they live and, in return, have a responsibility to generate knowledge for these societies. Particularly in the wealthy societies of the North, the professionalization of political science has been associated with the fading of a sense of societal responsibility and the loss of a concern for producing useful knowledge. It is time for academics to cast aside internal divisions that divert attention from this fundamental aspect of their mission.

This book owes much to many people. The impact of Jay Verkuilen is the most direct. Jay is coauthor of chapter 2, and we worked together on the EDI. Moreover, over the past nine years, I have sustained an ongoing discussion about measurement with Jay, and he has taught me a lot about methodology. I also owe much to two academic colleagues, David Collier and Guillermo O'Donnell. David's work on concept formation and measurement was the initial stimulus, back in the early 1990s, that got me thinking about the methodological issues addressed in this book. Guillermo introduced me to the UNDP, the organization that first gave me the opportunity to connect to discussions about politics outside an academic setting. Both before and after that gesture, his conceptualizations of democracy and efforts to grasp the specifics of Latin American cases have been a constant point of reference and insight for me. Finally, an acknowledgment of influences on the work that went into this book would be incomplete if I did not mention Dante Caputo. I have learned much from Dante, whom I initially encountered as coordinator of the UNDP report on *Democracy in Latin America* and with whom I continued to work after he became Under Secretary for Political Affairs at the OAS. From Dante, more than anyone else, I have gained an appreciation of the value of attempting to bridge the worlds of scholarship and politics.

I also received much encouragement, and useful feedback and assistance on individual chapters, from many people. On chapter 2, detailed and helpful comments were offered by Chris Achen, James Caporaso, David Collier, Michael Coppedge, James Kuklinski, Mark Lichbach, James Mahoney, Scott Mainwaring, Sebastián Mazzuca, Robert Pahre, Aníbal Pérez-Liñán, Cindy Skach, and Richard Snyder. Chapter 3 was motivated by a comment made by

Arturo Valenzuela when I made a presentation on the EDI at Georgetown University, and an earlier version of the chapter was improved as a result of extensive feedback by Richard Snyder.

The preparation of the EDI, which is discussed in chapter 4, was a lengthy process and involved extensive feedback. Three UNDP-sponsored conferences were held to discuss the EDI methodology and the EDI data on Latin America. An initial conference, at which various proposals for an index were discussed, was held in New York, on August 15–16, 2002. The attendants were Kenneth Bollen, Dante Caputo, Fernando Carrillo, Michael Coppedge, Enrique Ganuza, Freddy Justiniano, Fernando Medina, Mark Payne, Adam Przeworski, Arodys Robles Soro, Michael Smithson, and Oscar Yunovsky. A second conference, to discuss the EDI methodology and the values assigned to EDI for Latin America through 2002, was held in New York, on July 21, 2003. The participants, who graciously shared their expertise and experience, were Horacio Boneo, Hernando Gómez Buendia, Juan Fernando Londoño, Simón Pachano, Juan Rial, Elizabeth Spehar, Maria Hermínia Tavares, and José Woldenberg. Following this meeting, many additional useful suggestions to strengthen the index were offered by Horacio Boneo, Freddy Justiniano, and Myriam Méndez-Montalvo. Finally, a third seminar was held, to discuss the updating of the EDI through 2005, in Santo Domingo, Dominican Republic, on March 27, 2006. The participants at this meeting were Manuel Alcántara, David Altman, Ana Álvarez, Jorge Bernedo, Miguel Ceara Hatton, Michael Coppedge, Juan Pablo Corlazzoli, Miguel Ángel Encinas, Niky Fabiancic, Irene García, Jonathan Hartlyn, Dieter Nohlen, Mark Payne, Juan Rial, Rafael Roncagliolo, Oscar Sánchez, Claudio Tomasi, Rafael Toribio, and Adriana Velasco.

In addition, early versions of parts of the chapter were presented to the Kellogg Institute for International Studies, University of Notre Dame, on October 15, 2002; at a workshop at the University of Bocconi in Milan on March 21, 2003; on a panel at the International Congress of the Latin American Studies Association, in Dallas on March 27–29, 2003; at a conference on "Diagnosing Democracy: Methods of Analysis, Findings and Remedies," held in Santiago, Chile, on April 11–13, 2003; to the Department of Political Science at the University of California, Santa Barbara, on May 23, 2003; at a panel of the American Political Science Association annual convention, held in Philadelphia on August 28–31, 2003; and at the Center for Democracy and the Third Sector, at Georgetown University on October 3, 2003. Constructive comments were received from many people at these venues. In preparing the final version of this chapter, I benefited from feedback from Angela Hawken.

Finally, I received extensive and useful feedback at the OAS on an earlier version of chapter 5 from Mariclaire Acosta, Cesar Arias, Moisés Benamor, Dante Caputo, Steven Griner, Judith Lobos, Wendy Martinez, Katalina Montaña, Betilde Muñoz-Pogossian, Maria del Carmen Palau, Rubén Perina, and Elizabeth Spehar. In addition, Dexter Boniface offered assistance in the review of existing methodologies; Robert Ferguson collaborated in the analysis of a test case; and Angela Hawken, Jonathan Templin, and Jay Verkuilen gave helpful feedback and suggestions on various methodological issues discussed in this chapter.

Some of the chapters in this book draw on prior publications. Chapter 2 draws on an article published in *Comparative Political Studies* (2002); chapter 3 on a chapter published in Andreas Schedler (ed.), *Electoral Authoritarianism: The Dynamics of Unfree Competition* (Lynne Rienner, 2006); chapter 6 on a chapter published in Gerardo L. Munck (ed.), *Regimes and Democracy in Latin America: Theories and Methods* (Oxford University Press, 2007); and chapter 7 on part of a chapter published in Deepa Narayan (ed.), *Measuring Empowerment: Cross-Disciplinary Perspectives* (World Bank, 2005). All the chapters that rely on already published materials have been thoroughly revised with the intent of providing a coherent, integrated, and up-to-date text.

# Measuring Democracy

# ONE

# Bringing Knowledge to Bear on Politics

*The Uses and Misuses of Data in Democracy Promotion*

·······················································································

A fter the end of the cold war, the promotion of democracy became a concern of a broad spectrum of actors in global politics. Democracy promotion was born as an initiative of the U.S. government, but it grew to become a matter of interest of governments, intergovernmental organizations, and nongovernmental organizations (NGOs) around the world. Furthermore, although democracy promoters initially focused largely on the observation of elections, their scope of activities was subsequently expanded well beyond elections. Democracy promotion came to encompass an array of issues, intrinsic or closely related to democracy, such as the funding of political parties and political campaigns, the health of political parties, the working of parliaments and the judiciary, the corruption of state officials, public access to information and media freedom, and the capacity of states to implement public policies. Two decades after the collapse of the Berlin Wall, democracy promotion was a large and diverse field.

One distinctive and novel feature of current work to promote democracy is that it relies on data, understood here as quantitative or numerical representations linking concepts to empirical observations. Indeed, references to data on democracy have become commonplace in the discourse of democracy promoters. Data are used in practically all aspects of the work of democracy promotion organizations, from the setting of goals, the choice of means, and the evaluation of the results of actions. Data on democracy are a staple of reports by international organizations and NGOs, are regularly discussed in the media, and are invoked in policy debates. Measuring democracy has ceased to be solely an academic matter.

This chapter sets the context for the discussion about the measurement of democracy offered in the rest of the book. It focuses first on the rise of democracy promotion, placing emphasis on the formation of an extensive network of actors who work in the field of democracy promotion. It turns next to the uses of data by democracy promoters and shows how data on a wide array of aspects of democracy are used — enthusiastically and largely encouragingly — for a variety of purposes. Nonetheless, this chapter presents a cautious view regarding the promise of using data on democracy in the context of democracy promotion activities. As argued in the third section, many current practices in the use of data raise questions about their legitimacy. Because these practices curtail the potential for using data to invigorate a democratic agenda, they constitute a challenge for academics eager to contribute to the collective effort to bring knowledge to bear on politics. Thus, the conclusion touches on the role of engaged scholarship.

## 1.1. The Rise of Democracy Promotion

The promotion of democracy as an international activity started, in its current incarnation, as a U.S. government initiative during the Reagan administration in the early 1980s. This was certainly not the first time that democracy was presented as a key aim of U.S. foreign policy. Since 1917, when Woodrow Wilson declared that the United States' goal in World War I was "to make the world safe for democracy," a succession of U.S. presidents advocated fostering democracy abroad as a national interest. Moreover, as before, democracy was just one aspect of U.S. foreign policy, and, as analysts have repeatedly pointed out, the rhetoric and practice of U.S. foreign policy diverged, sometimes quite starkly.[1] However, the Reagan administration's policy to promote democracy — symbolically inaugurated in a speech President Reagan gave to the British Parliament in June 1982 — did introduce a shift in U.S. policy, which has had an enduring impact.

A sign of this policy was the development of an organizational infrastructure both within and outside the U.S. government oriented toward the promotion of democracy. The first step in this direction was the creation of the National Endowment for Democracy (NED), an organization funded by the U.S. Congress, and two organizations informally linked with the major U.S. parties, the National Democratic Institute for International Affairs (NDI) and the International Republican Institute (IRI), in 1983.[2] Later notable steps taken by the U.S. government after the end of the cold war included the establishment of the Office of Democracy and Governance within the United States Agency for International Development (USAID) and of the Bureau of Democracy, Human Rights and Labor within the U.S. State Department, both in 1994; and the founding of the Millennium Challenge Corporation—charged with administering the Millennium Challenge Account —within the U.S. State Department, in 2004.[3] Though the 9/11 attacks on the U.S. and developments particularly in the Middle East, most pointedly the second Iraq war and the situation in Palestine, have led to a questioning of U.S. democracy promotion initiatives both within and outside the United States, it is clear that democracy promotion has become institutionalized in the United States, and it seems safe to venture that U.S. democracy promotion is here to stay.[4]

Democracy promotion has also taken root beyond the United States. If democracy promotion was born in the United States in the early 1980s, the promotion of democracy was taken up in many countries and regions, and increasingly by intergovernmental organizations, beginning in the 1990s. In Europe, the old German government-funded party foundations and especially the Friedrich Ebert and Konrad Adenauer foundations—which had actually provided a model for the NED—were joined by new organizations, such as the Westminster Foundation for Democracy, established in 1992 by the British government, and the Netherlands Institute of Multiparty Democracy, established by parties representing the entire Dutch political spectrum in 2000. European regional intergovernmental organizations also embraced democracy promotion decidedly, with significant landmarks for the European Union (EU) being the approval of Copenhagen criteria, whereby democracy was identified as a condition for accession to the EU in 1993, and the creation of the European Initiative for Democracy and Human Rights, subsequently replaced by the European Instrument for Democracy and Human Rights, in 1994.[5]

Cross-regional intergovernmental organizations were likewise part of the trend. The Council of Europe, based in Strasbourg and encompassing all of Europe as well as extending to Central Asia and including Russia, established the European Commission for Democracy through Law—also known as the Venice Commission—in 1990. The Organization of Security and Cooperation in Europe, based in Vienna and covering all of Europe as well as extending to Central Asia and including Russia and also the United States, set up the Office for Free Elections, which later became the Office for Democratic Institutions and Human Rights, in 1990. The British Commonwealth, based in London and encompassing countries in six continents, committed itself to democratic principles in the Harare Commonwealth Declaration of 1991. International IDEA (Institute for Democracy and Electoral Assistance), a Stockholm-based intergovernmental organization, was established by governments from Europe and elsewhere in 1995.[6] And outside of Europe, the Organization of American States, based in Washington and encompassing North America, Latin America, and the Caribbean, established the Unit for the Promotion of Democracy, currently named the Secretariat for Political Affairs, in 1990.[7]

Finally, at the global level, the promotion of democracy grew in importance within the United Nations, even though the word *democracy* does not appear in the UN Charter (Rich 2001: 20), once the cold war ended. The UN Electoral Assistance Division, initially named the Electoral Assistance Unit, was established in 1991. The United Nations Development Programme (UNDP) focused more and more on issues of democratic governance starting in the 1990s. Moreover, a UN Democracy Caucus was formed and met for the first time in 2004, and a UN Democracy Fund was established the following year.[8]

This institutional thickening of the field of democracy promotion throughout the 1990s and into the 2000s has not been without its complications. With regard to some issues, a diverse set of organizations developed their practices in a more or less coordinated manner. This was particularly the case regarding international electoral observation, a practice that developed with the input from various intergovernmental organizations and NGOs (Bjornlund 2004: chs. 4 and 5), which have generated considerable consensus regarding how to conduct their monitoring activities.[9] On other issues of the broad democracy promotion agenda, however, the relationships within the democracy promotion community have been characterized by internal disagreement and some tension. Different approaches can be seen clearly in the way the United States and Europe have gone about promoting democracy (Whitehead 1996; Kopstein 2006). Important differences have been voiced regarding the political conditionality imposed by the World Bank, which is expressly prohibited by its charter from considering how a government came to power when making financing decisions, yet which has entered the field of democracy promotion under the guise of the "governance" rubric (Kapur and Webb 2000; Santiso 2004). The relationships between intergovernmental organizations and NGOs, especially those that focus on a single issue, have occasionally been strained as well. Nonetheless, developments since 1989 have made democracy promotion a global field, shaped by a large number of actors (the cursory overview presented here in no way pretends to be comprehensive) and by diverse types of actors— governments; regional, cross-regional, and global intergovernmental organizations; and NGOs. Though many challenges remain, these actors have undoubtedly constituted an extensive and active network that is a sign of the health and vitality of the field of democracy promotion.

## 1.2. The Uses of Data in Democracy Promotion

The work of democracy promotion is fundamentally political and hence a matter of advancing values, building coalitions of support to do so, and deciding among alternative courses of action to advance those values. In this regard, democracy promotion is not a new kind of activity. But one novel and distinctive feature of much work to promote democracy is that it has incorporated, sometimes as an essential element, a reliance on data in the form of quantitative measures. Data on a wide array of aspects of democracy have been used for a variety of purposes, which include the following five, increasingly demanding, uses: (1) describing the state of affairs, (2) monitoring compliance with standards and progress toward goals, (3) diagnosing countries and issuing early warnings, (4) evaluating programs, and (5) making decisions.

### 1.2.1. Describing the State of Affairs

One of the most basic uses of data in democracy promotion activities is to describe the state of affairs. Examples abound: the UNDP used data, generated by academics (Przeworski et al. 2000: ch. 1), to offer a picture of the state of democracy around the world in the *Human Development Report, 2002* (UNDP 2002: 10, 15); Transparency International, an NGO dedicated to the issue of corruption, undoubtedly closely related to democracy, releases the scores and ranking of its Corruption Perception Index every year; the Inter-Parliamentary Union presents data, updated on a continuous basis on its Web site, on the number of women elected to parliaments throughout the world. Moreover, the use of such data for the purpose of simply describing the state of affairs plays an important role. First, and probably most critically, it draws attention to certain issues in a powerful manner and hence places these issues on the agenda. Second, it offers a means to ground, and give precision to, the discussion about the strengths and weaknesses of democracy around the globe. Third, it implicitly rewards countries that do well and puts countries that do badly in a poor light.

### 1.2.2. Monitoring Compliance with Standards and Progress toward Goals

A second use of data on democracy is to describe how countries do relative to some specific standard or goal. An example of the use of data to assess compliance with standards is the parallel vote tabulation in the context of international electoral observation missions. Specifically, the parallel vote tabulation serves to verify whether the official vote totals diverge from those computed independently on the basis of the number of votes actually cast at polling stations and hence to ascertain whether elections meet the international standard that elections should be free of fraud (Bjornlund 2004: ch. 13). In turn, examples of the use of data to assess whether progress toward a preestablished goal is being made are offered by efforts to follow up on various UN conferences, such as the UN Commission on the Status of Women's monitoring of the implementation of the Beijing Platform for Action, adopted at the Fourth UN World Conference on Women, concerning the goal of attaining equality in access to public office (UNRISD 2005: ch. 9).

### 1.2.3. Diagnosing Countries and Issuing Early Warnings

A third use of data in democracy promotion is to offer a diagnostic of one or more countries. At the very least, such a use of data requires the development of a framework that encompasses all the different aspects of democracy and the collection of data with the aim of assessing where a country's strengths and weaknesses lie. Examples of such conceptual frameworks, and implementations of such frameworks using quantitative data, include those developed and/or sponsored by International IDEA (Beetham et al. 2001; Landman et al. 2006), the UNDP (2004a: 49–129; 2004b: 15–16), USAID (2000), and the World Bank (Kaufmann, Recanatini, and Biletsky 2002). More ambitiously, diagnostics have aimed at predicting an impending crisis and thus have required the development of an early-warning system, which is updated regularly with data.[10]

### 1.2.4. Evaluating Programs

A fourth use of data, which is gaining increased attention, aims at providing guidance about the impact of democracy promotion programs, that is, specific projects that are funded with the goal of advancing democracy. Such a use of data is very demanding, in that it requires not only collecting data on the program of interest and the sought-after outcome but also the design of a procedure to control for factors other than the program that could impact the outcome. Nonetheless, the growing need to assess whether the financial investments in democracy promotion are having the sought-after effect has led to numerous efforts to evaluate democracy promotion programs (Burnell 2007), the most ambitious to date being the pioneering work on USAID's Democracy and Governance programs (Bollen, Paxton, and Morishima 2005; Finkel, Pérez-Liñán, and Seligson 2007; Sarles 2007).

### 1.2.5. Making Decisions

Finally, data are used, quite directly, in the making of decisions. That is, in some cases the result of the analysis of data triggers, nearly automatically, a certain decision, rather than serving as an input in the debate or as one among various inputs into a process of deliberation leading to a decision. Such uses of data are rare. They are envisioned, though, when political conditionalities — that is, the requisite that certain political criteria are met — are legally mandated. One prominent case of such a use of data is the U.S. State Department's Millennium Challenge Account (Millennium Challenge Corporation 2007).

In sum, the promotion of democracy has included, as one of its ingredients, the use of data for a variety of purposes. Different actors — governments, intergovernmental organizations, and NGOs — have adopted this practice, and it is a truly novel practice. Statistics, which literally means the "science of the state," have long been used in matters of government. The generation of statistics on a wide range of economic, military, demographic, and social issues actually coincided with the consolidation of government administrative structures. But the availability of data on explicitly political matters and on the political process persistently lagged behind that on other aspects of society. Indeed, only recently have advances in the measurement of democracy and other political concepts enabled the use of data in the context of democracy promotion activities, an option that has been chosen with a considerable degree of enthusiasm.

## 1.3. The Misuses of Data in Democracy Promotion

The use of data in democracy promotion activities opens up a promising line of work. It is part of a broader endeavor to bring knowledge to bear on politics. It constitutes a trend that, for the most part, is encouraging and deserves to be supported. Nonetheless, many current practices in the use of data are highly questionable, and such practices strengthen the case of skeptics opposed as a matter of principle to the use of data in political affairs. Thus, it has become increasingly imperative to address, as part of the discussion of the uses of data in democracy promotion, some common and blatant misuses of data.

### 1.3.1. The Focus on the Others and Their Problems

A lot of the data in the field of democracy promotion is used to shine a light on other people's problems and, more specifically, is used by actors in wealthy countries to draw attention to problems in poorer countries. This is what happens, in effect, when election observation missions are sent to poor, usually small, countries to assess whether international standards are met but not to rich or big countries; when a German organization like the Bertlemann Foundation publishes data on democracy that covers most of the world except for Western Europe, North America, and Oceania; and when Transparency International, another organization based in Germany, publicizes data on corruption that characterizes as corrupt those countries where public officials accept bribes from foreign businesses but does not draw attention with the same diligence to those countries where the corrupting businesses are headquartered. This is, indeed, what happens when the majority of the data used in democracy promotion originates in wealthy countries and when these data either do not cover these wealthy countries or are never used to investigate problems there. Thus, it is hard to escape the impression that data ostensibly used to promote democracy are frequently used in a suspicious way — is it ever justified for someone to place themselves above the fray? —

and that the advocacy of democracy serves to deflect the public's attention from one's own problems or to protect particular interests.

### 1.3.2. Hiding Behind the Veil of Science

A second problem concerns the asymmetry between the ostensible use of much data to keep governments accountable and the practices followed by those who generate and use the data. A basic principle of scientific methodology is that the procedures used to generate the data and to reach results are public and hence open to scrutiny. But this principle is not followed in many cases. For example, two frequently used indices of corruption — Transparency International's Corruption Perception Index (CPI) and the World Bank's Control of Corruption Index (CCI) — have relied on commercial, nonpublic data sources.[11] Thus, the possibility of conducting independent tests to assess any potential bias in the data has been precluded. Similarly, though the World Bank's Country Policy and Institutional Assessments (CPIA) play a large role in the bank's allocation of aid to poor countries, the data of these CPIAs have not been made public and thus remain shielded from any challenges.[12] In other words, even though these organizations constantly demand transparency from the countries they are assessing, their own use of data on politics has not been characterized by transparency, a double standard that is particularly ironic in light of the principles of scientific methodology.

### 1.3.3. The Surreptitious Introduction of Ideological Bias

A third problem is the use of data in an ideologically biased manner or the use of data that carry an ideological bias embedded within them. The ideological use of data occurs frequently and is generally associated with the selective use of data. For example, a political leader might rely on data on the lack of political freedom in a country to which he is ideologically opposed in order to support a course of action, while ignoring similarly negative data on countries with which he feels an ideological affinity. The purposeful embedding of an ideological bias in the data themselves is a more complicated issue. In some instances, the indicators that are selected to measure a concept introduce certain sought-after conclusions. For example, the World Bank's rule-of-law measure is an index consisting of many indicators on private property, contracts, and business interests, but nothing similar on labor rights or discrimination against women and other groups (Kaufmann, Kraay, and Mastruzzi 2007: 74). Thus, on the one hand, countries that favor capitalism and are pro-business will be seen as respecting the rule of law, even if they do not recognize the rights of labor and other groups; and, on the other hand, the effort of countries that do recognize the rights of labor and other groups will not be acknowledged. In other instances, the introduction of an ideological position into the data occurs not conceptually but rather through the process whereby countries are coded, that is, assigned scores. An example of this is Freedom House's index of political rights, which during the cold war years systematically punished countries with leftist governments and favored countries that were allies of the United States (Scoble and Wiseberg 1981: 152–64; Bollen and Paxton 2000: 77; Mainwaring, Brinks, and Pérez-Liñán 2007: 145–47). When these data were used, conclusions regarding the respect for the rule of law and the democraticness of left-wing and right-wing governments were already embedded in the data. In other words, ideology was misleadingly presented as knowledge.

### 1.3.4. The Problem of Methodological Credibility

A fourth problem concerns the special status that is accorded to quantitative measures, given their association with science. Knowledge claims based on quantitative measures are commonly treated as though they had a distinct and superior status compared to claims based on other forms of information. Such data are seen as being generated through the application of a rigorous and tested methodology. Yet this assumption regarding the methodology that is used to generate data on politics is not always justified. In fact, sometimes the methodology is flawed. For example, though the indicators used by Freedom House to construct their index of political rights have changed over the years (compare Gastil 1991: 26 to Freedom House 1999: 547–48 and Freedom House: 2007a), when these methodological changes have been introduced, the scores assigned to previous years have not been revised to reflect the new methodology. Nonetheless, Freedom House claims that its index on political rights is comparable over time and uses it to analyze trends over time. In short, even if the three misuses of data identified above are avoided or set aside, the use of data by democracy promoters can be questioned in numerous cases because the data have been generated with an inappropriate methodology.

### 1.3.5. The Belief That Supporting a Value Is Enough

Finally, the most vexing problem in the use of data in democracy promotion activities concerns the links made between the data and values. Data on democracy are generally interpreted in a straightforward manner. Essentially, democracy is seen as a political value, and more democracy is seen as better than less democracy. Thus, democracy promoters who direct their activities toward the eradication of democratic deficits revealed by the data act confidently in the knowledge that they are doing good. But things are not that simple. The assumption that more democracy is better, in all places and under any circumstances, is justified if democracy is an absolute value or positively correlated with all other values. Yet both of these justifications can be questioned. It is hard to make a case that, some core human rights such as the right to life and to physical integrity excluded, democratic values should not be weighed relative to other values. In turn, the empirical evidence suggests that democratic progress is not always associated with an advance in other valued goals.[13] Thus, without giving in to relativism, democracy promoters must acknowledge that, because democracy is one among various competing values, data on democracy must be put in a broader perspective.

The use of data in democracy promotion is a recent phenomenon and practices concerning data use are evolving, as lessons are drawn from a process of trial and error. Nonetheless, the misuse of data in democracy promotion work entails serious costs. It gives critics a solid basis for arguing that the use of data in democracy promotion is frequently a modern Trojan horse, which hides the users' political interests. It taints the work that uses data properly. More broadly, it raises questions about the legitimacy of using data in the field of democracy promotion. Indeed, the misuse of data diminishes the likelihood that the use of data on democracy will be broadly supported in political circles and that the potential benefits of using data in politics will be attained.

## 1.4. Conclusion

The rise of democracy promotion and the use of data by democracy promoters have been largely salutary trends. The use of quantitative measures on democracy in the context of democracy promotion activities, however, must be evaluated with considerable caution. Although this development holds the promise of bringing knowledge to bear on politics, many current practices in the use of data are highly questionable. And, as a result, the potential for using data to invigorate a democratic agenda is, at the very least, curtailed.

The fulfillment of the promise associated with the use of data on democracy depends on many factors, including, very centrally, the continued support for its use among government officials, politicians, and national and international civil servants. But it also depends on academics. University-based research has played, and continues to play, an important role in the production and analysis of measures of democracy. Thus, academics have a role to play in ensuring that questionable practices in the use of data in democracy promotion are overcome and that the use of data on democracy in the world of politics flourishes. More specifically, the increased use and misuse of data in the field of democracy promotion prefigures a twofold challenge for academics.

One aspect of this challenge is purely scholarly and concerns the improvement of the quality of the data that are available. Academics can make an important contribution to this endeavor by drawing on their methodological skills. Indeed, knowledge about measurement methodology is a key skill that academics can bring to a discussion about politics. But it is certainly not the only skill required to produce good data. Knowledge of democratic theory is also essential, and detailed and extensive empirical knowledge of cases is likewise fundamental. Thus, academics must recognize that good data are produced through the combination of methods, theory, and empirics, and strive to combine these skills.

Another aspect of this challenge touches, in a deeper way, on the public mission of universities and academics. Generating rigorous, credible data about politics calls for an adherence to strict methodological criteria and hence an openness to discovering things that go against one's views. Thus, academics rightly worry about the impact of political involvements on scientific standards. But if academics are going to do their part to bring knowledge to bear on politics, they need to combine a proclivity for following ideas regardless of consequences with a reckoning of the consequences of their research. That is, scholars need to combine what Max Weber referred to as an "ethics of conviction" with an "ethics of responsibility,"[14] to think as social scientists *and* as citizens. Put in different words, academics need to listen more to politicians, to learn to see the world through the eyes of politicians, to embrace engaged scholarship, and to build a bridge between scholarship and politics.

# TWO

# Conceptualizing and Measuring Democracy

*An Evaluation of Alternative Indices*

with Jay Verkuilen

························································································································

The study of democracy — a core concern within comparative politics and international relations — increasingly has drawn upon sophisticated statistical methods of causal inference. This is a welcome development, and the contributions of this quantitative literature are significant. With a few notable exceptions,[1] however, quantitative researchers have paid sparse attention to the quality of the data on democracy that they analyze. Indeed, the data assessments that have been carried out are usually restricted to fairly informal discussions of alternative datasets and somewhat superficial examinations of correlations among aggregate data.[2] To a large extent, problems of causal inference have overshadowed the equally important problems of conceptualization and measurement.

Seeking to redress this oversight, this chapter provides a systematic assessment of the large-N datasets on democracy that are most frequently used in current statistical research.[3] Table 2.1, which compares these datasets in terms of their empirical scope, provides a first step in this direction. This is not a trivial matter because the common restriction of datasets to the post–World War II era and the exclusion of certain regions of the world limit the theories that they can be used to test. However, a thorough comparison and assessment of these datasets must move beyond a concern with empirical scope and tackle a range of methodological issues that complicate any effort to evaluate data on democracy.

The core problem is that the methodological issues that are relevant to the generation of data and that have a direct bearing on the quality of data on

TABLE 2.1. *Existing Datasets on Democracy: Empirical Scope*

| Name | Unit I: country | Unit II: year[a] |
|---|---|---|
| ACLP: Alvarez, Cheibub, Limongi, and Przeworski (1996: 23–30) | 141 | 1950–90[b] |
| Arat (1991: 136–66) | 152 | 1948–82 |
| Bollen (1980: 387–88; 1991: 16–19; 1993: 1227) | 113 | 1960 |
| | 123 | 1965 |
| | 153 | 1980 |
| Coppedge and Reinicke Polyarchy (Coppedge 2007) | 164 | 1985 |
| | 193 | 2000 |
| Freedom House (2007b) | All the world (number varies) | 1972–present |
| Gasiorowski Political Regime Change (1996: 480–82) | 97 | independence–1992[c] |
| Hadenius (1992: 61–69) | 132 | 1988 |
| Polity IV (Marshall and Jaggers 2007) | 161 | 1800–2004 |
| Vanhanen (2007) | 196 | 1810–2006 |

*Note:* The citations offered in this table contain the actual datasets.

[a] These indexes use countries as their unit of analysis and record one value per year. Thus, though these two aspects are disaggregated, the units of analysis are actually country-years.

[b] The ACLP dataset has been updated through 2002 by José Antonio Cheibub and Jennifer Gandhi (Cheibub and Gandhi 2004).

[c] Most datasets begin coding countries after a common year, including new cases as countries gained independence. Gasiorowski is an exception, starting the coding not at a common year but rather at the time independence was gained. Thus, his starting point varies widely, from 1747 to 1980. This index has been updated through 1998 and extended to encompass 147 countries by Reich (2002).

democracy are only partially addressed in the methodological literature. Although this literature provides some important clues concerning matters of conceptualization and measurement, it also suffers from some important gaps. Moreover, although the generation of data is affected by choices about a number of interrelated issues, little has been done to offer an integrated approach that shows how these issues are connected.

In order to make explicit and justify the criteria used to evaluate alternative democracy indices, this chapter addresses the distinctively methodological task of constructing a comprehensive and integrated framework for the analysis of data. The proposed framework, summarized in table 2.2 and developed throughout this chapter, distinguishes among three *challenges* that are sequentially addressed: conceptualization, measurement, and aggregation. Moreover, it identifies the specific choices or *tasks* analysts confront

TABLE 2.2.  *A Framework for the Analysis of Data: Conceptualization, Measurement, and Aggregation*

| Challenge | Task | Standard of assessment |
|---|---|---|
| Conceptualization | Identification of attributes | Concept specification: Avoid maximalist definitions (the inclusion of theoretically irrelevant attributes) or minimalist definitions (the exclusion of theoretically relevant attributes) |
| | Vertical organization of attributes by level of abstraction | Conceptual logic: Isolate the "leaves" of the concept "tree" and avoid the problems of redundancy and conflation |
| Measurement | Selection of indicators | Validity: Use multiple indicators and establish the cross-system equivalence of these indicators; use indicators that minimize measurement error and can be cross-checked through multiple sources<br>Reliability |
| | Selection of measurement level | Validity: Maximize homogeneity within measurement classes with the minimum number of necessary distinctions<br>Reliability |
| | Recording and publicizing of coding rules, coding process, and disaggregate data | Replicability |
| Aggregation | Selection of level of aggregation | Validity: Consider the relationship between the indicators used to measure a concept and the concept being measured and, when relevant, results of a test of dimensionality |
| | Selection of aggregation rule | Validity: Theorize the relationship among attributes, and ensure the correspondence between the theory of the relationship among attributes and the selected rule of aggregation<br>Robustness of aggregate data |
| | Recording and publicizing of aggregation rules and aggregate data | Replicability |

in tackling each of these challenges and the *standards of assessment* that pertain to each task.

The organization of the chapter follows directly from this framework. The three sections discuss the challenges of conceptualization, measurement, and aggregation, respectively. Each section elaborates the proposed framework, introduces the key methodological guidelines that analysts should consider, and assesses different democracy datasets in light of these guidelines. A final section offers an overall assessment of alternative datasets on democracy and stresses the value of efforts to evaluate existing datasets.

## 2.1. Conceptualization: Attributes and Logical Organization
......................................................................................................

The initial task in the construction of a dataset is the *identification of attributes* that are constitutive of the concept under consideration. This task, which amounts to a specification of the meaning of the concept, affects the entire process of data generation, given that it provides the anchor for all subsequent decisions. Thus, a natural and understandable impulse might be to find objective and unchanging criteria to guide this task. However, no hard-and-fast rule can be used to determine what attributes must be included in a definition of a certain concept. Because conceptualization is both intimately linked with theory and an open, evolving activity that is ultimately assessed in terms of the fruitfulness of the theories it helps to formulate (Kaplan 1964: 51–53, 71–78), "there is no point in arguing about what a 'correct' definition is" (Guttman 1994: 12; see also 295). Therefore, claims that disputes about how to specify a concept can be put to rest are inherently suspect, and the most useful — if admittedly flexible — methodological suggestion that can be offered is that scholars should avoid the extremes of including too much or too little in a definition.

The tendency to specify the meaning of a concept in a way that includes too many attributes — the problem of *maximalist definitions* — has the drawback of including extraneous attributes that correspond to other concepts and, hence, of not properly delimiting the concept under consideration. For example, if a market-based economic system is seen as a defining attribute of democracy, a feature of the economy is mistakenly used to characterize the distinct sphere of politics. As a result, the relationship between democracy and markets is obscured.

The effort to avoid the problem of maximalist definitions usually takes the form of *minimalist definitions,* which have the opposite drawback of failing to include attributes that are part of the meaning of the concept. For example, if democracy is defined only in terms of elections, other key features of democracy, such as the requirement that elected authorities have the power to set the agenda and are not removed unconstitutionally from office, would be left outside the concept. As a result, such an underdeveloped concept would most likely fail to register variation across cases, to the point of possibly mistaking nondemocracies for democracies if necessary attributes are erroneously considered to be sufficient. Thus, as a counterpart to the problem of maximalist definitions, analysts must also be sensitive to the problem of minimalist definitions.

Existing indices of democracy have addressed this first step in the construction of an index — the identification of attributes — with considerable acuity. In particular, the decision to draw, if to different degrees, on Robert Dahl's (1971: 4–6) influential insight that democracy consists of two attributes — contestation or competition and participation or inclusion — has done much to ensure that these measures of democracy are squarely focused on theoretically relevant attributes. This positive aspect notwithstanding, a systematic consideration of the attributes used by democracy indices (see table 2.3) reveals that they remain vulnerable to a number of criticisms.

Most constructors of indices subscribe to a procedural definition of democracy and thus avoid the problem of maximalist definitions. The only exception in this regard is Freedom House, which includes attributes that are more fruitfully seen as attributes of some other concept — for example, including "socioeconomic rights" as an aspect of its Civil Liberties index (Gastil 1991: 32–33; Ryan 1994: 10–11). In contrast, the problem of minimalist definitions is quite widespread.

One significant omission that affects various indices concerns one of the attributes Dahl highlights: participation. This omission is a particularly grave problem for the Polity index created by Ted Gurr and his associates (Marshall and Jaggers 2001). Because the scope of this dataset reaches back to 1800, this omission glosses over of a key feature of the experience with democratization in the nineteenth and early twentieth centuries as opposed to the late twentieth century: the gradual expansion of the right to vote. In contrast, this oversight is less significant in the cases of the "ACLP" index proposed by Michael Alvarez, José Antonio Cheibub, Fernando Limongi, and Adam Przeworski (Alvarez et al. 1996) and the index of Michael Coppedge and Wolfgang Reinicke (1991). The justification these authors offer —

TABLE 2.3. *Existing Datasets on Democracy: An Overview*

| Name of index | Attributes | Components of attributes | Measurement level | Aggregation rule |
|---|---|---|---|---|
| ACLP: Alvarez, Cheibub, Limongi, and Przeworski (1996) | Contestation Offices | { Election executive<br>{ Election legislature | Nominal<br>Nominal<br>Nominal | Multiplicative, at the level of components and attributes |
| Arat (1991) | Participation | { Executive selection<br>{ Legislative selection<br>{ Legislative effectiveness<br>{ Competitiveness of the nomination process | Ordinal<br>Ordinal<br>Ordinal<br>Ordinal | Additive, at the level of components; combined additive and multiplicative, at the level of attributes |
|  | Inclusiveness<br>Competitiveness | { Party legitimacy<br>{ Party competitiveness | Ordinal<br>Ordinal<br>Ordinal |  |
|  | Coerciveness |  | Interval |  |
| Bollen (1980) | Political liberties | { Press freedom<br>{ Freedom of group opposition<br>{ Government sanctions | Interval<br>Interval<br>Interval | Factor scores (weighted averages) |
|  | Popular sovereignty | { Fairness of elections<br>{ Executive selection<br>{ Legislative selection and effectiveness | Interval<br>Interval<br>Interval |  |
| Coppedge and Reinicke Polyarchy (1991) | Contestation | { Free and fair elections<br>{ Freedom of organization<br>{ Freedom of expression<br>{ Pluralism in the media | Ordinal<br>Ordinal<br>Ordinal<br>Ordinal | Guttman scale (hierarchical), at the level of components |
| Freedom House–Political Rights (Ryan 1994) | 9 attributes[a] |  | Ordinal | Additive, at the level of attributes |
| Freedom House–Civil Liberties (Ryan 1994) | 13 attributes[a] |  | Ordinal | Additive, at the level of attributes |

| Definition | Attributes | | Level of measurement | Aggregation |
|---|---|---|---|---|
| | | | Ordinal, with residual category[b] | None |
| Gasiorowski Political Regime Change (1996) | Competitiveness | | | None |
| | Inclusiveness | | | |
| | Civil and political liberties | | | |
| Hadenius (1992) | Elections | Suffrage | Interval | Combined additive and multiplicative (of weighted scores), at the level of components; additive, at the level of attributes |
| | | Elected offices | Interval | |
| | | Meaningful elections[c] [openness, fairness, and effectiveness] | Ordinal | |
| | Political freedoms | Freedom of organization | Ordinal | |
| | | Freedom of expression | Ordinal | |
| | | Freedom from coercion | Ordinal | |
| Polity IV (Marshall and Jaggers 2001) | Competitiveness of participation | | Ordinal | Additive (of weighted scores) |
| | Regulation of participation | | Ordinal | |
| | Competitiveness of executive recruitment | | Ordinal | |
| | Openness of executive recruitment | | Ordinal | |
| | Constraints on executive | | Ordinal | |
| Vanhanen (2000) | Competition | | Interval | Multiplicative |
| | Participation | | Interval | |

[a] For the list of attributes used by Freedom House, see Gastil (1991: 26, 32–33) and Ryan (1994: 10–11). This list has changed, problematically, over time; for the most recent list, see Freedom House (2007a).

[b] Though Gasiorowski offers a definition that disaggregates his main concept, he does not develop measures for his attributes. His choice of measurement level, thus, pertains to his main concept.

[c] The attributes in brackets constitute a third level of disaggregation and thus entail "subcomponents of attributes."

that they are concerned with gathering data only for the post–World War II period, that universal suffrage can be taken for granted in the post-1945 era, and thus that contestation is the most important aspect of the electoral process — is quite reasonable (Alvarez et al. 1996: 5, 19; Coppedge and Reinicke 1991: 51; Coppedge 1997: 181). Nonetheless, the exclusion of the attribute of participation remains problematic.[4] Although de jure restrictions on the right to vote are not found in current democracies, a whole battery of other restrictions, usually informal ones, curb the effective use of the formal right to vote and significantly distort the value of votes (Elklit 1994; Hadenius 1992: 40). Thus, the failure to include participation in its varied facets is a problem even for the study of democracy in recent times.[5]

Beyond this obviously relevant attribute of participation or inclusiveness, other significant omissions are noteworthy. One of the distinctive aspects of the ACLP dataset (Alvarez et al. 1996: 4–5) is that it includes an attribute called Offices that refers to the extent to which offices are filled by means of elections instead of some other procedure. This is an apt decision. After all, the concept of democracy seems inextricably linked with the notion of access to power, and, it is crucial to note, the set of government offices that are filled through elections has varied independently of the extent to which elections were contested and inclusive (Gehrlich 1973). Thus, the importance of Offices suggests that indices that have included only the attributes of contestation and/or participation (Coppedge and Reinicke, Gasiorowski, and Vanhanen) have omitted an important attribute.[6]

Relatedly, the suggestion that Offices is a relevant attribute raises the question about other attributes not linked so directly to the electoral process. For example, some authors have suggested that merely considering whether offices are elected is not sufficient to get at the essential question at stake — who exercises power? — and thus have included in their indices yet another attribute, called Legislative Effectiveness by Zehra Arat and Kenneth Bollen, Effectiveness of Elections by Axel Hadenius, and Constraints on the Chief Executive in the Polity IV dataset. As hard as this attribute may be to measure,[7] its relevance is difficult to dispute. Thus, indices that do not include such an attribute, which for the sake of convenience might be labeled the agenda-setting power of elected officials, suffer from a significant omission. In sum, the problem of minimalist definitions is quite widespread in existing indices of democracy.

Moving beyond the initial step of identifying *what* attributes are deemed to be constitutive of a concept, analysts must also consider *how* these

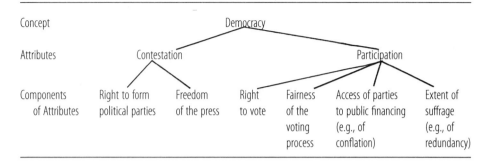

| Concept | | | Democracy | | | |
| --- | --- | --- | --- | --- | --- | --- |
| Attributes | | Contestation | | | Participation | |
| Components of Attributes | Right to form political parties | Freedom of the press | Right to vote | Fairness of the voting process | Access of parties to public financing (e.g., of conflation) | Extent of suffrage (e.g., of redundancy) |

FIGURE 2.1. The Logical Structure of Concepts

*Note:* This example has two levels of abstraction, labeled "attributes" and "components of attributes." One could introduce a third level of abstraction, called "subcomponents of attributes," and go even further. However, no matter how many levels of abstraction are introduced, attributes at the last level of abstraction, generically labeled as "leaves," are used as the starting point for the task of measurement. In this example, Right to form political parties is a "leaf."

attributes are related to each other and, more specifically, take explicit steps to ensure the *vertical organization of attributes by level of abstraction.* Though rarely addressed in standard discussions of methodology, this task has an impact on data generation by affecting the two subsequent challenges of measurement and aggregation. First, the specification of a concept's meaning frequently entails the identification of attributes that vary in terms of their level of abstractness. Thus, inasmuch as these attributes begin to form a bridge between the abstract level at which concepts are usually cast initially and the concrete level of observations, the identification of conceptual attributes affect — and can assist analysts in tackling — the distinct and subsequent challenge of measurement. To achieve this benefit, however, the various attributes must be organized vertically according to their level of abstraction. Indeed, by distinguishing attributes according to their level of abstraction, which for the sake of convenience are given different labels (attributes, components of attributes, subcomponent of attributes, etc.), analysts isolate the most concrete attributes, which can be labeled as "leaves" of the concept "tree" and serve as the point of departure for efforts at measurement (see figure 2.1).

Second, the identification of multiple attributes of a concept essentially amounts to a process of disaggregation, which immediately raises the question of how the disaggregate data might be aggregated. The challenge of aggregation can be carried out only once scores are assigned to each "leaf," that is, after the challenge of measurement has been tackled, which entails a complex set of issues. However, any discussion of aggregation presupposes that the attributes of a concept are organized in a way that follows two basic rules of conceptual logic. On the one hand, in organizing the attributes of a concept vertically, it is necessary that less abstract attributes be placed on the proper branch of the conceptual tree—that is, immediately subordinate to the more abstract attribute it helps to flesh out and make more concrete. Otherwise this attribute will be conjoined with attributes that are manifestations of a different overarching attribute and give rise to the problem of *conflation*. On the other hand, attributes at the same level of abstraction should tap into mutually exclusive aspects of the attribute at the immediately superior level of abstraction. Otherwise the analysis falls prey to the distinct logical problem of *redundancy* (for examples, see figure 2.1).[8]

Concerning this second task related to the challenge of conceptualization —the vertical organization of attributes by level of abstraction—all existing indices of democracy carefully distinguish the level of abstraction of their attributes and thus clearly isolate the leaves of their concept trees (see columns 2 and 3 in table 2.3). Nonetheless, these indices do not avoid basic problems of conceptual logic. Redundancy is evident in two indices. Polity IV falls prey to this problem because it identifies a pair of attributes (Competitiveness of Participation, and Regulation of Participation) that grasp only one aspect of democracy, the extent to which elections are competitive; and another pair of attributes (Competitiveness of Executive Recruitment, and Openness of Executive Recruitment) that also pertain to a single issue, whether offices are filled by means of elections or some other procedure. Likewise, Hadenius's subcomponent Openness of Elections is hard to distinguish from the three components into which he disaggregates his attribute Political Freedoms (see table 2.3).

The problem of conflation is even more common. Arat, for example, combines four components under a common overarching attribute Participation that actually relate logically to two different attributes: offices and agenda-setting power of elected officials. Similarly, Bollen (1980: 376) includes under his attribute Popular Sovereignty two components (Executive Selection, and Legislative Selection and Effectiveness) that grasp and thus very usefully disaggregate one single attribute, that is, whether key offices are elected, but he also includes a third component (Fairness of Elections) that seems more closely linked to a different attribute, such as participation. Likewise, Hadenius's index might be faulted for including under his attribute Elections an array of components and subcomponents that are clearly related to the electoral process (Suffrage, Openness, and Fairness) but also other components and subcomponents (Elected Offices, Effectiveness) that are best treated as aspects of other attributes such as offices and agenda setting. Finally, Freedom House includes so many attributes under its Political Rights and Civil Liberties indices (nine and thirteen, respectively) and does so with such little thought about the relationship among attributes—the attributes are presented as little more than a "checklist" (Ryan 1994: 10)—that it is hardly surprising that a large number of distinct or at best vaguely related aspects of democracy are lumped together (Bollen 1986: 584).

To be fair, constructors of democracy indices tend to be quite self-conscious about methodological issues. Thus, they all explicitly present their definitions of democracy, highlight the attributes they have identified, and clearly distinguish these attributes according to their level of abstraction. Moreover, a few indices are quite exemplary in terms of how they tackle specific tasks. In this sense, Hadenius is very insightful in identifying the attributes that are constitutive of the concept of democracy, as are ACLP with regard to how various attributes should be logically organized.[9] Nonetheless, there remains much room for improvement, with regard to both concept specification and conceptual logic.

## 2.2. Measurement: Indicators and Levels of Measurement

A second challenge in the generation of data is the formation of measures, which link the conceptual attributes identified and logically organized during the prior step with observations. The challenge of measurement takes as its starting point the attributes at the lowest level of abstraction, that is, the leaves of the concept tree. It is crucial to note, nonetheless, that even when concepts have been extremely well articulated, these leaves are rarely observable themselves. Hence, it is necessary to form measurement models relating unobservable "latent variables" to "observable variables" or indicators (Bollen 1989: ch. 6). This complex challenge requires consideration of a variety of issues. There is ample justification, though, for giving primacy to two tasks, the selection of indicators and measurement level, and to one standard of assessment, the *validity* of the measures (i.e., the extent to which the proposed measures actually measure what they are supposed to measure) (Carmines and Zeller 1979; Bollen 1989; Adcock and Collier 2001). Thus, these issues are addressed before turning to some others.

The first decision in the formation of measures is the *selection of indicators* that operationalize the leaves of a concept tree. Because there are no hard-and-fast rules for choosing valid indicators, this is one of the most elusive goals in the social sciences. However, some guidance can be derived from a consideration of the impact of two common pitfalls on the validity of measures. One is the failure to recognize the manifold empirical manifestations of a conceptual attribute and to properly use multiple indicators. This is probably one of the most difficult problems to avoid in the construction of large datasets, but the importance of these concerns is hard to overemphasize. On the one hand, the more one seeks to form measures for the purpose of cross-time and cross-space comparisons, the more necessary it becomes to avoid the potential biases associated with single indicators by using multiple indicators. On the other hand, the more multiple indicators are used, the more difficult the task becomes, as the analyst must establish the comparability of diverse indicators. Thus, an important guideline for maximizing the validity of indicators is to select multiple indicators but to do so in a way that explicitly addresses the need to establish the cross-system equivalence of these indicators (Przeworski and Teune 1970: chs. 5 and 6; Blalock 1982: chs. 3 and 4).

A second common pitfall associated with the selection of indicators is the failure to appreciate the inescapable nature of measurement error, which is usually thought of as having (at least) two basic components: systematic error (bias) and random error (noise). As a general rule, the choice of indicators is naturally and unavoidably guided in part by the availability or accessibility of data. Thus, it is understandable that such practical issues should affect the choice. But this represents a serious problem because the record left by history is inherently biased. For example, differences in levels of reported rapes might have more to do with changes in culture than the actual number of rapes. Likewise, increased evidence of corruption may be more a reflection of increased freedom of the press than an actual increase in corruption. This problem underscores the need for analysts to be aware of any systematic sources of measurement error and, specifically, to maximize the validity of their indicators by selecting indicators that are less likely to be affected by bias and that can be cross-checked through the use of multiple sources (Bollen 1986: 578–87; 1993). The level of random error in indicators may or may not be under the control of the investigator, depending on the nature of the variables; but, at a minimum, it is important to endeavor to understand likely sources of random error and reduce them whenever possible.[10]

Existing indices of democracy demonstrate significantly varying degrees of attention to the need for multiple indicators and the need to establish the cross-system equivalence of these indicators. ACLP (Alvarez et al. 1996: 7–13) and Hadenius (1992: 36–60) provide a detailed justification for their indicators that shows great sensitivity to context. However, in other cases, though indicators are presented explicitly, the lack of any detailed discussion makes it hard to understand how, or even if, they reflect differences in context. In yet other cases, the common practice of using data already coded by others is strongly associated with a tendency to simply sidestep the need to justify the choice of indicators (Arat 1991: ch. 2; Bollen 1980: 375–76). Finally, one of the most problematic examples concerning the choice of indicators is provided, somewhat ironically, by Tatu Vanhanen (1993: 303–8, 310), who defends the use of "simple quantitative indicators" and argues against measures that are "too complicated and have too many indicators . . . that . . . depend too much on subjective evaluations."

The problem with Vanhanen's position is that it overstates the contrast between subjective and objective indicators and consequently does not give much attention to the subjective judgments that shape the selection of "objective" indicators (see, however, Vanhanen 2000: 255). It is no surprise, then, that Vanhanen's decision to measure his attribute Competition in terms of the percentage of votes going to the largest party and his attribute Participation in terms of voter turnout has been criticized on the ground that these indicators not only constitute at best poor measures of the pertinent attribute but also introduce systematic bias (Bollen 1980: 373–74; 1986: 571–72; 1991: 4, 11; Hadenius 1992: 41, 43). Overall, democracy indices reflect insufficient sensitivity to the key issues involved in the choice of indicators.

When we turn to the second task in the formation of measures — the *selection of measurement level* — the concern with validity is again all-important. The selection of measurement level requires analysts to weigh competing considerations and make judicious decisions that reflect in-depth knowledge of the cases under consideration. Thus, there is no foundation to the widespread perception that the selection of measurement levels is something that is decided solely by reference to a priori assumptions. And there is no basis to the claim that, of the standard choice among nominal, ordinal, interval, or ratio scales, the choice of a level of measurement closest to a ratio scale — conventionally understood as the highest level of measurement in the sense that it makes the most precise distinctions — should be given preference on a priori grounds. Indeed, the best guidance is the more open-ended suggestion that the selection of a measurement level should be driven by the goal of maximizing homogeneity within measurement classes with the minimum number of necessary distinctions and should be seen as a process that requires both theoretical justification and empirical testing (Gifi 1990; Jacoby 1991, 1999).

From this perspective, the choice about measurement level might be seen as an attempt to avoid the excesses of introducing distinctions that are either too fine-grained, which would result in statements about measurement that are simply not plausible in light of the available information and the extent to which measurement error can be minimized, or too coarse-grained, which would result in cases that are well known to be different being placed together. This is no easy or mechanical task. Thus, the choice of measurement level should draw upon the insights of experts and be subjected to careful scrutiny. Moreover, this choice should be made in light of the availability of data and the likely extent of measurement error, and thus not take as a goal "measures that we cannot in fact obtain" (Kaplan 1964: 283). Finally, it should be open to testing, in the sense that analysts should consider the implications of different assumptions about the level of measurement and use an assessment of these implications in justifying choices.

The importance of this decision to the overall process of data generation notwithstanding, existing democracy indices probably pay even less attention to issues involved in the selection of measurement level than to the selection of indicators. As table 2.3 shows, different indices use nominal, ordinal, and interval scales. However, with rare exceptions, proponents of different levels of measurement hardly get beyond assertions about the inherent correctness of different measurement levels and thus do not properly assume the burden of proof of justifying and testing a particular choice (Collier and Adcock 1999). Unfortunately, the selection of measurement level is one of the weakest points of current democracy indices, and analysts have not fully acknowledged that "no variable comes with a measurement level obviously attached" and that any choice of "measurement level must be justified in the context of a specific problem" (Smithson and Verkuilen 2006: 28, emphasis in original removed).[11]

Beyond the concern with maximizing the validity of measures, two other basic standards of assessment deserve attention in the context of the challenge of measurement. One pertains to the *reliability* of measures, that is, the prospect that the same data collection process would always produce the same data. Efforts to ascertain a measure's reliability, which is typically assessed by the extent to which multiple coders produce the same codings, are useful in two senses. First, if tests of reliability prove weak, they alert analysts to potential problems in the measurement process. Second, if tests of reliability prove strong, they can be interpreted as an indication of the consensus garnered by the proposed measures. At the same time, it is important to note that these tests should not be interpreted as tests of the validity of measures. Weak reliability provides no clues as to which measures are more valid, only that there is disagreement about how cases are to be coded. In turn, strong reliability can be generated if all analysts suffer from the same biases and thus should not be interpreted as a sign of a measure's validity. In fact, one way to obtain very reliable measures is to adopt similar biases, something that is all too often done, even unconsciously. Thus, while reliability is obviously desirable in that it provides an indication of the extent to which a collectivity of scholars can arrive at agreement, it is important to acknowledge that there always might be systematic biases in measurement. Reliable measures need not be valid ones.

Another standard of assessment pertains to the *replicability* of measures, that is, the ability of a community of scholars to reproduce the process through which data were generated. This concern has little value in itself; the reason for worrying about replicability is that claims about either validity or reliability hinge upon the replicability of measures. Yet, because issues of measurement are inescapably subjective, involving a variety of judgments rather than objective criteria, it is absolutely vital that the community of scholars retain the ability to scrutinize and challenge the choices that shape the generation of data. Thus, in addressing the formation of measures, analysts should *record and make public:* (1) their *coding rules,* which should include, at the very minimum, a list of all indicators, the selected measurement level for each indicator, and sufficiently detailed information so that independent scholars can interpret the meaning of each scale; (2) the *coding process,* which should include the list of sources used in the coding process, the number of coders, and the results of any intercoder reliability tests; and (3) the *disaggregate data* generated on all indicators.

On their handling of these tasks, existing indices represent something of a mixed bag. With regard to coding rules, ACLP (Alvarez et al. 1996: 7–14), Hadenius (1992: 36–60), and Polity IV (Marshall and Jaggers 2001) are models of clarity, specifying their coding rules explicitly and in a fair amount of detail. Others are also quite explicit about their coding rules but do not provide as much detail and thus leave a fair amount of room for interpretation. Yet others, such as Freedom House and Mark Gasiorowski, never provide a clear set of coding rules and thus offer no basis for a real dialogue about how cases were coded.

With respect to the coding process, existing indices do quite poorly. All index creators provide some facts on the sources consulted in the coding process. However, the level of detail is such that an independent scholar would have a hard time reconstructing precisely what information the coder had in mind in assigning scores. Indeed, the type of information provided does not go beyond referring to titles of books or general sources such as *Keesing's Record of World Events,* without indicating what information was drawn from these sources, precisely where that information could be found, and what attribute was coded on the basis of what information. Moreover, existing indices are quite wanting when it comes to information about who did the coding, whether multiple coders were used, and, if so, whether tests of intercoder reliability were conducted. In a few isolated instances, the problem is as basic as not knowing who or how many people carried out the coding. Though in the majority of cases this information is provided, the common practice of using a single coder raises serious questions about the potential for significant bias. Finally, in some cases the potential gain associated with the use of multiple coders is denied due to the failure to conduct a test of intercoder reliability (Ryan 1994: 11, 7). Indeed, in only two cases — the Coppedge and Reinicke (1991: 55) index and Polity IV (Marshall and Jaggers 2001: 5–8) — were multiple coders used and tests of intercoder reliability conducted.[12]

Last, with regard to the availability of disaggregate data, existing democracy indices rate moderately well. A few index creators provide only aggregate data.[13] But many have either published their disaggregate data, published their aggregate data and also made the disaggregate data available upon request, or made the disaggregate data available over the Internet (see the sources in table 2.1).

As problematic as various indices are with respect to one or another task pertaining to the formation of measures, two of them stand out due to the unsatisfactory response they give to all three tasks involved in the measurement of a concept: the indices created by Gasiorowski and Freedom House. The first problem with Gasiorowski's index is that no effort to measure and code was ever conducted at the level of attributes. That is, even though definitions for the index's three attributes are introduced, the effort at measurement formally bypasses the disaggregated attributes and focuses directly on the most aggregate level, negating the basic rationale for disaggregating a concept. At the aggregate level, Gasiorowski (1996: 471–72) proposes a three-point ordinal scale — distinguishing among democracy, semidemocracy, and authoritarianism — with a residual category for transitional regimes. This choice is well rooted in the literature, but no explicit discussion of indicators and no coding rules are ever offered. Finally, even though Gasiorowski identifies the sources he uses and has gone even further by making the narrative summaries he used in coding cases publicly available, there is no way an independent researcher could attempt to replicate the coding, something that is particularly necessary in light of the fact that the coding was all done by a single person, Gasiorowski himself (1996: 473–75).

The problems with the Freedom House indices start with the selection of indicators. Though Freedom House shows an awareness of the need to use different indicators in different countries (Gastil 1991: 25–26), this sensitivity to context has not gone hand in hand with an effort to establish the equivalence of different indicators.[14] Concerning the selection of the level of measurement, the problems continue. Each of the attributes listed in Freedom House's checklist (Gastil 1991: 26, 32–33; Ryan 1994: 10–11) is measured on an ordinal five-point scale. This might very well be a reasonable choice, but no justification for adopting this level of measurement is provided. Indeed, a concern with symmetry rather than a consideration of theory and/or the structure of the data seems to drive this choice. Finally, very little is done to open the process of measurement to public scrutiny, which obscures the entire exercise. Because no set of coding rules is provided, independent scholars are left in the dark as to what distinguishing features would lead a case to receive a score of 0, 1, 2, 3, or 4 points. Furthermore, the sources of information are not identified with enough precision so that independent scholars could reanalyze them. And, to make matters even worse, the failure to make public the disaggregated data (until 2006) has ensured that a scholarly, public debate about issues of measurement is virtually impossible. In the end, the aggregate data offered by Freedom House has to be accepted largely on faith.[15]

In sum, existing indices of democracy have not tackled the challenge of measurement very well. A few positive aspects can be rescued. Valuable insights concerning the selection of indicators can be gleaned from ACLP and Hadenius. Moreover, concerning the recording and publicizing of the coding rules, the coding process, and the disaggregate data, ACLP, Coppedge and Reinicke, and Polity IV set a high standard. But the broader trend is clearly negative. The cases of Gasiorowski and Freedom House are examples of deeply flawed approaches to issues of measurement. More generally, it is fair to state that existing indices fail on numerous grounds. They do little to select indicators that reflect a sensitivity to context, problems of equivalence, and measurement error. They tend to rely on a fairly unsophisticated approach to the selection of measurement level. And they do not take adequate steps to ensure replicability. The need for a more careful approach to issues of measurement is readily apparent.

## 2.3. Aggregation: Levels and Rules of Aggregation

Once the process of measurement is completed with the assignment of scores to each of the leaves of the concept tree, analysts face a third challenge: to determine *whether* to reverse the process of disaggregation that was carried out during the conceptualization stage and *how* to generate a single score or index from disaggregate scores.[16] As important as this step is for the validity of measures, it has not received much attention in the literature on measurement methodology in political science.

The first task that must be confronted — the *selection of the level of aggregation* — can be considered from different perspectives. In the conventional view, taken largely from psychometrics, aggregation involves a delicate balancing act. The rationale for aggregating disaggregate scores is given by the sheer amount of attributes and data that can be associated with a richly developed, thick concept. A large amount of data makes research conducted at the most disaggregate level somewhat unwieldy and hence analysts might consider that some effort at trimming is appropriate. After all, a more parsimonious concept is likely to be more analytically tractable and facilitate theorizing and testing. Yet, within this view, the gains to be accrued from aggregation must be weighted against the potential loss in information about systematic variation among the cases. Specifically, aggregation is seen as justified inasmuch as the lower levels of aggregation tap into a unidimensional phenomenon, a matter that can be tested through common procedures such as the Spearman factor model (McDonald 1999).

A different rationale for aggregating disaggregate scores is that the disaggregate scores, taken by themselves, are parts of a whole and that their meaning is understood only when the parts are considered in context or, in other words, when the parts are combined to form a whole.[17] From this perspective, the dimensionality of the disaggregate scores is not relevant to the choice of level of aggregation. Indeed, the conventional assumption that aggregation operates on multiple parallel measurements is simply not made when the disaggregate scores being aggregated are considered parts of a whole. Thus, in tackling the decision to generate an index, analysts should first specify how they think about the relationship between the indicators used to measure a concept and the concept being measured and, specifically, which of these two perspectives they adopt.[18]

The conventional perspective is self-consciously adopted by Coppedge and Reinicke (1991: 52–53; Coppedge 1997: 180–84), who tackle the process of aggregation by constructing a Guttman scale. The advantage of such a scale is that the process of aggregation can be carried out without losing information in the process of moving from a lower to a higher level of aggregation and without having to assign weights to each component. The problem, however, is that a Guttman scale can be constructed only if the multiple components move in tandem and measure the same underlying dimension, which does not seem to be quite the case with the components used in the Coppedge and Reinicke index.[19] The limit to the usefulness of Guttman scales in this context notwithstanding, Coppedge and Reinicke demonstrate an exemplary sensitivity about the possible loss of information that can occur in the process of aggregation in light of the empirical dimensionality of a concept.

The creators of the other indices adopt, more or less consciously, the less conventional perspective,[20] and thus had to confront a second task, the *selection of an aggregation rule* that specifies the relationship among the disaggregate scores that are to be aggregated. This task assumes as a key prerequisite that a concept's attributes have been logically organized in an explicit fashion, a point addressed previously. Indeed, because the selection of an aggregation rule requires the clear identification of what attributes are to be aggregated and in what order, as shown in figure 2.2, this task hinges on the prior resolution of any problems of conceptual logic. But the selection of a rule of aggregation proper is a distinct task driven by the concern with formalizing the theoretical understanding of the links among the attributes — and, where relevant, the components and subcomponents of attributes — which have been identified in the process of disaggregating a concept.

This task involves a two-step process. First, the analyst must make explicit the theory of the relationship among attributes, components, and subcomponents. Second, the analyst must ensure that there is a correspondence

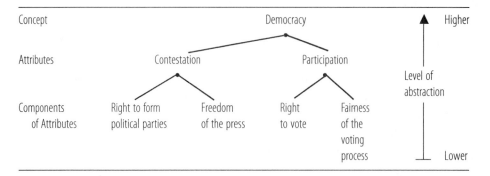

FIGURE 2.2. The Process of Aggregation

*Note:* A node is represented by a dot (•). Aggregation starts at the lowest level of abstraction, where scores are assigned to "leaves," and moves to higher levels of abstraction. Moreover, aggregation requires the use of rules of aggregation, which specify the theoretical link between attributes that are at the same level of abstraction and are connected to the same overarching attribute (by means of a node). In this example, the selection of aggregation rules would first have to focus on the relationship between the Right to form political parties and Freedom of the press, so as to define a score for Contestation, and between Right to vote and Fairness of the voting process, so as to generate a score for Participation. Thereafter, if a decision is made to move to the next level of aggregation, represented here by Democracy, the focus would shift to the relationship between Contestation and Participation.

between this theory and the selected aggregation rule, that is, that the aggregation rule is actually the equivalent formal expression of the posited relationship.[21] For example, if the aggregation of two attributes is at issue and one's theory indicates that there is no interaction among the attributes, one would simply add the scores of both attributes. If one's theory indicates that the two attributes are both necessary conditions, one could multiply both scores. And, if one's theory indicates that the two attributes are sufficient conditions, one could take the score of the attribute with the highest value. In this regard, it is crucial that researchers be sensitive to the multitude of ways in which attributes might be linked and avoid the tendency to limit themselves by adherence to defaults, such as additivity.

The importance of theory as a guide in the selection of aggregation rules notwithstanding, much as with the selection of measurement levels, it is still critical to stress that such choices should be open to testing. Thus, analysts should consider what results would follow from applying different aggregation rules and gain a sense of the *robustness* of the aggregate data, that is, the degree to which changes in the aggregation rule result in changes in the aggregate data. Furthermore, as a way to enable other researchers to replicate the process of aggregation and carry out tests pertaining to aggregation rules, analysts should *record and publicize the aggregation rules and aggregate data.*

With regard to these various tasks, existing datasets on democracy once again are less than adequate. In the case of the Freedom House indices, the selected aggregation rule is clear and explicit: scores for the two indices — of Political Rights and Civil Liberties — are generated by adding up the scores assigned to each of its respective attributes.[22] As innocent an operation as this may appear, it is fraught with problems. First, because the bewilderingly long list of attributes used in the Freedom House indices are not presented as a theoretically connected set of attributes but only as a checklist (Ryan 1994: 10), no theoretical justification for this choice of aggregation rule is offered. Second, the equal weighting of each attribute that is implied by this aggregation through addition seems patently inadequate in light of the content of the components. To give but one example, it seems unfounded to give the issue of decentralization of power (attribute 9 of the Political Rights index) the same weight and significance for democracy as the actual power exercised by elected representatives (attribute 4 of the Political Rights index) (Ryan 1994: 10). Third, even though independent scholars have good reason to question the aggregation rule used by Freedom House, they have been unable to test the implications of different aggregation rules due to the failure of Freedom House (until 2006) to make public the disaggregate data. In short, the numerous conceptual and measurement problems that weaken the Freedom House indices are compounded by the blatant disregard of the challenge of aggregation.

Only slightly better than the Freedom House indices in this regard are the Vanhanen and Polity IV indices. Vanhanen (2000: 255–57) proposes a clear and simple aggregation rule: aggregate scores are generated by multiplying the scores of his two attributes. However, little is done to offer a theoretical justification for the weight thus assigned to each attribute, and no effort to test the implications of different aggregation rules is made. The only redeeming point of this arbitrary and ad hoc approach to the process of aggregation is that Vanhanen, in contrast to Freedom House, at least provides the data on his disaggregated attributes. Thus, others can independently test how different aggregation rules would affect the aggregate scores.

The Polity IV index, in turn, is based on an explicit but nonetheless quite convoluted aggregation rule (Marshall and Jaggers 2001: 11–14). First, the index's five attributes are weighted differently because different scales, with a variable number of points, are used for each attribute. Although weighted scores provide a legitimate way of acknowledging the greater or lesser theoretical import of different attributes, a problem already crops up at this step in that no justification is provided for the weighting scheme. Second, the scores assigned to the five attributes are added to generate either two scores (a democracy and an autocracy score) or a single score (a Polity score), giving rise to yet more problems. Not only is virtually no theoretical justification for this operation provided, but it also is open to criticism due to the index's problems of conceptual logic. Indeed, as discussed previously, Polity IV includes a pair of redundant attributes, and this leads to a fair amount of double counting that is never acknowledged or explained. A positive quality of the Polity IV index, however, is that the disaggregate data are publicly available, thus ensuring that independent scholars can assess the implications of different aggregation rules and potentially suggest more appropriate aggregation rules.

Other indices offer more lucid approaches to the process of aggregation but are still not problem-free. Arat (1991: 26) presents a formal aggregation rule that is quite complex. However, though the aggregation rule is plausible, it is not justified. Moreover, the proposed aggregation rule is never tested and the opportunity for other scholars to carry out independent tests is denied, because the disaggregate data are not made available. In contrast, ACLP (Alvarez et al. 1996: 14) explicitly offer a rationale for considering a country as democratic only if the chief executive and the legislature are elected in contested races and, if they fail to formalize their theoretical understanding of the connection between their attributes, they do make it clear that positive scores on their three attributes are individually necessary and jointly sufficient to classify a regime as democratic. Still, they do not consider the implications of using different aggregation rules and do not provide all the information needed to enable scholars to conduct such tests themselves. Thus, in comparison to other datasets, Hadenius's index is especially noteworthy. He proposes a complex aggregation rule, yet both justifies it explicitly and extensively by reference to democratic theory and formalizes it. Moreover, he displays a sensitivity about the implications of different aggregation rules, and not only offers the necessary information for others to test the implications of different aggregation rules but actually carries out a test of robustness of his proposed aggregation rule (Hadenius 1992: 61, 70–71). Indeed, in light of the poor standard set by many other indices, Hadenius's approach to the challenge of aggregation rules is exemplary.

In sum, with a few notable exceptions, existing democracy indices have displayed a fairly low level of sophistication concerning the process of aggregation. Index constructors have tended to use aggregation rules in a fairly ad hoc manner, neither offering an explicit theory concerning the relationship between attributes nor putting much effort into ensuring the correspondence between the theoretical understanding of the relationship among attributes and the selected aggregation rules. Likewise, virtually no effort is put into testing and assessing the implications of different aggregation rules. The challenge of aggregation is undoubtedly a weak point of many existing democracy indices.

## 2.4. Conclusion

This review of existing democracy indices underscores two key points. First, index creators have demonstrated widely divergent levels of sophistication in tackling the challenges of conceptualization, measurement, and aggregation. To highlight only the most notable strengths and weaknesses, praise is most justified in the cases of ACLP (Alvarez et al. 1996), who are particularly insightful concerning the selection of indicators and especially clear and detailed concerning coding rules; Coppedge and Reinicke (1991), who display a concern with coder reliability and sensitivity on the question of levels of aggregation; and Hadenius (1992), who offers a compelling conceptualization of democracy, an appropriate choice of indicators, and a sophisticated use of aggregation rules. Datasets that are unfortunately so problematic as to require explicit mention include those compiled by Freedom House (2007b), Gasiorowski (1996), and Vanhanen (2000, 2007), which exemplify problems in all three areas of conceptualization, measurement, and aggregation (see table 2.4).

Second, this review shows that no single index offers a satisfactory response to all three challenges of conceptualization, measurement, and aggregation. Indeed, even the strongest indices suffer from weaknesses of some importance. Thus, the ACLP index is based on a fairly narrow conception of democracy and is quite weak when it comes to the selection of measurement level; the Coppedge and Reinicke index also offers a fairly narrow conception of democracy; and Hadenius's index suffers from numerous problems of

TABLE 2.4.  *Existing Datasets on Democracy: An Evaluation*

| Name | Strengths | Weaknesses |
|---|---|---|
| ACLP: Alvarez, Cheibub, Limongi, and Przeworski (1996) | Identification of attributes: offices<br>Conceptual logic<br>Appropriate selection of indicators<br>Clear and detailed coding rules | Minimalist definition: omission of participation and agenda setting |
| Arat (1991) | Identification of attributes: offices and agenda setting | Conceptual logic: problem of conflation |
| Bollen (1980) | Identification of attributes: offices, agenda setting, and fairness | Minimalist definition: omission of participation<br>Conceptual logic: problem of conflation<br>Restricted empirical (temporal) scope |
| Coppedge and Reinicke Polyarchy (1991) | Identification of attributes: fairness<br>Test of intercoder reliability<br>Sophisticated aggregation procedure | Minimalist definition: omission of participation, offices, and agenda setting<br>Restricted empirical (temporal) scope |
| Freedom House (Ryan 1994) | Comprehensive empirical (spatial) scope | Maximalist definition<br>Conceptual logic: problem of conflation<br>Multiple problems of measurement<br>Inappropriate aggregation procedure |
| Gasiorowski Political Regime Change (1996) | Comprehensive empirical scope | Minimalist definition: omission of offices and agenda setting<br>Multiple problems of measurement |
| Hadenius (1992) | Identification of attributes: offices, agenda setting, and fairness<br>Appropriate selection of indicators<br>Clear and detailed coding rules<br>Sophisticated aggregation procedure | Conceptual logic: problems of redundancy and conflation<br>Restricted empirical (temporal) scope |
| Polity IV (Marshall and Jaggers 2001) | Identification of attributes: offices and agenda setting<br>Clear and detailed coding rules<br>Test of intercoder reliability<br>Comprehensive empirical scope | Minimalist definition: omission of participation<br>Conceptual logic: problem of redundancy<br>Inappropriate aggregation procedure |
| Vanhanen (2000a) | Clear coding rules<br>Comprehensive empirical scope<br>Replicability | Minimalist definition: omission of offices and agenda setting<br>Questionable indicators<br>Inappropriate aggregation procedure |

conceptual logic. Moreover, the best indices are also fairly restricted in their scope (see table 2.1), while the indices with the broadest scope, with the partial exception of Polity IV, are not among the strongest on issues of conceptualization, measurement, and aggregation. In short, as important a contribution as these indices represent, there remains much room for improving the quality of data on democracy.

This critical assessment, it bears stressing, is not aimed at discouraging efforts at causal assessment using large-N datasets. Having a dataset on democracy, even if it is partially flawed, is better than not having any dataset at all, and scholars should use what they have at their disposal. Thus, it is unreasonable to declare a moratorium on statistical tests until the problems highlighted in this chapter are resolved. But it is equally important to emphasize that the careful development of measures constitutes the foundation for efforts at drawing causal inferences and is a critical task in itself.

The need for the sort of detailed analysis of measures this chapter offers is not always clearly recognized. Indeed, analysts many times overlook the fact that mathematical statistics — which develops the relationship between theory, data, and inference — presumes that the relationship between theory, observation, and data has been well established. Thus, one cannot slight the task of measurement, hoping that mathematical statistics will somehow offer a solution to a problem it is not designed to tackle (Jacoby 1991). In this sense, the basic goal and contribution of this chapter can be put as follows. By offering a comprehensive framework for the generation and/or analysis of data, it draws attention to the complex issues raised by an aspect of research that underpins causal inference. Moreover, by applying this framework to existing measures of democracy and hence responding to Bollen's (1986: 589) call for "better analyses of existing measures," this chapter seeks to identify distinct areas in which attempts to improve the quality of data on democracy might fruitfully be focused. Ultimately, the value of analyses of measures has to be assessed in terms of the ability to generate better measuring instruments and better data, a challenge addressed in subsequent chapters (see chapters 4 and 5). Nonetheless, it is important to recognize the independent value of evaluations of existing datasets, especially in the case of datasets, such as the democracy indices discussed here, that are frequently used in causal assessments in both international relations and comparative politics but have been the subject of little in-depth attention.

# THREE

# Drawing Boundaries

*The Crafting of Intermediate Regime Categories*

..............................................................................................................

The notion of convergence around a single political model, a matter of much discussion in the heady days of 1989, increasingly seems to run counter to political realities in the post–cold war era. Thus, even as scholars have recognized the unprecedented shift toward democracy — for the first time in history it is credible to claim that more than half the countries in the world fulfill the requisites of a minimalist definition of democracy — they have also grappled with the variety of ways that politics is practiced around the globe. One important strand of thinking has focused on the quality of democracy (O'Donnell 2004b; Munck 2004: 450–56; Diamond and Morlino 2005). Another potentially fruitful literature, which serves as the point of reference for this chapter, has focused on cases that have been variously characterized as instances of semidemocracy (Case 1996), illiberal democracy (Zakaria 1997), semiauthoritarianism (Ottaway 2003), authoritarian democracy (Sakwa 1998), competitive authoritarianism (Levitsky and Way 2002), electoral authoritarianism (Schedler 2002) or, more generically, hybrid regimes (Karl 1995; Diamond 2002).

This literature on hybrid regimes seeks to exploit a key insight: a considerable number of countries seem to be neither fully democratic nor blatantly authoritarian and thus are best characterized with intermediate categories. Yet, even as this literature calls attention to the broad variety of current political regimes and exposes the limitations of concepts that are conventionally used to describe political practices, it suffers from its own problems. Methodologically, it tends to ignore standard practices that have been refined in the literature on measurement and that for some time have been used to generate large-N datasets on regimes and democracy. Substantively, it largely overlooks an established theoretical literature on democracy and political parties that offers key insights relevant to the methodological choices involved in the creation of measures that envisage intermediate categories. In short, though this literature focuses on a real-world problem of great import, it has still not proposed a clear and methodologically appropriate way to generate data, let alone presented systematic data that could be used to conduct a rigorous empirical analysis.

This chapter seeks to show how the insight at the heart of the literature on hybrid regimes might be developed by focusing on the methodological issues involved in crafting intermediary categories of political regime. It emphasizes basic issues regarding the methodology of measurement but also argues that new thinking about core methodological issues is called for. Specifically, the central point of this chapter is that the measurement of each regime dimension requires an appreciation of the fundamental role of equivalence-difference relationships that upsets the deeply ingrained perception that researchers must choose between measures that highlight distinctions of kind or of degree. A secondary point is that more attention needs to be given to the decisions involved in the aggregation of measures of multiple regime dimensions and, specifically, to the way in which these decisions revolve around a distinct type of part-whole relationship. These are complicated matters, and it is important to be sensitive to the manner in which methodological discussions can turn into a long detour that slows down progress in responding to pressing questions about politics. Yet it is equally important to recognize that circumventing methodological issues most likely leads to unwarranted knowledge claims. Thus, it is advisable to tackle these methodological questions head on and to build on the accomplishments of existing scholarship, drawing whenever possible on clues offered in the substantive literature as to how various methodological choices might be confronted.

## 3.1. Boundaries and Intermediate Categories: Some Preliminary Considerations

From a methodological perspective, a central issue raised by the recent literature on hybrid regimes concerns the identification of thresholds that establish boundaries between categories and between cases and, relatedly, the development of measures that include multiple thresholds and thus entail intermediate categories and cases. This is, of course, not a new issue in political science. After all, Aristotle's classical typology is based on a trichotomous distinction regarding the number of power holders (one vs. few vs. many) and a dichotomous distinction regarding the use of power (the common good vs. private interest). Yet students of political regimes have still to address in a satisfactory way the methodological issues that are relevant to drawing boundaries and exploring intermediate categories.

One of the main obstacles to devising better measures of political regimes — and, hence, to improving our ability to describe regimes in a systematic and nuanced manner — is the widely held view that scholars face a choice between generating dichotomous and continuous measures (Collier and Adcock 1999). The oft-repeated phrase that there are distinctions "of kind" and "of degree," and that they should not be confused, indicates how deeply this stark choice is ingrained in current thinking. Even self-consciously methodological discussions of measurement focus on the pros and cons of choosing dichotomous or continuous measures without ever addressing the wisdom of this dichotomous choice. Yet this supposedly critical choice is based on a false-dilemma fallacy.

This fallacy is rooted in a failure to grasp a deceptively simple point: the most basic decision in measurement, the drawing of a boundary that establishes an equivalence-difference relationship, underlies *each and every level of measurement* that could possibly be used in constructing a scale. Indeed, all measures involve, first and foremost, classifications that distinguish between cases that are relatively similar to each other and relatively different from other cases in terms of some category. Understanding this point is critical to grasping why scholars do not have to weigh the virtues of dichotomous versus continuous measures and why, as Carl Hempel (1952: 54–57) argued, it is always preferable — whether it is attainable is another matter — to have more advanced, higher-level measures.

Put in different terms, measurement *is* quantification because it consists of assigning numbers to objects according to rules. Yet measurement is also necessarily qualitative, because each number, inasmuch as it is theoretically interpretable, can always be linked to a class of phenomena. Thus, the proper distinction to draw among scales concerns not whether the scales are qualitative (i.e., "of kind") or quantitative (i.e., "of degree") — efforts to distinguish between qualitative and quantitative scales lack meaning and are based on arbitrary choices[1] — but rather the mathematical properties of the relationship among the numbers. And, as a consequence, even if we should not strive to "replace qualitative distinctions by quantitative ones" (Cohen and Nagel 1934: 290) — inasmuch as quantitative distinctions are necessarily rooted in

FIGURE 3.1.  Dahl's Regime Property Space: An Adaptation
*Source:* Dahl (1971: 6–7).

qualitative ones, this advice does not make sense — we should strive to develop higher-level measures because they offer more information than lower-level measures.

With these basic points about measurement in mind, the following discussion seeks to show how this false-dilemma fallacy can be overcome. It focuses on Robert Dahl's (1971: 6–7) concept of political regime, disaggregated into the twin dimensions of participation and contestation (figure 3.1). Thus, it takes the choice of conceptual attributes used to define a political regime as a given. Moreover, the discussion is further circumscribed because it treats participation and contestation in fairly narrow terms, as involving the right of suffrage and the right to compete in elections respectively. But the point is not to offer a full assessment of how to measure political regimes. Rather, the purpose of the following discussion is to highlight how the introduction of thresholds, or cutoff points, generates categories that provide a foundation for increasingly more powerful scales of participation and contestation.

## 3.2. Disaggregate Measures:
## Building on Equivalence-Difference Relationships

### 3.2.1. Participation: The Right of Suffrage

The construction of a scale of participation that uses the right of suffrage as an indicator can take as its starting point a threshold that distinguishes cases that do not allow elections or do not recognize the right of suffrage from

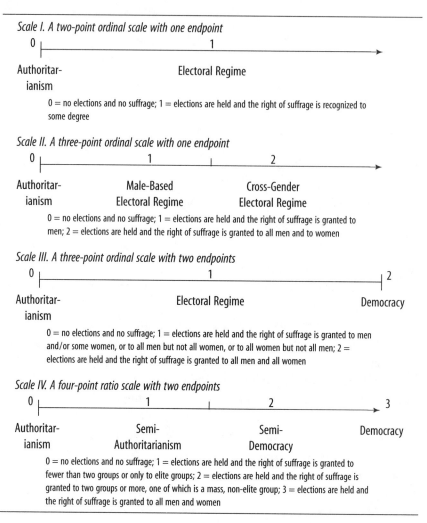

Scale I. A two-point ordinal scale with one endpoint

0 ——————————————————————— 1 ————————→

Authoritar-
ianism                              Electoral Regime

0 = no elections and no suffrage; 1 = elections are held and the right of suffrage is recognized to
some degree

Scale II. A three-point ordinal scale with one endpoint

0 ——————————— 1 ——————— 2 ————→

Authoritar-            Male-Based              Cross-Gender
ianism                Electoral Regime        Electoral Regime

0 = no elections and no suffrage; 1 = elections are held and the right of suffrage is granted to
men; 2 = elections are held and the right of suffrage is granted to all men and to women

Scale III. A three-point ordinal scale with two endpoints

0 ———————————————————— 1 ———————————— 2

Authoritar-                 Electoral Regime              Democracy
ianism

0 = no elections and no suffrage; 1 = elections are held and the right of suffrage is granted to men
and/or some women, or to all men but not all women, or to all women but not all men; 2 =
elections are held and the right of suffrage is granted to all men and all women

Scale IV. A four-point ratio scale with two endpoints

0 ——————————— 1 ——————— 2 ——————→ 3

Authoritar-           Semi-                 Semi-              Democracy
ianism               Authoritarianism       Democracy

0 = no elections and no suffrage; 1 = elections are held and the right of suffrage is granted to
fewer than two groups or only to elite groups; 2 = elections are held and the right of suffrage is
granted to two groups or more, one of which is a mass, non-elite group; 3 = elections are held and
the right of suffrage is granted to all men and women

FIGURE 3.2. Participation Scales

cases that allow elections and recognize the right of suffrage to some degree
(see scale I in figure 3.2). Note that this is not a simple dichotomy, in that it
includes information about order, and is also based on the identification of
an endpoint, the absence of the right of suffrage.[2] But this two-point ordinal
scale with an endpoint has a stark limitation: it relies on a definition *a con-
trario* (i.e., by contrast), and thus generates a residual category — "electoral
regime" — that does not differentiate among varieties of electoral regimes. It
is quite easy, however, to improve on this simple scale.

More-nuanced scales can be built by adding points to this ordinal scale. One way to do this is by identifying thresholds that subdivide the category of electoral regime. For example, by using universal male suffrage as a threshold, the category of electoral regime can be replaced by two, more-informative categories: "male-based electoral regime" and "cross-gender electoral regime." Another way to build a more discriminating scale is to add a second endpoint, the full presence of the right of suffrage.[3] In this case, the resulting scale is a closed scale, anchored at either endpoint by the categories of authoritarianism and democracy, electoral regime serving as an intermediate category. Thus, starting with an ordinal scale with just one endpoint, improvements are made by either subdividing the category of electoral regime or setting an upper bound to it (see scales II and III in figure 3.2).

These two basic strategies — building ordinal scales with either one or two endpoints — can be pushed further by introducing more thresholds and thus developing ordinal scales that include further information. Indeed, fairly sophisticated measures can be obtained using these relatively simple strategies. But neither strategy can be used to identify the threshold that marks a boundary between authoritarian and democratic levels of participation. This boundary has long figured prominently in theorizing about democratization and has a special status. Thus, the need for even more powerful scales is apparent.

The task of identifying a threshold separating authoritarian from democratic levels of participation can be articulated easily. What is needed is a new type of scale, one that involves not just ordered categories but, more demandingly, categories that are separated by *equal intervals of distance*. Or, more specifically, what is needed is the identification of a midpoint between the endpoints defined by the absence and full presence of the right of suffrage. The practical difficulties of identifying this threshold are significant, however.

These difficulties can be seen in a cursory review of just a few efforts to determine at what point the extent of the right of suffrage crosses from an authoritarian to a democratic level. On the low end are proposals that this threshold should be established at 25 or 30 percent of the adult population or, more precisely, when the proportion of adult males with the right to vote reaches 50 percent (Huntington 1991: 16; Boix 2003: 66) or 60 percent (Rueschemeyer, Stephens, and Stephens 1992: 303). On the high end are suggestions that the threshold should be set at 90 percent of all adults (Dahl 1971: 232–33, 246–48).[4] In light of these disparate views and the explicit claim by some authors that their choice of threshold is arbitrary (Vanhanen 2000: 257),[5] one might legitimately wonder whether it is possible to build a scale that distinguishes authoritarian from democratic levels of participation. But we do have some useful leads for dealing with this thorny problem.

First, the literature offers some guidance concerning the most vital issue: the theoretical grounds for making a decision about the location of the threshold that distinguishes authoritarian from democratic levels of participation. What is at stake in the extension of the right of suffrage is whether the views of groups likely to have conflicting interests are included or excluded from the political process (Dahl 1971: 28–29, 246–47; 1998: 76–78; Valenzuela 1985: 28–35; 2001: 251–56). Moreover, democratic theory provides good reasons for defining the threshold separating authoritarian from democratic levels of participation in terms of the extension of the right to vote to *two groups*, one of which must be a mass, nonelite group. These are important insights and they can be formalized in a fairly simple coding rule (see scale IV in figure 3.2).

Second, various attempts at measurement offer lessons regarding how this core insight might be further operationalized. In this regard, it is important to emphasize a shortcoming of the standard approach, which is to pinpoint the key threshold in terms of a fixed percentage of citizens who enjoy the right to vote. The problem is that such a landmark is unlikely to travel well across countries, for what is at stake is not just a certain percentage of potential adult voters or male adult voters, or even the extension of the right to vote to a certain percentage of the working class.[6] Indeed, cross-national variation in the structure of societies and the relative salience of nonclass cleavages will alter the precise percentage of enfranchisement that would guarantee that the right to vote has been extended to at least two groups, one of which is a mass, nonelite group. Thus, establishing equivalent indicators requires that we get beyond the commonly employed, yet deceptively simple, criterion of identifying a certain percentage of the adult population that can vote.[7]

### 3.2.2. Contestation: The Right to Compete

Measuring contestation, understood here in terms of the right to compete in elections, involves a distinct set of challenges, and responding adequately to these challenges is central to research on regimes. Contestation is the aspect of regimes that is at the heart of some of the most significant contemporary

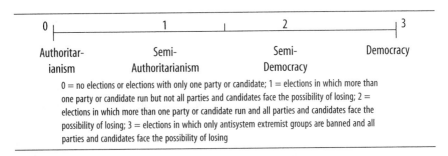

FIGURE 3.3. Contestation: A Four-Point Ratio Scale with Two Endpoints

political struggles. As formal and overt restrictions on the right of suffrage have become harder to sustain politically, variation in political regimes today appears to hinge increasingly on the rules and conditions under which actors compete for access to political power (Przeworski 1991: 10; Przeworski et al. 2000: 15–16).[8]

By moving directly to the task of constructing a scale of contestation with two endpoints, it is relatively easy to anchor the scale by defining the absence and full presence of contestation. On the one hand, the absence of the right to compete in elections is indicated by the lack of elections or, alternatively, by elections in which candidates from only one party can run.[9] On the other hand, the full presence of contestation is denoted by elections in which only antisystem extremist groups are banned.[10] However, building a scale of contestation that adds further information is a complicated task.

Some important insights can be drawn from the literature, especially with regard to a criterion for establishing the halfway point between these two endpoints. As various authors have stressed, the critical threshold that distinguishes authoritarian from democratic patterns of contestation hinges not only on parties and candidates losing elections but, more precisely, on the *possibility* of all parties and candidates losing elections.[11] This point clarifies what is theoretically at stake and offers a handy way to define coding rules (see figure 3.3). Moreover, by highlighting how measurement decisions ultimately rest on an assessment of a "nonevent" — usually framed as the possibility of an incumbent's electoral defeat that did not, in fact, transpire — it also offers a basis for distinguishing unproductive from fruitful attempts to measure contestation.[12]

An example of an unproductive proposal is one that seeks to pinpoint this key threshold in terms of the percentage of votes garnered by the winning party. Such a proposal fails because it simply does not capture the concept of interest, confusing competition with competitiveness (Sartori 1976: 218–19). In addition, such a proposal is likely to lead to frequent misclassifications, either by counting as competitive elections that are not or by counting as noncompetitive elections that actually are competitive.[13] In contrast, an example of a fruitful attempt to measure contestation is Giovanni Sartori's (1976: 192–201, 230–38, 283) distinction between systems with a "hegemonic party" that permits other parties to exist but only as "second class, licensed parties," thus foreclosing the possibility of an electoral loss by the hegemonic party, and a "predominant party system," where parties other than the predominant party exist and contest elections, yet, in spite of the possibility of winning elections, fail to defeat the incumbent party.[14] Thus, this clarification of what needs to be measured helps researchers avoid dead ends and identify contributions that provide a foundation that can be built on.[15]

These important leads notwithstanding, two important challenges remain. One concerns the basis for judging whether the possibility of a loss by incumbents exists. Adam Przeworski and his collaborators (2000: 23–28) offer a useful discussion of the difficulties of making coding decisions in the absence of clear observables, and their proposed coding rule for getting around this problem — the "alternation rule" — is a valuable point of reference. Yet it falls short of providing a solid basis for coding. Specifically, the proposal to use information in a retroactive manner gives more weight to the certainty of the information at hand than to the direct relevance of the information.[16] Indeed, it would probably be a mistake to use the indisputable evidence that the Institutional Revolutionary Party relinquished power in Mexico in 2000 to infer that it was equally willing to give up power in the past, despite obvious evidence to the contrary, such as the reports of fraud in 1988. Thus, with regard to the central issue of assessing whether the possibility of a loss by incumbents exists, further work is needed to establish criteria for systematically using all the available information and to weigh the reliability of this information.

A second challenge concerns the development of a scale of contestation that adequately distinguishes among degrees of contestation that lie on the democratic side of the threshold separating authoritarian from democratic levels of contestation. This is a significant gap in current research. After all, existing scales either simply distinguish contested from noncontested elections (Przeworski et al. 2000: 28–29) or, if they go further, introduce distinctions only among cases with nondemocratic forms of contestation (Sartori 1976: 283; Hermet 1982: 27–29). Yet the need for such nuanced measures is suggested by the multiple ways in which contestation can be restricted short of totally preventing the possibility of an electoral loss by incumbents. Some restrictions operate through legal restrictions on parties and candidates, including bans on the formation of parties or on their right to compete in elections, bans on certain classes of candidates (e.g., based on class, racial, or gender characteristics), and bans on specific candidates. Others manifest themselves in failures by the state to guarantee the conditions for contested elections, such as the physical safety of candidates and their right to campaign throughout the entire territory of a country. All these restrictions undercut the democratic principle that all citizens should be eligible to be both electors and candidates and, in turn, that all candidates should have the opportunity to reach voters with their message and run for office on a level playing field. Thus, the implications of these restrictions for a scale of contestation cannot be taken lightly.

The range of variation produced by these restrictions is unlikely to fit easily in the category of "semidemocratic" contestation (see figure 3.3). For example, the banning of the Communist party in Chile in the late 1940s and early 1950s was different in scope from the banning of the Peronist party in Argentina and of APRA (American Popular Revolutionary Alliance) in Peru in many elections from the 1930s through the 1960s. Likewise, the assassination of presidential front-runners, such as Galán in Colombia in 1989 or Colosio in Mexico in 1994, had an impact different from the assassination of party activists. To capture such distinctions, a scale with further thresholds would have to be constructed. Yet how such new thresholds might be best established remains largely an unexplored matter.[17]

In sum, the development of scales of participation and contestation hinges on complex methodological choices, many of which can be illuminated by an established theoretical literature and many of which remain to be addressed in future work. The tasks at hand are demanding, but the pitfalls of shortcuts, usually associated with the identification of an easily observable quantitative milestone, are also apparent. Unless the methodological choices discussed here are consciously confronted and each decision is duly justified, one of the most basic goals of the social sciences—the elaboration of theoretically meaningful and systematic descriptions—will not be fulfilled.

## 3.3. Aggregate Measures:
## Adding Part-Whole Relationships to the Picture

Measurement can involve, in addition to the construction of scales, as those just discussed, the creation of indices, that is, aggregate measures that combine multiple measures. The reason for constructing an index is straightforward. When the concept being measured has multiple attributes, and especially inasmuch as these attributes are measured with higher-level scales, it is simply hard to develop a composite measure in a clear and tractable manner without an index. Indeed, the limits of typologies, a basic tool in qualitative research that is useful for thinking about concepts with two conceptual attributes and low-level measures, are rapidly reached and more powerful quantitative tools are called for.[18]

The construction of indices that can be used to distinguish democracies from nondemocracies introduces a new complication into the discussion of the measurement of political regimes. The development of democracy indices, as seen in chapter 2, frequently, but not always, involves the choice of an aggregation rule (see section 2.3). Yet, if the goal is to interpret the index in terms of the concept of democracy, such an index must include a threshold that separates countries that deserve to be characterized as democracies from those that do not deserve such a label and, for this reason, the use of a theoretically derived aggregation rule is inevitable. The ability to interpret an index in terms of certain concepts depends on the vertical relationships between a concept and its conceptual attributes as well as any interactions among conceptual attributes that take a concept as their point of reference, and not on the horizontal relationships among indicators (see figure 3.4). In other words, the issue at stake is not a matter of scalability, that is, whether the multiple indicators used to measure a concept vary in a parallel or otherwise orderly fashion. And because of this, the construction of an index cannot be based solely on an empirical analysis of the disaggregate data using scaling techniques. Indeed, such a procedure would amount to putting the statistical cart before the theoretical horse.

The choice of aggregation rule hinges on the understanding of what the parts into which a concept has been disaggregated contribute to the whole, that is, the way in which the impact of a concept's multiple indicators on the concept itself is theorized. Specifically, the analyst must decide (1) whether a high score on one indicator is dragged down or is insulated from the low

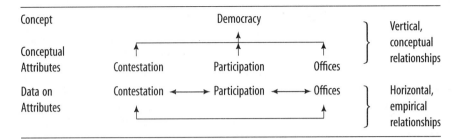

FIGURE 3.4. Conceptual and Empirical Relationships

score on another indicator; and (2) whether a high score on one indicator can compensate or make up for a low score on another indicator. These choices — whether the relationship across indicators is interactive or noninteractive, and compensatory or noncompensatory — have a big effect on the index, determining whether the positive or negative scores of each individual indicator are assigned greater or lesser weight. Thus, they must be justified in terms of the theoretical status of each conceptual attribute. Otherwise, even if an index is constructed using scales that distinguish authoritarian from democratic patterns, the index cannot be interpreted in terms of the concept of democracy using, as a rule of thumb, the middle point of an index (0.5 on a 0.0–1.0 index scale).

To give an example, if the attributes of a concept are considered to have an interactive, noncompensatory relationship — as Dahl (1971: 2) implicitly posits when he argues that competition and participation are necessary conditions of democracy — the choice of the corresponding aggregation rule would be multiplication. And if this aggregation rule is applied to conceptual attributes measured with scales designed with a midpoint that distinguishes authoritarian from democratic patterns of competition and participation, the result would be an index with a middle point that can be interpreted as the threshold separating democracies from nondemocracies (see the row that starts with "Interactive, noncompensatory" in table 3.1). At the same time, it is hard to overemphasize how the choice of aggregation rule can make a big difference and that other theoretical assumptions and associated aggregation rules would yield quite different index values (compare the row that starts with "Interactive, noncompensatory" to other rows in table 3.1). In short, the inevitable question about the theoretical status of each conceptual attribute is a matter of critical importance in the interpretation of an index and

TABLE 3.1.  *Conceptual Relationships, Aggregation Rules, and Index Values*

| Relationships among conceptual attributes | Aggregation rule | Index value[a] | | | | |
|---|---|---|---|---|---|---|
| | | Data: 0.0, 0.5, 1.0 | Data: 0.5, 0.5, 1.0 | Data: 0.5, 1.0, 1.0 | Data: 0.75, 1.0, 1.0 | Data: 1.0, 1.0, 1.0 |
| Interactive, noncompensatory | Multiplication | 0.00 | 0.25 | 0.50 | 0.75 | 1.00 |
| Noninteractive, noncompensatory | Minimum | 0.00 | 0.50 | 0.50 | 0.75 | 1.00 |
| Interactive, partially compensatory | Geometric mean | 0.00 | 0.63 | 0.79 | 0.91 | 1.00 |
| Noninteractive, partially compensatory | Arithmetic mean | 0.50 | 0.66 | 0.83 | 0.92 | 1.00 |
| Noninteractive, compensatory | Maximum | 1.00 | 1.00 | 1.00 | 1.00 | 1.00 |

*Note:* Conceptual attributes that are characterized by an interactive, noncompensatory relationship are conventionally labeled "necessary conditions."

[a] The index values are calculated using disaggregate data for three attributes measured using 0–1 scales with two endpoints and a halfway point that distinguishes authoritarian from democratic patterns.

thus deserves to be addressed with all deliberate care in the initial step of index construction, the act of concept formation.

As important as the choice of aggregation rule is to the interpretation of indices in terms of the concept of democracy, existing efforts to develop measures of democracy have rarely addressed this issue with much care. One exception is the index created by Przeworski and his collaborators (2000: ch. 1). This index is consciously created to distinguish democracies from nondemocracies by focusing on a small number of attributes that are considered necessary conditions of democracy, by creating dichotomous scales designed to distinguish democratic from nondemocratic patterns, and by selecting an aggregation rule — multiplication — that corresponds to the theory that each conceptual attribute being aggregated is a necessary condition of democracy. But other indices, which encompass more attributes and/or rely on higher-level scales, do not yield indices interpretable in terms of the concept of democracy.

Probably most problematic among all these indices is the Freedom House political rights index (Freedom House 2007a). In this case, the measures that are aggregated are based on five-point ordinal scales that were not designed with the explicit intent of distinguishing democratic from nondemocratic patterns. Moreover, the choice of addition as the rule of aggregation implies that the index treats attributes such as the determination of the head of government, and the choice of members of the national legislature, through free and fair elections as nonnecessary conditions, a view that runs contrary to a large body of democratic theory.[19] But the problems are quite generalized and affect most available indices. Thus, the development of indices, especially ones that include a considerable number of conceptual attributes and rely on high-level scales, which can be interpreted in terms of the concept of democracy, remains a key challenge.

## 3.4. Conclusion

Abraham Kaplan (1964: 24–25) warned about "the myth of methodology," the view that "the most serious difficulties which confront behavioral sciences are 'methodological,' " and he associated this myth with an unhealthy diversion of efforts from substantive to methodological problems. This warning may, in many circumstances, be relevant, and the statement that "methodology is very far from being a sufficient condition for scientific achievement" is certainly accurate (Kaplan 1964: 24). There is plenty of methodologically sophisticated work that is substantively flat and offers superficial, trivial results. But Kaplan's (1964: 24) admonition to resist "the notion that the cultivation of methodology is . . . necessary . . . for successful scientific endeavor" goes too far. Indeed, good research depends on the marriage of methodological and substantive knowledge and, thus, one of the necessary conditions for scientific progress is the availability and proper use of adequate methodological tools.

The implications of the methodological questions addressed in this chapter are quite direct, affecting how we describe the world, and hence the questions we choose to ask, and the way we learn about these questions. For a long time, the literature on regimes and democracy has insisted that scholars face a choice between analyzing democratization with dichotomous or continuous measures. And this choice has led to the development of two literatures that do not talk to each other very much. Yet this choice is a false dilemma that, with due attention to certain methodological issues, can be overcome. Although there is merit to the claim that the transition from an authoritarian to a democratic regime is distinctive and marks a kind of political quantum leap, acknowledging this point does not require that democracy be treated as a dichotomous variable. Rather, the insight behind this notion of a quantum leap can be retained at the same time that we develop more nuanced measures that allow us to analyze democratization as a process consisting of multiple thresholds. To do this, however, it is critical to remember that measurement should not be delinked from the task of defining, in an organized manner, the meaning of the concept to be measured or, in other words, that measurement depends on concept formation.

# FOUR

# Producing and Validating Political Data

*The Case of the Electoral Democracy Index*

..................................................................................................................

This chapter seeks to contribute to the ongoing effort to produce data on politics by focusing on the electoral democracy index (EDI), a new index developed to study Latin American countries. The EDI, created by the author in collaboration with Jay Verkuilen for the United Nations Development Programme (UNDP), and introduced in the UNDP's report *Democracy in Latin America* (UNDP 2004a: 207–13; 2004b: 21–33), is largely an outgrowth of the assessment of democracy indices provided in chapter 2. That is, the EDI is a measuring instrument that takes previous research as a point of reference and seeks to implement the lessons drawn from existing work on the measurement of democracy, trying to retain insights developed by scholars who have sought to measure democracy and to introduce various improvements.

The chief goal of this chapter is to consider the validity of the EDI. Although discussions of types of validity can be cumbersome, validity is a simple concept. In the context of measurement, it refers to whether a measure actually measures the concept it is intended to measure. But validating a measure is a complex task. Data should be validated by reference to theory and empirical tests. Moreover, inasmuch as multiple measures of the same concept are available, validation should not rely solely on an internal analysis, that is, a self-referential analysis focused strictly on the measure under consideration (the EDI in this analysis). In addition, it should be based on an external analysis, that is, a comparison between the measure under consideration and other measures. After all, if more than one measure of a certain concept is available, a validity assessment is essentially a matter of ascertaining which of these measures does a better job of measuring the concept. In short, the validation of measures is a difficult, multifaceted task.

The chapter is divided into three main sections. The first section discusses the measuring instrument used to produce the EDI and focuses on three core features: its conceptual attributes, measurement scales, and aggregation rule. The theoretical justification for the key choices that go into the making of the EDI is addressed, and the implication of a test of the robustness of various aggregation rules is considered.[1] In different ways, the EDI is shown to be a measure that adequately corresponds to the theory behind the concept of electoral democracy, that this theory is strong enough to justify the design of the measuring instrument used to produce the EDI and, therefore, that the EDI is theoretically interpretable as a measure of electoral democracy.

In the second section, the EDI is compared to other democracy indices. This analysis places an overwhelming emphasis on empirical tests, a common feature of the literature on democracy indices. But the validation methodology departs from the standard practice of simply reporting correlations among aggregate measures of democracy and interpreting high correlations as evidence of validity. The standard test is flawed, among other reasons, because its assumption that the same concept is being measured with different methodologies does not hold. In contrast to standard practice, the reported tests focus on distinct features of the measuring instruments, draw attention to differences in the concept being measured, and, where possible, use disaggregate data. These tests demonstrate that, contrary to current views, the concept measured with different measuring instruments differs considerably and that these differences are reflected in the measures that are produced. But the analysis shows not only that the various indices are different, but also that some, including the EDI, are more valid than others.

The third section addresses the role of coders. This is an essential feature of the way in which the EDI is produced, as it is of many other measures of democracy, and it introduces an important potential source of measurement error. Nonetheless, the burden placed on coders varies considerably across indices. It is not possible to test the impact of this variable burden, due to a lack of data. Thus, this analysis is merely suggestive. Nevertheless, there are good reasons to suspect that some indices are more susceptible than others to coder-induced error and to argue that the EDI avoids some of the problems of other indices.

## 4.1. The Electoral Democracy Index

Any assessment of the validity of measures should include a consideration of the theoretical justification for the choices that go into the making of a measuring instrument. Testing is an essential part of validation. Indeed, as shown in this and the next section, testing is as integral to an evaluation of measures as it is to causal assessment. It is also important to consider not just how a measuring instrument is designed but how it is used, a matter discussed in the third section, on the role of coders. However, before moving on to those matters, it is crucial to consider the theoretical basis for the choices made regarding, at the very least, three central features of a measuring instrument: its conceptual attributes, measurement scales, and aggregation procedure (see chapter 2). Thus, as a first step in the evaluation of the EDI, this section discusses what decisions went into the design of the EDI and why these decisions were made.

### 4.1.1. Conceptual Attributes

The EDI consists of four conceptual attributes: the right to vote, clean elections, free elections, and elected public offices. These attributes refer to the right of citizens to vote in elections, to cast a vote free of pressures and to have that vote counted accurately, to run for office, and to elect the holders of all main public offices (see figure 4.1). Thus, they tap into distinct aspects of a broad process and highlight the specific roles of voters, candidates, and elected governments.

The choice of attributes included and excluded from the EDI rests on a well-developed corpus of theory on democracy (Schumpeter 1942: 240–73; Rokkan et al. 1970: ch. 4; Dahl 1989: chs. 8 and 9; Sartori 1987a: 184–85; Przeworski et al. 2000: 28–29, 57; O'Donnell 2001: 10, 12). This theoretical work provides a strong basis for understanding the concept of electoral democracy as referring to procedures pertaining to the access to state offices. And it makes a case for including each of the four conceptual attributes as parts of the concept of electoral democracy and, furthermore, for considering them as necessary conditions of electoral democracy.

The exclusion of other attributes also has a theoretical basis. First, because the concept of electoral democracy is understood as referring to procedures pertaining to access to state offices, procedures relevant to other

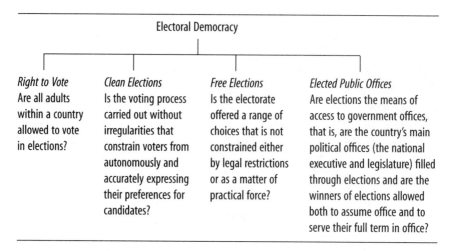

FIGURE 4.1.  The Four Conceptual Attributes of Electoral Democracy

aspects of the state, such as corruption in decision making, are excluded. Likewise, outcomes of state action, such as the torture of citizens by state agents and respect for property rights or poverty rates, are excluded. Second, to facilitate the index's interpretation, a series of aspects that do pertain to access to state offices are also excluded. Thus, issues that have an unclear implication for the democraticness of the procedures regulating access to state offices, such as the rules for allocating seats (the proportional vs. majoritarian rules distinction) and the mode of election of the chief executive officer (the presidentialism vs. parliamentarism distinction), are not included. Even issues that have a clear implication for the democraticness of the procedures regulating access to state offices were excluded, either if they are not necessary conditions of electoral democracy, such as party internal democracy, or if they are less the state's responsibility to uphold than a reflection of citizens' actions, such as voter turnout. In short, in addition to the inclusion and exclusion of conceptual attributes on theoretical grounds, to enhance the interpretability of the index in theoretical terms, the design of the EDI puts a premium on theoretical tractability.

### 4.1.2. Measurement Scales

The measurement of the EDI's four conceptual attributes relies on three five-point ordinal scales, and one three-point ordinal scale, with endpoints (see table 4.1),[2] which, for the purposes of aggregation, are normalized, that is, translated into a common metric, through a simple linear norming to the unit interval (normed value = raw value / maximum raw value).

The design of the measurement scales is driven, first, by the imperative to ensure that what are, in effect, operational definitions of the EDI's conceptual attributes do not surreptitiously drop some of the content of these conceptual attributes or add indicators of some extraneous concept. After all, the point of offering a theoretically based rationale for including certain conceptual attributes in an index, and excluding other attributes from an index, is lost when suitable empirical indicators for all these attributes are not developed. Thus, to ensure that the design of scales does not undermine the theoretical foundation for the EDI, the endpoints of each scale are defined in such a way as to capture the full range of variation of each attribute, and each point on the scale is defined in terms that are tightly linked to the corresponding conceptual attribute.

The choice of metric involves a more complex matter. Unfortunately, nearly any option would be somewhat tentative; there is, as yet, no widely accepted unit of electoral democracy comparable to units such as kilogram or dollar. Moreover, a major objection is likely to be that the scales are simply ordinal scales and that norming into the unit interval is a case of inadmissible "meaningless" mathematics. However, this choice of normalization procedure is justifiable. All the scales have theoretically meaningful endpoints, with 0 indicating a total lack of the property and 1 indicating full possession of the property. For example, a case with right to vote = 0 has no suffrage at all, while a case with right to vote = 1 after norming has complete adult suffrage, the theoretically established standard. Thus, the problem of distance relates only to the points between the endpoints. Yet, to meet this concern, the scales were constructed by initially determining theoretically meaningful endpoints and then identifying distinct scale values as far apart conceptually as possible, starting with the midpoint.[3] Though the proposed metric is a matter calling for further discussion, it is defensible.

### 4.1.3. Aggregation

Finally, in aggregating the EDI's four conceptual attributes, each attribute is held to be a necessary condition — in the terminology introduced in chapter 3 (see section 3.3), the relationship across indicators is interactive and

*Right to Vote.* The component responds to the question whether all adults within a country are allowed to vote in elections. Beyond the holding of elections, the measure does not include procedures that might hamper the effective use of the right to vote, such as access to the polls.

0 = no election is held to install the government;
1 = only some men have the right to vote (there are restrictions related to property, gender, and literacy);
2 = most men enjoy the right to vote (there are restrictions related to gender and literacy);
3 = most men and most women enjoy the right to vote (there are restrictions related to literacy);
4 = the right to vote is universally recognized. However, even in countries with universal suffrage some restrictions may exist, affecting groups such as the military, the police, the clergy, foreign residents, and citizens living abroad.

*Clean Elections.* This component responds to the question whether the voting process is carried out without irregularities that constrain voters from autonomously and accurately expressing their preferences for candidates. It does not include issues related to the competitiveness of the elections or even if the winner of an election is allowed to assume office and if all the offices are elected.

0 = major irregularities in the voting process that have a determinative effect on the result of elections (e.g., alteration in the election for the national executive and/or the balance of power in parliament);
1 = significant irregularities in the voting process (e.g., intimidation of voters, violence against voters, electoral fraud), which do not, however, have a determinative effect on the result of elections;
2 = lack of significant irregularities in the voting process (e.g., elections that might include "technical" irregularities but not any systematic bias of considerable weight).

*Free Elections.* This component responds to the question whether the electorate is offered a range of choices that is not constrained either by legal restrictions or as a matter of practical force. The measure does not include factors that affect the ability of parties and candidates to compete in equality of conditions, such as public financing, access to the mass media, and the use of public resources.

0 = single party system;
1 = ban on major party;
2 = ban on minor party;
3 = restrictions of a legal or practical nature that significantly affect the ability of potential candidates to run for office and/or the formation of political parties (e.g., systematic assassinations and intimidation of candidates, ban on popular candidates, legal or practical restrictions that prevent the formation of parties or that lead parties to boycott the elections);
4 = essentially unrestricted conditions for the presentation of candidates and the formation of parties.

*Elected Public Offices.* This component responds to the question whether elections are the means of access to government offices, that is, whether the country's main political offices (i.e., the national executive and legislature) are filled through elections and the winners of elections are allowed both to assume office and serve their full term in office. When elected officeholders are removed, the form of removal and selection of a replacement is considered.

0 = none of the main political offices are filled through elections, or all of the elected officeholders are forcefully displaced from office and replaced by unconstitutional rulers;
1= a few political offices are filled by winners of elections, or most of the elected office holders are forcefully displaced from office and replaced by unconstitutional rulers;
2 = the president or the parliament is not elected; or, if elected, they are forcefully displaced from office and replaced by unconstitutional rulers;
3 = the president or the parliament is elected, but the president is displaced from office and/or replaced by semiconstitutional means; or a significant number of parliamentarians are not elected or, if they were elected, are forcefully displaced from office;
4 = all of the main political offices are filled by elections, and none of the elected officeholders are displaced from office unless their removal from office and their replacement are based on strictly constitutional grounds.

noncompensatory. Hence, the EDI's aggregation rule relies on a simple rule, the multiplication of the values of all four attributes:

EDI = Right to Vote × Clean Elections ×
Free Elections × Elected Public Offices[4]

Once again, theory offers a basis for this key feature of the EDI. Specifically, the core insight used in justifying this aggregation rule is the well-established view that the EDI's four attributes are parts that constitute a system by virtue of the way in which they combine together and, moreover, that these four attributes are so fundamental that the absence of any one would simply render the system nondemocratic. For example, the fact that Soviet-type systems had elections with full suffrage was meaningless, from the perspective of democracy, because the electorate did not have a choice among alternative candidates. As noted, the four attributes of the EDI are posited as individually necessary conditions,[5] which means that these attributes interact with each other and cannot substitute for each other.

Going beyond theoretical arguments, a test of the robustness of various aggregation rules shows that there is some difference in the means of the EDI when it is calculated with different aggregation rules. The arithmetic and geometric means of the EDI's four attributes have means of 0.93 and 0.92, respectively. In contrast, the minimum value and the product (the selected operator) of the EDI's four attributes have means of 0.86 and 0.84, respectively. But this difference is not large. Moreover, the results also show that no matter which rule is used, the rank correlations are all very high (0.99–1.00), indicating that the general ordering of cases is preserved. Thus, this test shows that the EDI is relatively robust to modifications in the aggregation rule, a fact that adds more credibility to the theoretical choice of aggregation rule.[6]

### 4.1.4. Conclusions

A case can be made, thus, that the EDI is a theoretically meaningful measure of electoral democracy.[7] Theory has a key role in justifying the choice of conceptual attributes. Thereafter, the theoretical content of the concept is not lost or contaminated through the way it is operationalized in each measurement scale. Finally, theory serves to justify the way the relationship among conceptual attributes is formulated. In addition, the empirical test of the robustness of the EDI to changes in aggregation rule shows that the theoretical assumptions made in the selection of the aggregation rule do not have large consequences, which suggests that the strength of the theory is sufficient to justify the choice of aggregation rule.

This self-contained, internal analysis is critical but limited. It is critical because it shows that the measures produced with this measuring instrument adequately correspond with the theory of the concept of electoral democracy and that this theory is relatively strong. Indeed, in the absence of a considerable degree of confidence that the EDI is theoretically interpretable as a measure of electoral democracy, there would be little point in proceeding further with the discussion. But this analysis is also limited, because it does not provide an external perspective on the EDI, as is afforded by a comparison of the EDI to other measures of democracy. Such comparisons are important, in that they offer the opportunity for more testing than is possible within the context of an internal analysis. As the next section shows, such tests add texture and nuance to the assessment of the EDI.

## 4.2. The Electoral Democracy Index in Comparative Perspective

The comparison among measures produced with different measuring instruments is frequently a key aspect of the validation of data. After all, inasmuch as multiple measures of a concept are available, validity is a relative matter. That is, the question is not just, Is a certain measure valid? but, rather, the more pointed query, Is a certain measure more valid than others, and hence preferable to others?

The latter, comparative question is of considerable relevance in the context of a discussion of the concept of democracy, given that many alternative measures of democracy have been proposed. But the literature on the measurement of democracy still has not addressed this question appropriately. Comparisons among alternative measures have increasingly been made and have frequently included tests. Nonetheless, these tests shed little light on the core issue of the relative validity of alternative measures. Indeed, the choice of test used in such comparisons has rarely been well justified, and the results of such tests have routinely been misinterpreted.

The most common test used in validations of democracy indices has been a simple correlation among aggregate measures, and the usual interpretation of this test has been that high correlations are evidence of validity.[8] Hence, efforts to test the validity of measures of democracy make a basic assumption: that the *same concept* is being measured with *different methods* and that a convergent validation test is thus called for (Campbell and Fiske 1959). But a quick comparison of some common democracy indices reveals that they are not measuring the same thing (see table 4.2).[9] The measuring instruments used to produce these measures of democracy differ considerably in terms of their conceptual attributes. They also differ in terms of the operational definitions used in their measurement scales and the choice of aggregation rule, two other key aspects that are closely connected to the conceptual content of a measuring instrument. Thus, whether or not the same label "democracy" is appended to these measures, there are important differences across the indices in terms of what they are measuring.

The degree of convergence among measures is also not always very high and robust. The correlations among indices vary from a low of 0.494 to a high of 0.755 (see table 4.3).[10] These results actually make sense in light of the mix of similarities and differences of these indices' conceptual attributes, measurement scales, and aggregation rules. That is, one would not expect these measures to converge, the (implicit) hypothesis underlying the usual interpretation of high correlations as evidence of validity, but rather expect only a partial convergence. But these results also draw attention to the limitations of this standard test — a correlation of aggregate scores interpreted as a test of convergence — as a means of validation. Because the compared measures of democracy are produced with different methodologies but the concepts being measured are partly similar and partly different, such a test simply does not serve to assess the validity of these measures of democracy. The test reported in table 4.3 is at best inconclusive and certainly offers no basis for determining whether a certain measure is preferable to others.

Seeking to overcome the shortcoming of the standard test used in validations of democracy indices, this section proposes a different approach that, within the limits set by data availability, relies on tests that focus on the distinct features of measuring instruments. Most broadly, the analysis highlights differences in the design of measuring instruments and hence explores the association between these differences and differences — rather than similarities — in the measures produced with various measuring instruments. And, more specifically, the analysis focuses on the key features of measuring instruments — the conceptual attributes, measurement scales, and aggregation rule — and seeks to estimate and interpret their impact on the strictness, and discriminating power, of measuring instruments.

TABLE 4.2. *Overview of the Electoral Democracy Index and Other Democracy Indices*

| Name of index | Conceptual attributes | Measurement scales | | Aggregation rule |
|---|---|---|---|---|
| | | Lowest score description | Highest score description | |
| Electoral Democracy Index (EDI) | Right to vote | • No election is held to install the government. | • The right to vote is universally recognized. | Multiplication |
| | Clean elections | • Major irregularities in the voting process that have a determinative effect on the result of elections. | • Lack of significant irregularities is found in the voting process. | |
| | Free elections | • Single party system. | • Essentially unrestricted conditions exist for the presentation of candidates and the formation of parties. | |
| | Elected public offices | • None of the main political offices are filled through elections, or all of the elected office holders are forcefully displaced from office and replaced by unconstitutional rulers. | • All of the main political offices are filled by elections and none of elected officeholders are displaced from office unless their removal from office and their replacement are based on strictly constitutional grounds. | |
| Consolidation of Democracy Index (Schneider and Schmitter 2004a, 2004b) | Parties that challenge the constitution | — | • No significant political party advocates major change in the existing constitution. | Addition[a] |
| | Regular elections and respect for electoral outcomes | — | • Regular elections are held, and their outcomes are respected by those in position of public authority and major or opposition parties. | |
| | Free and fair elections | — | • Elections have been free and fair. | |
| | Acceptance of electoral conditions | — | • No significant parties or groups reject previous electoral conditions. | |
| | Electoral volatility | — | • Electoral volatility has diminished significantly. | |

| | | | Aggregation |
|---|---|---|---|
| Nonelected veto group within country | — | Elected officials and representatives are not constrained in their behavior by non-elected veto groups within the country. | |
| Alternation in power (first time) | — | A first rotation-in-power or significant shift in alliances of parties has occurred within the rules already established. | |
| Alternation in power (second time) | — | A second rotation-in-power or significant shift in alliances of parties has occurred within the rules already established. | |
| Agreement on association formation and behavior | — | Agreement, formal and informal, has been reached on the rules governing the association formation and behavior. | |
| Agreement on executive format | — | Agreement, formal and informal, has been reached on the rules governing the executive format. | |
| Agreement on territorial division of competencies | — | Agreement, formal and informal, has been reached on the rules governing the territorial division of competencies. | |
| Agreement on rules of ownership and access to media | — | Agreement, formal and informal, has been reached on the rules governing the rules of ownership and access to mass media. | |
| Freedom House Political Rights (Piano and Puddington 2005)[b] | | | Addition, followed by collapsing of variation (from 40 to 7 points) by proportional segments |
| Free and fair elections for head of state and/or head of government | — | The head of state and/or head of government or other chief authority are elected through free and fair elections. | |
| Free and fair elections for legislative representatives | — | Legislative representatives elected through free and fair elections. | |

*continued*

TABLE 4.2. *Continued*

| | | Measurement scales | | |
|---|---|---|---|---|
| Name of index | Conceptual attributes | Lowest score description | Highest score description | Aggregation rule |
| | Fair electoral laws, equal campaigning opportunities, fair polling, and honest tabulation of ballots | — | • There are fair electoral laws, equal campaigning opportunities, fair polling, and honest tabulation of ballots. | |
| | Right to organize parties | — | • People have the right to organize in different political parties or other competitive political groupings of their choice, and the system is open to the rise and fall of these competing parties or groupings. | |
| | Opposition power and possibilities | — | • There is a significant opposition vote, de facto opposition power, and a realistic possibility for the opposition to increase its support or gain power through elections. | |
| | Impact of unelected actors on people's political choices | — | • People's political choices are free from domination by the military, foreign powers, totalitarian parties, religious hierarchies, economic oligarchies, or any other powerful group. | |
| | Rights of cultural, ethnic, religious, and other minority groups | — | • Cultural, ethnic, religious, and other minority groups have reasonable self-determination, self-government, autonomy, or participation through informal consensus in the decision-making process. | |

| | | | |
|---|---|---|---|
| Impact of unelected actors on government policies | — | • Freely elected representatives determine the policies of the government. | Multiplication, followed by collapsing of all intermediary points to 1 point |
| Government corruption | — | • The government is free from pervasive corruption. | |
| Government accountability and transparency | — | • The government is accountable to the electorate between elections, and operates with openness and transparency. | |
| Latin American Democracies (Mainwaring, Brinks, and Pérez-Liñán 2007) Elections for the legislature and the executive | • The head of government or the legislature is not elected; the government uses its resources (patronage, repression, or a combination of both) to ensure electoral victory; or the government makes it impossible for a wide gamut of parties to compete (or if they do compete, to take office) through fraud, manipulation, or outright repression. | • The head of government and the legislature are chosen in free and fair elections. | |
| Franchise | • A large part of the adult population is disenfranchised on ethnic, class, gender, or educational grounds in ways that are likely to prevent very different electoral outcomes (or so it is widely believed), are unusually exclusionary for that historical period, or trigger mass social protests. | • The franchise is broad compared to other countries in the same historical period, and disenfranchised social categories are not seen as politically excluded groups with distinctive electoral preferences. | |
| Civil liberties | • There are gross human rights violations or censorship against opposition media occuring systematically, or political parties are not free to organize—i.e., most major parties | • Violations of human rights are uncommon, parties are free to organize, and the government respects constitutional guarantees. | |

*continued*

TABLE 4.2. *Continued*

| Name of index | Conceptual attributes | Measurement scales | | Aggregation rule |
|---|---|---|---|---|
| | | Lowest score description | Highest score description | |
| | Civilian control | are banned, just a single party is allowed to exist, or a few parties are tightly controlled by the government.<br>• Military leaders or the military as an institution openly dominates major policy areas not strictly related to the armed forces, or the elected head of government is a puppet, such that the electoral process does not really determine who governs. | • Military leaders and the military as an institution have negligible or minor influence in policies other than military policy, and their preferences do not substantively affect the chances of presidential candidates. | |
| Polity IV–Democracy (Marshall and Jaggers 2005)[c] | Competitiveness of executive recruitment | • Dual executives rule in which one is chosen by hereditary succession, the other by competitive election. Such rule is also used for transitional arrangements between selection (ascription and/or designation) and competitive election. | • Chief executives are typically chosen in or through competitive elections matching two or more major parties or candidates. (Elections may be popular or by an elected assembly.) | Addition (of weighted scores)[d] |
| | Openness of executive recruitment | — | • Chief executives are chosen by elite designation, competitive election, or transitional arrangements between designation and election; or hereditary succession plus electoral selection of an effective chief minister. | |
| | Executive constraints | • Intermediate category between "There are some real but limited restraints on the executive" and "The executive has more effective | • Accountability groups have effective authority equal to or greater than the executive in most areas of activity. | |

| | | | Multiplication |
|---|---|---|---|
| Competitiveness of political participation | authority than any accountability group but is subject to substantial constraints by them." <br> • Polities with parochial or ethnic-based political factions regularly compete for political influence in order to promote particularist agendas and favor group members to the detriment of common, secular, or cross-cutting agendas. | • There are relatively stable and enduring political groups that compete for political influence at the national level. | |
| Political Regimes Classification (Przeworski, Alvarez, Cheibub and Limongi 2000: ch. 1, as updated by Cheibub and Gandhi 2004) Contestation | — | • There is more than one party, understood as an independent list of candidates, and the opposition has a real possibility of winning elections and assuming office. | |
| Election executive | — | • The chief executive is directly or indirectly (if the electors are themselves elected) elected in popular elections and is responsible only directly to voters or to a legislature elected by voters. | |
| Election legislature | — | • The legislature is elected. | |

*Note:* — = no descriptive text is provided.

[a] Though Schneider and Schmitter discuss another index of consolidation of democracy, the focus here is on their simpler scale that relies on the sum of the scores of twelve attributes (Schneider and Schmitter 2004a: 68, 81–86).

[b] Freedom House does not offer any specific language to describe the five-point scales of its Political Rights index. Thus, its discussion of each conceptual attribute is used to describe the highest possible score. The Freedom House criteria have changed over the years; the criteria discussed here correspond to those used by Freedom House in its index for 2005.

[c] Though the Polity scales have more points, these are the only ones used for the purpose of calculating the Polity IV-Democracy index. In some cases, the lowest point in scales used for the Polity IV-Democracy index correspond to intermediate categories.

[d] The one exception is that the score received on "competitiveness of executive recruitment" determines whether the attribute "openness of executive recruitment" is included in the index.

TABLE 4.3. *Pearson Correlations of Five Democracy Indices, 1990–2000*

| | Electoral Democracy Index (EDI) | Consolidation of Democracy Index | Freedom House Political Rights | Latin American Democracies | Polity IV– Democracy |
|---|---|---|---|---|---|
| Electoral Democracy Index (EDI) | 1.000 (198) | | | | |
| Consolidation of Democracy Index | 0.704 (99) | 1.000 (99) | | | |
| Freedom House Political Rights | 0.494 (198) | 0.571 (99) | 1.000 (198) | | |
| Latin American Democracies | 0.596 (198) | 0.601 (99) | 0.735 (198) | 1.000 (198) | |
| Polity IV– Democracy | 0.496 (197) | 0.749 (98) | 0.755 (197) | 0.676 (197) | 1.000 (197) |

*Note:* All correlations are significant at the 0.01 level. The figures in parentheses are the N or number of cases. All the indices were normalized by setting their lowest possible value at zero (0) and dividing all measures by their maximum possible value. For sources, see table 4.2.

### 4.2.1. The Strictness of Measuring Instruments

One obvious way to compare democracy indices is in terms of the breadth of the conceptual attributes measured by different instruments. As mentioned, although the data produced with the instruments introduced here are routinely treated as measures of the same concept, these instruments actually measure quite different conceptual attributes. Indeed, they vary considerably in their conceptual breadth (see table 4.4). Some indices, such as the Political Regimes Classification index and the EDI, are relatively narrow in conceptual scope. Others, such as the Consolidation of Democracy Index and the Freedom House Political Rights index, are relatively broad. These differences should be reflected in the data produced by using these measuring instruments. Specifically, the mean values of conceptually broader indices should be lower than those of conceptually narrower indices. That is, the expectation to be assessed is whether instruments that are stricter, in the sense of embodying a higher normative standard, have lower scores on average.

The results of such a comparison offer considerable support for the hypothesis that the mean values of conceptually broader indices are lower than the mean values of conceptually narrower indices. The conceptual differences among indices are not always clear, and it is not possible to

TABLE 4.4. *Conceptual Breadth of the Electoral Democracy Index and Other Democracy Indices*

| | Concepts included in index | | | | | | | | | | | |
| | Access to state offices | | | | Decision making within state offices | | | | Others | | | |
| Name of index | Elected offices | Electoral competition | Voting rights | Voting process | Power of elected officials | Checks and balances | Corruption | Transparency | Agendas of political actors | State action on society | Time factor | Actors' attitudes |
|---|---|---|---|---|---|---|---|---|---|---|---|---|
| Political Regimes Classification | x | x | | | | | | | | | | |
| Electoral Democracy Index (EDI) | x | x | x | x | | | | | | | | |
| Polity IV–Democracy | x | x | | | | x | | | x | | | |
| Latin American Democracies | x | x | x | x | x | | | | | x | | |
| Consolidation of Democracy Index | x | x | ? | ? | x | | | | | | x | x |
| Freedom House Political Rights | x | x | x | x | x | | x | x | | x | | |

*Note:* Though one of the items included in the Consolidation of Democracy Index refers to "free and fair elections" (Schneider and Schmitter 2004a: 68), it is unclear whether this phrase encompasses, as is customary, issues such as voting rights and electoral fraud.

TABLE 4.5. *Strictness of Measuring Instruments I: Conceptual Attributes and Aggregation Rules*

| Name of index | Conceptual attributes: conceptual breadth | Aggregation rules: severity rating | Means (1990–2000) | |
|---|---|---|---|---|
| Consolidation of Democracy Index (CDI) | > PRC | Moderately lenient (addition) | 0.661 | Low |
| Freedom House Political Rights (FH PR) | > PRC, EDI, LAD | Moderately lenient (addition) | 0.734 | |
| Polity IV–Democracy (Polity IV-D) | > PRC | Moderately lenient (addition) | 0.737 | |
| Latin American Democracies (LAD) | > PRC, EDI <br> < FH PR | Severe (multiplication) | 0.788 | |
| Political Regimes Classification (PRC) | < CDI, FH PR, LAD, Polity IV-D, EDI | Severe (multiplication) | 0.833 | |
| Electoral Democracy Index (EDI) | > PRC <br> < LAD, FH PR | Severe (multiplication) | 0.885 | High |

*Note:* > = broader than, < = narrower than. This ordering of indices in terms of conceptual breadth draws on table 4.4. Because the indices were normalized for purposes of this comparison, the indices that use addition as a rule of aggregation were actually computed using the arithmetic mean, a closely related rule of aggregation. For a comparison of aggregation rulers in terms of their severity, see table 4.6.

unambiguously rank each index relative to the other indices. Yet, it is possible to rank some indices. And a comparison of these indices suggests that the conceptual breadth and the mean value of indices are closely associated (see table 4.5). Contrary to expectations, the EDI has a higher mean than the Political Regimes Classification index. But, otherwise, the evidence is consistent with expectations. The EDI has a higher mean than the Latin American Democracies and the Freedom House Political Rights indices, and all the other expectations are confirmed.

Another way to compare democracy indices is in terms of the aggregation rule used by different instruments. Much as the breadth of the conceptual attributes affects the strictness of a measuring instrument, aggregation rules have two characteristics that make them more severe or lenient (see table 4.6). They can allow for a high score on one conceptual attribute to compensate or make up for a low score on another attribute. Moreover, they can allow the scores on various conceptual attributes to interact with each other, either insulating the high score on one conceptual attribute from the low score on another attribute or allowing a low score on one conceptual attribute to drag down the high score on another attribute. In

TABLE 4.6. *Severity of Aggregation Rules I: Characteristics and Examples*

| Aggregation rule | Characteristics | | Severity rating | Example 1 | | Example 2 | |
|---|---|---|---|---|---|---|---|
| | | | | Disaggregate values | Index value | Disaggregate values | Index value |
| Multiplication (product) | Noncompensatory | Interactive | Severe | 0.0, 0.2, 0.5, 1.0 | 0.0 | 0.3, 0.5, 0.6, 0.8 | 0.1 |
| Minimum | Noncompensatory | Noninteractive | ↕ | | 0.0 | | 0.3 |
| Geometric mean | Partially compensatory | Interactive | | | 0.0 | | 0.5 |
| Arithmetic mean (average) | Partially compensatory | Noninteractive | | | 0.4 | | 0.6 |
| Maximum | Compensatory | Noninteractive | Lenient | | 1.0 | | 0.8 |

*Note:* An aggregation rule is compensatory when a positive score (higher scores in the examples) can make up for or lift up other negative scores (lower scores in the examples), increasing thus the weight of this positive score. An aggregation rule is interactive when a negative score has a negative implication for the other scores, increasing thus the weight of this negative score.

TABLE 4.7. *Severity of Aggregation Rules II: Some Democracy Indices*

| Name of index | Means on Indices (1990–2000), by aggregation rule | | | | |
| --- | --- | --- | --- | --- | --- |
| | Multiplication | Minimum | Geometric mean | Arithmetic mean | Maximum |
| Electoral Democracy Index | **0.885** | 0.907 | 0.966 | 0.969 | 1.000 |
| Consolidation of Democracy Index | 0.035 | 0.035 | 0.066 | **0.661** | 0.959 |
| Polity IV–Democracy | 0.428 | 0.533 | 0.722 | **0.737** | 0.986 |

*Note:* The actual aggregation operator used in each index is highlighted in bold.

sum, aggregation rules can be compensatory or noncompensatory, and interactive or noninteractive, and assign greater or lesser weight to the positive or negative scores received by individual conceptual attributes.

The impact of aggregation rules on different measures of democracy, a matter discussed above in the context of the EDI, can be shown more broadly. Using disaggregate data (for those indices that provide these data) and hence controlling for other factors, it is easy to confirm that the same data aggregated according to different rules generates sometimes quite different measures that, as expected, are lowest when aggregation is conducted through multiplication and highest when the maximum aggregation operator is used (see table 4.7).

At the same time, the impact of aggregation rules gives added force to the argument that the differences in mean scores correspond to differences in the conceptual breadth of the index. Because the aggregation rule of the three conceptually narrower indices — the EDI, the Latin American Democracies index, and the Political Regimes Classification index — are all equally severe, and the aggregation rule of the other three indices are equally lenient (see table 4.5), the implication of aggregation rules for the analysis of the association between conceptual breadth and mean value is straightforward. Were we to control for the severity of the aggregation rule, not only would the ordering of indices according to their mean values remain unaltered. In addition, the difference in means between the narrower and broader indices would be even greater and offer stronger support for the hypotheses that the mean value of indices are associated, as expected, with the conceptual breadth of the index.

Still, the strictness of the different measuring instruments does not appear to be fully explained by the breadth of their conceptual attributes and

TABLE 4.8. *Strictness of Measuring Instruments II: Some Comparisons with Disaggregate Data*

| Name of index | Conceptual attributes: conceptual breadth | Aggregation rules: severity rating | Means (1990–2000) | |
|---|---|---|---|---|
| Consolidation of Democracy Index Reduced (CDI-R) | Elected offices + Electoral competition | Severe (multiplication) | 0.801 | Low |
| Political Regimes Classification (PRC) | | | 0.833 | ↑ |
| Polity IV–Democracy Reduced (Polity IV-D-R) | | | 0.855 | |
| Electoral Democracy Index Reduced (EDI-R) | | | 0.938 | High |

*Note:* To make the CDI, Polity IV-D and EDI conceptually relatively equivalent to the PRC, the scores of some attributes were excluded. The CDI-R was calculated using the attributes "Regular elections and respect for electoral outcomes" and "Free and fair elections." For Polity IV-D, the attributes "Competitiveness of executive recruitment" and "Openness of executive recruitment" were used; and, to remove the reference to agendas of political actors, "Regulation of participation" was dichotomized, turning scores of 3 and above into a 1 and 2 and below into a 0. Finally, the EDI-R consists of the attributes "Free elections" and "Elected public offices." See table 4.2 for the full list of attributes of these indices.

the severity of their aggregation rules. This is apparent when one compares the mean values of different indices, reworked using disaggregate data so as to control for the breadth of the conceptual attributes and the severity of aggregation rules (see table 4.8). As shown, the means of the four indices that are analyzed vary from 0.801 to 0.938, even though they are measures of the same conceptual attributes combined using the same aggregation rule. Thus, there are grounds for thinking that part of the difference in mean values of indices might be due to another feature of the measuring instruments, the measurement scales and, more specifically, where thresholds are placed on these scales. There is a lot of variability in terms of how the literature of democracy has defined key thresholds (see section 3.2). And the language used to describe the points on the scales of the indices under consideration also shows some variability, which could be associated with differences not accounted for by the breadth of their conceptual attributes and the severity of their aggregation rules. Nonetheless, rather than discuss the link between measurement scales and the mean values of indices here, because the issue is so wrapped up with process of coding, it is addressed below, when the role of coders is discussed.

### 4.2.2. The Discriminating Power of Measuring Instruments

Much as the measuring instruments vary in level of strictness, so too do they differ in their discriminating power. That is, the measures produced with different instruments are more or less tightly clustered around the mean. Moreover, much as the mean values of the indices were shown to be associated with certain features of the measuring instruments, so too can a link be established between the standard deviations of the indices and three features of the instruments: the number of conceptual attributes, the number of points on the measurement scales, and the aggregation rule. These three features determine the number of points of the index scale. And, as would be expected, more or less mechanically, the instruments with scales with fewer points show a greater dispersion of their values compared to the scales with more points (see table 4.9).

The dispersion around the mean is reduced when the value of an index is very low or very high. Thus, it is particularly striking that the Latin American Democracies and the Political Regimes Classification indices, two of the indices with the highest means (see table 4.5), end up nonetheless with the highest standard deviation measures. These two cases show that the tendency toward greater dispersal is strongly associated with measurement scales that consist of dichotomies, and especially with indices in which the combined effect of the number of conceptual attributes, the number of points on the measurement scales, and the aggregation rule yields an index scale with very few points.

### 4.2.3. Conclusions

The results of the tests presented in this section are somewhat tentative due to data limitations. Indeed, without disaggregate data, some important questions cannot be answered empirically. Nonetheless, some conclusions can be drawn regarding the validity of the measures generated with different measuring instruments.

One conclusion is that, to a large extent, the concept measured by various measuring instruments differs considerably, and these differences, as expected, are reflected in differences in the measures that are generated with the different measuring instruments. In other words, the measuring instruments vary in terms of their strictness — some instruments measure broader concepts than others and hence use a higher standard — and stricter measuring

TABLE 4.9. *Discriminating Power of Measuring Instruments*

| Name of index | Conceptual attributes: no. of attributes | Scales: no. of points on scales | Aggregation rules | No. of points on index scale | Standard deviations (1990–2000) | |
|---|---|---|---|---|---|---|
| Political Regimes Classification | 3 | 2 | Multiplication | 2 | 0.374 | High |
| Latin American Democracies | 4 | 3 | Multiplication, followed by the collapsing of all 79 intermediary points to 1 point | 3 | 0.267 | |
| Consolidation of Democracy Index | 12 | 2[a] | Addition | 12 (24)[a] | 0.211 | |
| Polity IV–Democracy | 4 | 2, 2, 3, 4 | Addition | 11 | 0.195 | |
| Freedom House Political Rights | 10 | 5 | Addition, followed by reduction of 41 possible points by 6-point (and one 5-point) segments | 7 (reduced from a space of 41 points) | 0.178 | |
| Electoral Democracy Index | 4 | 3, 5, 5, 5[b] | Multiplication | 375 (15.379)[b] | 0.177 | Low |

[a] An intermediate point was also used. Hence the total number of points is greater than 12.

[b] Pluses and minuses were used to record intermediary situations. Hence the total number of points is greater than 375.

instruments produce lower mean values. This result suggests that the various measuring instruments are not better or worse than each other but, rather, that they are simply measuring different concepts. Nonetheless, this analysis has two important implications. First, the concept being measured should not be read exclusively from the term used in labeling the index. Rather, an interpretation of indices of democracy must focus on the conceptual attributes, the measurement scales, and the aggregation rule used in each index. Second, the assumption that different indices of democracy are interchangeable, an assumption implicit in much of the substantive and methodological literature on democracy, is not correct.

Another conclusion is that the methodology of measurement has an impact on the measures produced by different measuring instruments and hence that a portion of the variance in the values of indices is due to error. This is seen most clearly with regard to the choice of scales and, specifically, the number of points of each measurement scale and the index scale. As has been noted, "No variable comes with a measurement level obviously attached" (Smithson and Verkuilen 2006: 28). Yet, a strong case can be made that two- and three-point measurement scales and index scales do not appropriately capture significant, verifiable differences among cases and hence unnecessarily compress the measurement space and artificially magnify the spread across cases.

Finally, conclusions can be drawn regarding the EDI in particular. The EDI's conceptual attributes are derived from a well-developed body of theorizing on democracy and, as expected, the EDI's mean value is higher than conceptually broader indices (see table 4.5). The EDI's aggregation rule is also selected in light of a well-established argument in democracy theory; moreover, because the robustness of the EDI to changes in aggregation rule is greater than that of other indices (see table 4.7), the theoretical justification for the EDI's aggregation rule is less questionable than the theoretical justification that could be offered for other indices. And the EDI's measurement scales and index scale are designed so as to be theoretically interpretable and go further than the other indices in avoiding the shortcomings of scales that do not match the nuanced information currently available and hence truncate, a priori, the choices open to coders (see table 4.9). In sum, the EDI is arguably a more valid measure than alternative indices of democracy.

One remaining key aspect in assessing the validity of the EDI concerns the way in which the values of its conceptual attributes are assigned. The EDI, as mentioned previously, is based on expert coding. That is, the values assigned to each country on the various measurement scales are choices made by people who are considered to be particularly knowledgeable about the countries being measured. Such a procedure is common in the measurement of democracy and is a distinct source of potential measurement error. Thus, this section addresses the role of coders in the production of the EDI and the other indices of democracy introduced in the previous section.

The role of coders in expert-coded data is significant. Even when coding rules are well developed and contribute to the operationalization of the concepts being measured, there remains a considerable distance between the concepts used in describing each point of a measurement scale and the information gathered to carry out a coding exercise. Coding rules cannot and should not include instructions regarding how every possible event and circumstance maps onto each point on every measurement scale. An attempt to do so would be incredibly cumbersome and would result in an instrument that still would not capture evolving practices and new ways in which democratic rights might be restricted. Instead, the coding rules attached to measurement scales might be thought of as legislation that is deliberately worded in abstract terms so as to encompass multiple and even unanticipated acts. Thus, the job of coders is necessarily a complicated one. Essentially, they must assess the conceptual equivalence of variegated acts and situations, inevitably interpret the information they have at their disposal, and make judgments when they code cases.

Expert-coded indices vary nonetheless in terms of the burden placed on coders — which might be thought of as a ratio between the amount of guidance offered coders relative to the difficulty of the tasks coders confront — and hence are more or less susceptible to coder-induced error. For example, the EDI's scales include descriptions of relatively concrete events and situations that correspond to each point on the scales (see table 4.1). Moreover, the EDI's scales mostly consist of five-point scales and hence offer at least a moderate range of specifically described options.[11] But other indices, especially the Freedom House Political Rights index, the Consolidation of Democracy index, and Political Regimes Classification index, provide considerably less guidance to coders (see table 4.10).

Freedom House provides apparently well-developed scales, in that they are five-point scales. But beyond a description of each of the conceptual attributes that are included in its Political Rights index, no help is offered to coders. No specifics are offered regarding each of the five points on the scales used in coding each attribute. Hence, it is entirely up to the coder to decide what each point on the scales means. Likewise, the Consolidation of Democracy index and the Political Regimes Classification index rely on scales that are hard to code. The meaning of the conceptual attributes is explained. But coders are offered a choice between only two options, and the coding rules are vague as to where the cutoff between the two possible values—yes and no—is located. These indices require coders, in essence, to code cases and also to construct scales, that is, to determine the standards to be applied in distinguishing among cases.

The level of difficulty of the coding exercise is affected by other factors beyond the extent to which measurement scales specify what each point on a scale means and offer a range of options to coders. Indices vary in terms of the number of conceptual attributes for which good information is difficult to come by. And they also vary in terms of the scope of the coding exercise, in the sense of both the conceptual breadth of the index and the number of cases for which data are produced.[12] In the case of the Freedom House Political Rights index in particular, it is hard to avoid wondering about the errors introduced by coders whose knowledge of many cases is surely quite thin and whose overall knowledge is of inconsistent quality.

It is not possible to estimate the impact of coders on the indices under consideration. To do this, data by multiple coders — or, more specifically, data on the same concept using the same methodology except for the identity of the coder—are needed. And such data are not available.[13] But there are reasons to suspect that indices that impose a greater burden on coders are more error prone. Indeed, we have strong evidence of coder-induced error (Hutchinson 1985), including in the measurement of democracy (Bollen and Paxton 2000). Thus, inasmuch as data are generated using coders, it is important to consider whether coders are more or less lenient and more or less prone to magnify or reduce the differences across cases. In short, even though we cannot estimate the magnitude and direction of coder-induced error, coders are likely to be another source, in addition to those features of the measuring instruments discussed previously, of variance in the values of indices.

**TABLE 4.10. The Coder Factor**

| Name of index | Development of measurement scales | No. of hard-to-measure conceptual attributes | Scope of coding exercise | | Burden of coder |
| --- | --- | --- | --- | --- | --- |
| | | | Conceptual breadth | No. of cases | |
| Freedom House – Political Rights | Low: 5-point scales, with no descriptive text | 3: Impact of unelected actors on government policies; government corruption; government accountability and transparency | Broad | 192 (Global) | High |
| Consolidation of Democracy Index | Low: 2-point scales[a] | 5: Free and fair elections; agreement on association formation and behavior; agreement on executive format; agreement on territorial division of competencies; agreement on rules of ownership and access to media | Broad | 31 (Multiple regions) | ↑ |
| Polity IV– Democracy | Medium: 1 2-, 1 3-, and 1 4-point scale | 1: Competitiveness of participation | Somewhat broad | 164 (Global) | |
| Political Regimes Classification | Low: 2-point scales | 1: Contestation | Narrow | 199 (Global) | |
| Latin American Democracies | Medium: 3-point scales | 1: Civilian control | Somewhat broad | 20 (Latin America) | ↓ |
| Electoral Democracy Index | High: 1 3- and 2 5-point scales[b] | 1: Clean elections | Somewhat narrow | 18 (Latin America) | Low |

[a] An intermediate point was also used.
[b] Pluses and minuses were used to record intermediary situations.

## 4.4. Conclusion

This chapter has analyzed the methodology used to produce the electoral democracy index and compared measures of the EDI to other measures of democracy. The importance of a theoretical justification of the methodology used to produce measures, and of tests to validate measures, has been stressed. And the multiple features of measuring instruments, and the role of coders, have been addressed. The results of some empirical tests are tentative, due to data limitations. Yet the internal and external analyses, with their supplementary emphases on theory and tests, do offer considerable support for the view that the EDI actually measures what it purports to measure, the concept of electoral democracy, and that, in many respects, it is a better, more valid measure than alternative ones. In short, this chapter offers a basis for arguing that the EDI measures should be used in the study of electoral democracy in Latin America.

The EDI is a measure of a relatively narrow concept, and the EDI data cover only one region of the world during a relatively short period of time. Thus, this chapter has addressed only a part of the challenge of developing good measures of democracy *tout court*. Nonetheless, it has sought to provide an in-depth discussion of the production and validation of political data that has broad implications. As shown, good data are the result of a complex research process that involves a series of methodological choices, many of which are seldom seriously discussed, and the way these choices are resolved hinges heavily on the state of theory and country knowledge as well as prior efforts at measurement. Furthermore, as chapter 7 discusses, the lessons that can be drawn from the exercise of measuring electoral democracy in Latin America are relevant to the research strategy adopted to produce, and the methods used to validate, data on a broad range of political concepts.

### Appendix: The Electoral Democracy Index Data

Tables 4.11–4.15 follow on pp. 81–85.

TABLE 4.11. The Electoral Democracy Index, 1960, 1977, 1985, 1990–2005

| Country | 1960 | 1977 | 1985 | 1990 | 1991 | 1992 | 1993 | 1994 | 1995 | 1996 | 1997 | 1998 | 1999 | 2000 | 2001 | 2002 | 2003 | 2004 | 2005 |
|---|---|---|---|---|---|---|---|---|---|---|---|---|---|---|---|---|---|---|---|
| Argentina | 0.25 | 0.00 | 1.00 | 1.00 | 1.00 | 1.00 | 1.00 | 1.00 | 1.00 | 1.00 | 1.00 | 1.00 | 1.00 | 1.00 | 0.92 | 1.00 | 1.00 | 1.00 | 1.00 |
| Bolivia | 1.00 | 0.00 | 0.75 | 1.00 | 1.00 | 1.00 | 1.00 | 1.00 | 1.00 | 1.00 | 1.00 | 1.00 | 1.00 | 1.00 | 1.00 | 1.00 | 0.75 | 0.75 | 0.75 |
| Brazil | 0.69 | 0.26 | 0.40 | 1.00 | 1.00 | 1.00 | 1.00 | 1.00 | 1.00 | 1.00 | 1.00 | 1.00 | 1.00 | 1.00 | 1.00 | 1.00 | 1.00 | 1.00 | 1.00 |
| Chile | 0.75 | 0.00 | 0.00 | 0.75 | 0.75 | 0.75 | 0.75 | 0.75 | 0.75 | 0.75 | 0.75 | 0.75 | 0.75 | 0.75 | 0.75 | 0.75 | 0.75 | 0.75 | 0.75 |
| Colombia | 0.75 | 0.83 | 1.00 | 0.56 | 0.56 | 0.56 | 0.56 | 0.56 | 0.56 | 0.56 | 0.56 | 0.56 | 0.56 | 0.56 | 0.56 | 0.69 | 0.69 | 0.69 | 0.69 |
| Costa Rica | 1.00 | 1.00 | 1.00 | 1.00 | 1.00 | 1.00 | 1.00 | 1.00 | 1.00 | 1.00 | 1.00 | 1.00 | 1.00 | 1.00 | 1.00 | 1.00 | 1.00 | 1.00 | 1.00 |
| Dominican Republic | 0.08 | 0.08 | 1.00 | 0.83 | 0.83 | 0.83 | 0.83 | 0.50 | 0.50 | 1.00 | 1.00 | 1.00 | 1.00 | 1.00 | 1.00 | 1.00 | 1.00 | 1.00 | 1.00 |
| Ecuador | 0.75 | 0.00 | 1.00 | 1.00 | 1.00 | 1.00 | 0.75 | 1.00 | 1.00 | 1.00 | 0.83 | 1.00 | 1.00 | 0.75 | 0.75 | 0.75 | 1.00 | 1.00 | 0.75 |
| El Salvador | 0.00 | 0.69 | 0.56 | 0.56 | 0.75 | 0.75 | 0.75 | 1.00 | 1.00 | 1.00 | 1.00 | 1.00 | 1.00 | 1.00 | 1.00 | 1.00 | 1.00 | 1.00 | 1.00 |
| Guatemala | 0.56 | 0.56 | 0.00 | 0.56 | 0.56 | 0.56 | 0.42 | 0.56 | 0.56 | 0.56 | 0.56 | 0.56 | 0.56 | 1.00 | 1.00 | 1.00 | 1.00 | 0.84 | 0.84 |
| Honduras | 1.00 | 0.00 | 0.92 | 1.00 | 1.00 | 1.00 | 1.00 | 1.00 | 1.00 | 1.00 | 1.00 | 1.00 | 1.00 | 1.00 | 1.00 | 1.00 | 1.00 | 1.00 | 1.00 |
| Mexico | 0.56 | 0.56 | 0.75 | 0.42 | 0.42 | 0.50 | 0.50 | 0.50 | 1.00 | 1.00 | 1.00 | 1.00 | 1.00 | 1.00 | 1.00 | 1.00 | 1.00 | 1.00 | 1.00 |
| Nicaragua | 0.06 | 0.06 | 0.75 | 1.00 | 1.00 | 1.00 | 1.00 | 1.00 | 1.00 | 1.00 | 1.00 | 1.00 | 1.00 | 1.00 | 0.92 | 0.92 | 0.92 | 0.92 | 0.84 |
| Panama | 0.75 | 0.00 | 0.54 | 1.00 | 1.00 | 1.00 | 1.00 | 1.00 | 1.00 | 1.00 | 1.00 | 1.00 | 0.58 | 1.00 | 1.00 | 1.00 | 1.00 | 1.00 | 1.00 |
| Paraguay | 0.03 | 0.06 | 0.06 | 0.75 | 0.75 | 0.75 | 0.75 | 0.75 | 0.75 | 0.75 | 0.75 | 0.75 | 0.75 | 0.38 | 1.00 | 1.00 | 1.00 | 1.00 | 1.00 |
| Peru | 0.19 | 0.00 | 1.00 | 1.00 | 1.00 | 0.50 | 1.00 | 1.00 | 1.00 | 1.00 | 1.00 | 1.00 | 0.75 | 0.38 | 1.00 | 1.00 | 1.00 | 1.00 | 1.00 |
| Uruguay | 1.00 | 0.00 | 0.75 | 1.00 | 1.00 | 1.00 | 1.00 | 1.00 | 1.00 | 1.00 | 1.00 | 1.00 | 1.00 | 1.00 | 1.00 | 1.00 | 1.00 | 1.00 | 1.00 |
| Venezuela | 1.00 | 1.00 | 1.00 | 1.00 | 1.00 | 1.00 | 1.00 | 1.00 | 1.00 | 1.00 | 1.00 | 1.00 | 1.00 | 1.00 | 1.00 | 0.67 | 1.00 | 0.84 | 0.84 |

TABLE 4.12.  Components of the Electoral Democracy Index I: Right to Vote, 1960, 1977, 1985, 1990–2005

| Country | 1960 | 1977 | 1985 | Previous | Election | 1990 | 1991 | 1992 | 1993 | 1994 | 1995 | 1996 | 1997 | 1998 | 1999 | 2000 | 2001 | 2002 | 2003 | 2004 | 2005 |
|---|---|---|---|---|---|---|---|---|---|---|---|---|---|---|---|---|---|---|---|---|---|
| Argentina | 4 | 0 | 4 | 1989 | 4 | | 4 | | | | 4 | | | | 4 | | 4 | | 4 | | 4 |
| Bolivia | 4 | 0 | 4 | 1989 | 4 | | | | 4 | | | | 4 | | | | | 4 | | | 4 |
| Brazil | 3 | 3 | 3 | 1989 | 4 | 4 | | | | 4 | | | | 4 | | | | 4 | | | |
| Chile | 3 | 0 | 0 | 1989 | 4 | | | | 4 | | | | 4 | | | | 4 | | | | 4 |
| Colombia | 4 | 4 | 4 | 1986 | 4 | 4 | 4 | | | 4 | | | | 4 | | | | 4 | | | |
| Costa Rica | 4 | 4 | 4 | 1986 | 4 | 4 | | | | 4 | | | | 4 | | | | 4 | | | |
| Dominican Republic | 4 | 4 | 4 | 1986 | 4 | 4 | | | | 4 | | 4 | | 4 | | 4 | | 4 | | 4 | |
| Ecuador | 3 | 0 | 4 | 1988 | 4 | | | 4 | | | | 4 | | 4 | | | | 4 | | | |
| El Salvador | 0 | 4 | 4 | 1989 | 4 | | 4 | | | 4 | | | 4 | | 4 | 4 | | | 4 | 4 | |
| Guatemala | 4 | 4 | 4 | 1985 | 4 | 4 | | | | 4 | 4 | | | | 4 | | | | 4 | | |
| Honduras | 4 | 0 | 4 | 1989 | 4 | | | | 4 | | | | 4 | | | | 4 | | | | 4 |
| Mexico | 4 | 4 | 4 | 1988 | 4 | | 4 | | | 4 | | | 4 | | | 4 | | | 4 | | |
| Nicaragua | 4 | 4 | 4 | 1984 | 4 | 4 | | | | | | 4 | | | | | 4 | | | | |
| Panama | 4 | 0 | 4 | 1989 | 4 | | | | | 4 | | | | | 4 | | | | | 4 | |
| Paraguay | 2 | 4 | 4 | 1989 | 4 | | | | 4 | | | | | 4 | | | | | 4 | | |
| Peru | 3 | 0 | 4 | 1985 | 4 | 4 | | 4 | | | 4 | | | | | 4 | 4 | | | | |
| Uruguay | 4 | 0 | 4 | 1989 | 4 | | | | | 4 | | | | | 4 | | | | | 4 | |
| Venezuela | 4 | 4 | 4 | 1988 | 4 | | | | 4 | | | | | 4 | | 4 | | | | | 4 |

*Note:* The right to vote component of the EDI responds to the question whether all adults within a country are allowed to vote in elections. Beyond the holding of elections, the measure does not include procedures that might hamper the effective use of the right to vote, such as access to the polls. This component is coded according to the following rules: 0 = no election is held to install the government; 1 = only some men have the right to vote (there are restrictions related to property, gender, and literacy); 2 = most men enjoy the right to vote (there are restrictions related to gender and literacy); 3 = most men and most women enjoy the right to vote (there are restrictions related to literacy); 4 = the right to vote is universally recognized. However, even in countries with universal suffrage some restrictions may exist, affecting groups such as the military, the police, the clergy, foreign residents, and citizens living abroad.

TABLE 4.13. *Components of the Electoral Democracy Index II: Clean Elections, 1960, 1977, 1985, 1990–2005*

| Country | 1960 | 1977 | 1985 | Previous | Election | 1990 | 1991 | 1992 | 1993 | 1994 | 1995 | 1996 | 1997 | 1998 | 1999 | 2000 | 2001 | 2002 | 2003 | 2004 | 2005 |
|---|---|---|---|---|---|---|---|---|---|---|---|---|---|---|---|---|---|---|---|---|---|
| Argentina | 2 | – | 2 | 1989 | 2 | | 2 | | 2 | | 2 | | 2 | | 2 | | 2 | | 2 | | 2 |
| Bolivia | 2 | – | 2 | 1989 | 2 | | | | 2 | | | | 2 | | | | | 2 | | | 2 |
| Brazil | 2 | 2– | 2 | 1989 | 2 | | | | | 2 | | | | 2 | | | | 2 | | | |
| Chile | 2 | – | – | 1989 | 2 | | | | 2 | | | | 2 | | | 2 | | | | | 2 |
| Colombia | 2 | 2 | 2 | 1986 | 2 | 1 | 1 | | | 1 | | | | 1 | | | | 2– | | | |
| Costa Rica | 2 | 2 | 2 | 1986 | 2 | 2 | | | | 2 | | | | 2 | | | | 2 | | | |
| Dominican Republic | 2 | 2 | 2 | 1986 | 2 | 1–* | | | | 0* | | 2 | | 2 | | 2 | | 2 | | 2 | |
| Ecuador | 2 | – | 2 | 1988 | 2 | | | 2 | | 2 | | 2 | | 2 | | | | | | | |
| El Salvador | | 1 | 1 | 1989 | 1 | | 2 | | | 2 | | | 2 | | 2 | 2 | | | 2 | 2 | |
| Guatemala | 2 | 1 | 1 | 1985 | 1 | 1 | | | | 1 | 1 | | | | 2 | | | | 2– | | |
| Honduras | 2 | – | 2 | 1989 | 2 | | | | 2 | | | | 2 | | | | 2 | | | | 2 |
| Mexico | 1 | 1 | 2 | 1988 | 0+** | | 2– | | | 2 | | | 2 | | | 2 | | | 2 | | |
| Nicaragua | 1 | 1 | 2 | 1984 | 2 | 2 | | | | | | 2 | | | | | 2 | | | | |
| Panama | 2 | – | 0+* | 1989 | 2 | | | | | 2 | | | | | 2 | | | | | 2 | |
| Paraguay | 1 | 1 | 1 | 1989 | 2 | | | | 1 | | | | | 2 | | | | | 2 | | |
| Peru | 2 | – | 2 | 1985 | 2 | 2 | | 2 | | | 1 | | | | | 0* | 2 | | | | |
| Uruguay | 2 | – | 2 | 1989 | 2 | | | | | 2 | | | | | 2 | | | | | 2 | |
| Venezuela | 2 | 2 | 2 | 1988 | 2 | | | | 2 | | | | | 2 | | 2 | | | | 1+ | 2– |

*Note:* The clean elections component of the EDI responds to the question of whether the voting process is carried out without irregularities that constrain voters from autonomously and accurately expressing their preferences for candidates. It does not include issues related to the competitiveness of the elections or even if the winner of an election is allowed to assume office and if all the offices are elected. This component is coded according to the following rules: 0 = major irregularities in the voting process that have a determinative effect on the result of elections (e.g., alteration in the election for the national executive and/or the balance of power in parliament); 1 = significant irregularities in the voting process (e.g., intimidation of voters, violence against voters, electoral fraud), which do not, however, have a determinative effect on the result of elections; 2 = lack of significant irregularities in the voting process (e.g., elections that might include "technical" irregularities but not any systematic bias of considerable weight). If the government is nonelected, this component is not applicable, as indicated by a dash (–). Pluses and minuses, which are given the value of 0.33, are used to record intermediary situations. When elections for both president and the legislature are held in the same year and the irregularities apply only to the elections for the executive office, this situation is indicated with an asterisk (*). In those instances, the value for the legislative elections is a 1. Two asterisks (**) are used to indicate that the score for the legislative elections is a 1.

TABLE 4.14.  Components of the Electoral Democracy Index III: Free Elections, 1960, 1977, 1985, 1990–2005

| Country | 1960 | 1977 | 1985 | Previous | Election | 1990 | 1991 | 1992 | 1993 | 1994 | 1995 | 1996 | 1997 | 1998 | 1999 | 2000 | 2001 | 2002 | 2003 | 2004 | 2005 |
|---|---|---|---|---|---|---|---|---|---|---|---|---|---|---|---|---|---|---|---|---|---|
| Argentina | 1 | — | 4 | 1989 | 4 | | 4 | | 4 | | 4 | | 4 | | 4 | | 4 | | 4 | | 4 |
| Bolivia | 4 | — | 4 | 1989 | 4 | | | | 4 | | | | 4 | | | | | 4 | | | 4 |
| Brazil | 4— | 3 | 4— | 1989 | 4 | 4 | | | | 4 | | | | 4 | | | | 4 | | | |
| Chile | 4 | — | — | 1989 | 4 | | | | 4 | | | | 4 | | 4 | | 4 | | | | 4 |
| Colombia | 3 | 3+ | 4 | 1986 | 4 | 3 | 3 | | | 3 | | | | 3 | | | | 3 | | | |
| Costa Rica | 4 | 4 | 4 | 1986 | 4 | 4 | | | | 4 | | | | 4 | | | | 4 | | | |
| Dominican Republic | 0+ | 0+ | 4 | 1986 | 4 | 4 | | | | 4 | | 4 | | 4 | | 4 | | 4 | | 4 | |
| Ecuador | 4 | — | 4 | 1988 | 4 | | | 4 | | | | 4 | | 4 | | | | 4 | | | |
| El Salvador | — | 4— | 3 | 1989 | 3 | | 3 | | | 4 | | | 4 | | 4 | 4 | | | 4 | 4 | |
| Guatemala | 3 | 3 | 3 | 1985 | 3 | 3 | | | | 3 | 3 | | | | 4 | | | | 4— | | |
| Honduras | 4 | — | 4— | 1989 | 4 | | | | 4 | | | | 4 | | | | 4 | | | | 4 |
| Mexico | 0+ | 3 | 4 | 1988 | 4 | | 4 | | | 4 | | | 4 | | | 4 | | | 4 | | |
| Nicaragua | 3 | 0+ | 3 | 1984 | 3 | 4 | | | | | | 4 | | | | | 4— | | | | |
| Panama | 3 | — | 4 | 1989 | 4 | | | | | 4 | | | | | 4 | | | | | 4 | |
| Paraguay | 0+ | 0+ | 0+ | 1989 | 3 | | | | 4 | | | | | 4 | | | | | 4 | | |
| Peru | 1 | — | 4 | 1985 | 4 | 4 | | 3 | | | 4 | | | | | 3 | 4 | | | | |
| Uruguay | 4 | — | 3 | 1989 | 4 | | | | | 4 | | | | | 4 | | | | | 4 | |
| Venezuela | 4 | 4 | 4 | 1988 | 4 | | | | 4 | | | | | 4 | | 4 | | | | 4— | 4 |

Note: The free elections component of the EDI responds to the question whether the electorate is offered a range of choices that is not constrained either by legal restrictions or as a matter of practical force. The measure does not include factors that affect the ability of parties and candidates to compete in equality of conditions, such as public financing, access to the mass media and the use of public resources. This component is coded according to the following rules: 0 = single party system; 1 = ban on major party; 2 = ban on minor party; 3 = restrictions of a legal or practical nature that significantly affect the ability of potential candidates to run for office and/or the formation of political parties (e.g., systematic assassinations and intimidation of candidates, ban on popular candidates, legal or practical restrictions that prevent the formation of parties or that lead parties to boycott the elections); 4 = essentially unrestricted conditions for the presentation of candidates and the formation of parties. If the government is nonelected, this component is not applicable, as indicated by a dash (—). Pluses and minuses, which are given the value of 0.33, are used to record intermediary situations.

Table 4.15. *Components of the Electoral Democracy Index IV: Elected Public Offices, 1960, 1977, 1985, 1990–2005*

| Country | 1960 | 1977 | 1985 | 1990 | 1991 | 1992 | 1993 | 1994 | 1995 | 1996 | 1997 | 1998 | 1999 | 2000 | 2001 | 2002 | 2003 | 2004 | 2005 |
|---|---|---|---|---|---|---|---|---|---|---|---|---|---|---|---|---|---|---|---|
| Argentina | 4 | 0 | 4 | 4 | 4 | 4 | 4 | 4 | 4 | 4 | 4 | 4 | 4 | 4 | 4− | 4 | 4 | 4 | 4 |
| Bolivia | 4 | 0 | 3 | 4 | 4 | 4 | 4 | 4 | 4 | 4 | 4 | 4 | 4 | 4 | 4 | 4 | 3 | 3 | 3 |
| Brazil | 4 | 2 | 2+ | 4 | 4 | 4 | 4 | 4 | 4 | 4 | 4 | 4 | 4 | 4 | 4 | 4 | 4 | 4 | 4 |
| Chile | 4 | 0 | 0 | 3 | 3 | 3 | 3 | 3 | 3 | 3 | 3 | 3 | 3 | 3 | 3 | 3 | 3 | 3 | 3 |
| Colombia | 4 | 4 | 4 | 4 | 4 | 4 | 4 | 4 | 4 | 4 | 4 | 4 | 4 | 4 | 4 | 4 | 4 | 4 | 4 |
| Costa Rica | 4 | 4 | 4 | 4 | 4 | 4 | 4 | 4 | 4 | 4 | 4 | 4 | 4 | 4 | 4 | 4 | 4 | 4 | 4 |
| Dominican Republic | 4 | 4 | 4 | 4 | 4 | 4 | 4 | 4 | 4 | 4 | 4 | 4 | 4 | 4 | 4 | 4 | 4 | 4 | 4 |
| Ecuador | 0 | 0 | 4 | 4 | 4 | 4 | 4 | 4 | 4 | 4 | 3+ | 4 | 4 | 3 | 3 | 3 | 4 | 4 | 3 |
| El Salvador | 4 | 4 | 4 | 4 | 4 | 4 | 4 | 4 | 4 | 4 | 4 | 4 | 4 | 4 | 4 | 4 | 4 | 4 | 4 |
| Guatemala | 4 | 4 | 4 | 4 | 4 | 4 | 3 | 4 | 4 | 4 | 4 | 4 | 4 | 4 | 4 | 4 | 4 | 4 | 4 |
| Honduras | 4 | 0 | 4 | 4 | 4 | 4 | 4 | 4 | 4 | 4 | 4 | 4 | 4 | 4 | 4 | 4 | 4 | 4 | 4 |
| Mexico | 4 | 4 | 4 | 4 | 4 | 4 | 4 | 4 | 4 | 4 | 4 | 4 | 4 | 4 | 4 | 4 | 4 | 4 | 4 |
| Nicaragua | 4 | 4 | 4 | 4 | 4 | 4 | 4 | 4 | 4 | 4 | 4 | 4 | 4 | 4 | 4 | 4 | 4 | 4 | 4− |
| Panama | 4 | 0 | 4 | 4 | 4 | 4 | 4 | 4 | 4 | 4 | 4 | 4 | 4 | 4 | 4 | 4 | 4 | 4 | 4 |
| Paraguay | 4 | 4 | 4 | 4 | 4 | 2 | 4 | 4 | 4 | 4 | 4 | 4 | 2+ | 4 | 4 | 4 | 4 | 4 | 4 |
| Peru | 4 | 0 | 4 | 4 | 4 | 2 | 4 | 4 | 4 | 4 | 4 | 4 | 4 | 4 | 4 | 4 | 4 | 4 | 4 |
| Uruguay | 4 | 0 | 4 | 4 | 4 | 4 | 4 | 4 | 4 | 4 | 4 | 4 | 4 | 4 | 4 | 4 | 4 | 4 | 4 |
| Venezuela | 4 | 4 | 4 | 4 | 4 | 4 | 4 | 4 | 4 | 4 | 4 | 4 | 4 | 4 | 4 | 3− | 4 | 4 | 4 |

*Note:* The elected public offices component of the EDI responds to the question whether elections are the means of access to government offices, that is, whether the country's main political offices (i.e., the national executive and legislature) are filled through elections and the winners of elections are allowed both to assume office and serve their full term in office. When elected office holders are removed, the form of removal and selection of a replacement is considered. This component is coded according to the following rules: 0 = none of the main political offices are filled through elections or all of the elected officeholders are forcefully displaced from office and replaced by unconstitutional rulers; 1 = a few political offices are filled by winners of elections or most of the elected officeholders are forcefully displaced from office and replaced by unconstitutional rulers; 2 = the president or the parliament are not elected or, if they were elected, are forcefully displaced from office and replaced by unconstitutional means; or a significant number of parliamentarians are not elected or, if they were elected, are forcefully displaced from office; 3 = the president or the parliament is elected but the president is displaced from office and/or replaced by semiconstitutional means; 4 = all of the main political offices are filled by elections and none of the elected officeholders are displaced from office unless their removal from office and their replacement are based on strictly constitutional grounds. Pluses and minuses, which are given the value of 0.33, are used to record intermediary situations.

85

# FIVE

# Assessing Elections

*A Methodology for Election Observation Missions*

.............................................................................................................

D emocracy is about more than elections. Yet elections are not a distinctive feature of democracies. After all, the usual reference to "free and fair" elections indicates that the elections that are part of democratic systems are characterized by a series of features that serve to distinguish democratic from nondemocratic elections. Much rides on this distinction. Indeed, election observation missions around the world routinely make pronouncements about the quality of elections—categorizing them as "genuine," "acceptable," or "flawed"—and such pronouncements can be highly consequential.

As election observation has become more widespread since 1990, to the point of becoming a common aspect of electoral processes, the need for an explicitly formulated and well-justified methodology to assess elections has been increasingly recognized. Many international organizations have produced handbooks, which provide guidelines regarding what things election observers should scrutinize in their attempt to discern whether elections live up to standards developed by the international community. Moreover, some academics have sought to elaborate methodologies that can be used for the same purpose. The task at hand is complicated, and much work remains to be done to develop a suitable methodology to assess elections. But the recognition of the need for election observers to rely on transparent procedures is an important step.

This chapter presents a methodology to assess elections designed for use by election observation missions of the Organization of American States (OAS).[1] The first section defines the concept of democratic elections in light of standards regarding electoral processes recognized in a series of instruments of the Inter-American system, such as the Inter-American Democratic Charter. This initial focus on matters of definition is essential. A definition that explicitly states what is to be assessed serves as a touchstone when confronting various complex methodological choices involved in the development of measures of democratic elections. Moreover, an effort at measurement cannot proceed with clarity if the constituent elements of the concept of interest are presented as little more than a list of elements — a common practice in election observation methodologies — and have not been fleshed out in a logically organized manner. Indeed, an adequate resolution of these conceptual issues is inextricably linked to the successful development of measures (see section 2.1).

The second section discusses two tools for gathering information to measure the concept of democratic elections. One tool is the election day questionnaire for electoral observers. This instrument is designed to gather valuable information based on firsthand observations about events on election day, a time when election observation missions deploy their largest number of observers throughout the territory of the country where elections are held. The other tool is a guide for collecting information on the electoral process. This tool responds to the imperative to assess elections as a process that begins well before election day and that extends beyond this day. It is also geared to facilitating the presentation of information gathered by various specialists of election observation missions in an orderly fashion.

The third section turns to the challenge of arriving at an overall, quantitative assessment of an election. As mentioned, election observation missions routinely offer pronouncements on the overall quality of elections, using a variety of adjectives and qualifiers. But, even though election observation missions rely on methodologies to conduct important aspects of their work, such overall judgments have as yet not relied on a transparent methodology consistently applied across elections. Thus, to fill a key gap in the methodology of election observation, an Index of Democratic Elections that uses the information gathered in the course of election observation is proposed.

## 5.1. The Concept of Democratic Elections

The methodology to assess elections presented in this chapter focuses on rights established in key international democracy instruments. These instruments — in the context of the Americas, the instruments of the Inter-American system such as the Inter-American Democratic Charter, developed and subscribed to by the OAS's member countries, are the most relevant — explicitly uphold the status of democracy as an essential value; the importance of periodic, free and fair elections as a core aspect of democracy; and a range of rights associated with electoral processes (see appendix B).[2] In other words, these instruments articulate the standards that serve as an obligatory point of reference in any attempt to evaluate elections. Nonetheless, a mere listing of rights does not constitute an adequate framework for an evaluation of elections. Thus, the first task in the development of a methodology to assess elections is the crafting of a definition of democratic elections. Developing measures that can be used to determine whether elections are democratic is not possible without a clear sense of what is meant by the concept of democratic election.[3]

Taking the standards articulated in various instruments of the Inter-American system as a point of reference but also seeking to offer the foundation for a methodology to assess elections, this chapter advances the thesis that elections can be considered democratic when they fulfill four basic conditions. First, elections must be *inclusive,* that is, all citizens must be effectively enabled to exercise their right to vote in the electoral process. Second, elections must be *clean;* in other words, voters' preferences must be respected and faithfully registered. Third, elections must be *competitive,* that is, they must offer the electorate an unbiased choice among alternatives. Finally, the main *public offices* must be accessed through periodic elections, and the results expressed through the citizens' votes must not be reversed. As a first approximation, elections are democratic when they are inclusive, clean, and competitive and constitute the means of access to high public offices (see table 5.1).

This succinct definition can be clarified by spelling out what is encompassed by each of its four core conceptual attributes. With respect to inclusive elections, it is important that the right to universal and equal suffrage is legally recognized and the use of the right to vote is facilitated in practice. With respect to clean elections, the key issue is ensuring the integrity of voters' preferences, as well as the faithful recording of these preferences. With respect to competitive elections, the driving concern is whether citizens have the right to run for public offices, but also whether candidates running for office are able to do so without concerns for their security and with equal opportunities in a context of respect for civil rights, such as freedom of the press, free access to information, and freedom of association, assembly, expression, and movement. Finally, the attribute regarding elective public

TABLE 5.1. *The Concept of Democratic Elections I: A First Approximation*

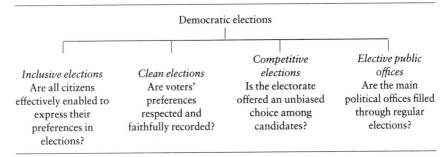

| | Democratic elections | | |
|---|---|---|---|
| *Inclusive elections* Are all citizens effectively enabled to express their preferences in elections? | *Clean elections* Are voters' preferences respected and faithfully recorded? | *Competitive elections* Is the electorate offered an unbiased choice among candidates? | *Elective public offices* Are the main political offices filled through regular elections? |

offices is concerned with the access to all the main political offices through periodic elections and the irreversibility of the results of the elections. As table 5.2 shows, the elements of this more detailed definition can be formally identified as components and subcomponents of the four core attributes of democratic elections, a step that shows how the concept is logically organized and further clarified by specifying what is at stake in each of the elements of this definition.

Another way to clarify the definition of the concept of democratic elections is to state what is not included in the definition. After all, a central desideratum in the formation of a concept is the establishment of its boundaries. Such an exercise is particularly useful inasmuch as it touches on conceptually proximate elements that are nonetheless excluded from the definition.

Focusing on the concept of democratic elections from this perspective, a number of exclusions are worth highlighting. First, this definition does not include a range of aspects of the electoral process, such as abstentionism, whether voting is compulsory, the electoral formula used for translating votes into seats, and the presence of territorial chambers. Though each of these elements is important, we still lack unambiguous or agreed-upon standards regarding what practices are preferable from the point of view of democracy.

Second, this definition excludes other aspects of the electoral process such as the independence of electoral authorities and the confidence that different actors exhibit in the electoral process and election results. Evidently, the actions of electoral authorities have a big impact on the electoral process and hence are an integral part of an assessment of the quality of elections. Similarly, it is very desirable that the results of the elections be widely accepted, as long as these results are correct. Nevertheless, the ways in which

TABLE 5.2. *The Concept of Democratic Elections II: A More Elaborate Approximation*

| Attributes | Components and subcomponents of attributes | Issue at stake |
|---|---|---|
| I. Inclusive Elections | 1. Universal and equal suffrage | Who is legally allowed to vote? |
| | 2. Conditions for the use of the right to vote | |
| | i. Registration | Are there significant legal or other hurdles to register to vote? |
| | ii. Electoral roll | Is the information in the electoral roll accurate? |
| | iii. Polling station access | Are there significant legal or other hurdles to get to a polling station or otherwise cast a vote? |
| | iv. Vote casting | Are all eligible and willing voters able to cast their vote and do so as intended? |
| II. Clean Elections | 3. Integrity of voter preferences | Are voters able to vote without any outside pressure or fear of reprisals? |
| | 4. Faithful recording of voter preferences | Are all ballots scrutinized (i.e., checked and counted) and/or tabulated (i.e., aggregated) impartially and accurately? |
| III. Competitive Elections | 5. Right to run for office | Are there unreasonable legal hurdles to become a candidate? |
| | 6. Basic guarantees for an electoral campaign | |
| | i. Equal security | Is the physical security of all candidates and party personnel guaranteed? |
| | ii. Equal opportunity | Do candidates compete on a level playing field? |
| | iii. Right to a free press and to information | Do the voters have access to the information needed to make an informed choice when they cast their votes? |
| | iv. Freedom of association, assembly, expression, and movement | Are candidates for office and the electorate allowed to organize and interact freely? |
| IV. Elective Public Offices | 7. Regular elections for top national offices | Are the main political offices (i.e., the national executive and legislature) filled through regular elections? |
| | 8. Irreversibility of electoral results | Are the winners of elections duly installed in office? |

*Note:* The terms *attributes*, *components*, and *subcomponents* are used to distinguish the level of abstraction of each of the conceptual elements.

the electoral authorities are constituted (whether by personnel who are part of the executive branch, by representatives of political parties, or by independent professionals), and the attitudes of politicians and citizens toward electoral results, are best considered as possible causes or consequences of the quality of electoral processes. Thus, they are not elements that should form part of an evaluation strictly focused on the quality of the electoral process.[4]

Third, this definition does not cover a multitude of topics that are commonly identified as challenges to democratic governance. In fact, though the electoral process is more than an election day event, the actions of elected government officials largely pertain to a wider discussion about democracy. Thus, this definition does not extend beyond the goal of a successfully completed electoral process, that is, the assumption of office by the victors of elections.

In sum, the proposed definition of democratic elections consists of four core conceptual attributes: two focused on voters and their intent to signal a preference for a candidate or position (inclusive and clean elections), one primarily on candidates and their need to reach potential supporters (competitive elections), and another on the stakes of the electoral process (elective public offices).[5] In these terms, elections are considered democratic when all citizens are enabled to vote, when voters are able to express their preferences through the ballot box without being pressured and when their votes are faithfully recorded, when citizens are free to run for office and candidates can reach potential voters with their message, and when the winners of elections are duly installed in office.

## 5.2. Tools for Gathering Information

The information required to measure this concept of democratic elections and to carry out an assessment of an electoral process is extensive. One by-now traditional source of information is the quick count or parallel vote tabulation. This quantitative information is valuable inasmuch as it serves to detect irregularities in one key aspect of the electoral process, the totalization of votes cast at each polling station.[6] In addition, the methodology developed for the OAS includes two other, supplementary tools for gathering information: an election day questionnaire for electoral observers and a guide for collecting information on the electoral process.[7]

### 5.2.1. The Election Day Questionnaire for Electoral Observers

Election day is the moment when election observation missions deploy their largest number of observers throughout the territory of the country where elections are held and provides a unique opportunity for election observation missions to gather firsthand observations about events at polling stations. In addition, because most election observers are usually engaged in the task of collecting data for a quick count and are assigned to observe polling stations that constitute part of a representative statistical sample, it is possible to gather information that has an important degree of representativeness.[8] Thus, one important source of systematic and valuable information about the electoral process is a questionnaire administered on election day and filled out by electoral observers.

The questionnaire consists of four parts and requires that observers visit the same polling station at three times during the day — at the opening of the polls, around midday, and at the closing of the polls — to be able to offer an in-depth accounting of the voting process at one location (see parts A, B, and C in table 5.3). Moreover, a fourth part of the questionnaire is designed to obtain a thorough evaluation of the overall electoral process at the specific polling station visited on three occasions (see part D in table 5.4).[9]

The information gathered through the questionnaire administered on election day is valuable, inasmuch as it is based on firsthand observations and a representative sample. But it is limited in scope. This questionnaire provides information that is relevant only to assess whether elections are inclusive and clean (see table 5.2). And even in this respect it offers only part of the relevant information. Indeed, whether an election lives up to democratic standards is largely determined by what happens in the run-up to election day, many times months in advance. Moreover, an election can be determined by what happens after the day of the elections, when the totalization of the vote is usually completed, when legal challenges are considered, when the results of elections are confirmed (and in some cases even announced), and when elected members are to be duly installed in office. Thus, an assessment of elections must also rely on information gathered by means other than the election day questionnaire for electoral observers.

TABLE 5.3.  *Election Day Questionnaire for Electoral Observers I*

| A | Questions regarding the opening of the polling station | Answer (mark your response with a circle or write in your answer) | | |
|---|---|---|---|---|
| 1 | At what time did the polling station open? | Did not open | Time: | |
| 2 | Were all the indispensible electoral materials available at the polling station? | Yes | No | |
| 3 | Were all the designated polling officials present at the opening of the polling station? | Yes | No | |
| 4 | Were representatives of the following parties present at the polling station? | Party acronyms here | | |
| 5 | Were domestic election observers present at the polling station? | Yes | No | |
| 6 | Is the space at the polling station adequate? | Yes | No | |
| 7 | Were members of the security forces present in the polling center? | Yes | No | |
| 8 | Is the electoral roll on display? | Yes | No | NA (Not applicable) |
| 9 | Do the voters have adequate information about the location of their polling station? | Yes | No | |

| B | Voting process, at approximately 1 p.m. | Answer (mark your response with a circle or write in your answer) | |
|---|---|---|---|
| 1 | How many voters are there on the voting roll? | Number: | |
| 2 | How many voters have cast a ballot by 1:00 p.m.? | Number: | |
| 3 | How many minutes does each voter take to cast their ballot? | Number of minutes: | |
| 4 | Were representatives of the following parties present at the polling station? | Party acronyms here | |
| 5 | Were domestic election observers present at the polling station at 1:00 p.m.? | Yes | No |
| 6 | Did you observe any of the following practices at the polling station? | | |
| | i. Voters on the electoral roll were not allowed to vote | Yes | No |
| | ii. Long lines of voters waiting to vote | Yes | No |
| | iii. Interruptions in the voting process | Yes | No |
| | iv. Restrictions to the right to a secret vote | Yes | No |
| | v. Electoral campaigning | Yes | No |
| | vi. Incidences of violence | Yes | No |
| | vii. Others (indicate which) | Yes | No |

*continued*

TABLE 5.3. *Continued*

| B | Voting process, at approximately 1 p.m. | Answer (mark your response with a circle or write in your answer) | | |
|---|---|---|---|---|
| 7 | Are there any other issues or observations not covered in the questions that you consider significant? | | | |

| C | Closing of polling station and vote counting | Answer (mark your response with a circle or write in your answer) | | |
|---|---|---|---|---|
| 1 | At what time did the polling station close? | Time: | | |
| 2 | Were any voters left in line at the moment of the closing of the polling station not allowed to vote? | Yes | No | |
| 3 | Were representatives of the following parties present at the polling station? | Party acronyms here | | |
| 4 | Were domestic election observers present at the polling station? | Yes | No | |
| 5 | Did the counting of the ballots follow legal procedures? | Yes | No | |
| 6 | Were there any administrative or organizational defects or problems in the counting of the ballots? | Yes | No | |
| 7 | Were there intentional acts to alter the expressed preferences of voters during the vote counting? | Yes | No | |
| 8 | Were claims and disputes related to the vote counting addressed in a fair and quick manner? | Yes | No | NA (Not applicable) |
| 9 | How many voters are there on the voting roll? | Number: | | |
| 10 | What is the total number of votes cast in the presidential (or otherwise, in the parliamentary) election? | Number: | | |
| 11 | How many votes in the presidential (or otherwise, in the parliamentary) election were declared null? | Number: | | |
| 12 | Was the voting returns protocol challenged? | Yes | No | |
| 13 | Was a copy of the voting returns protocol provided to party representatives? | Yes | No | |
| 14 | At what time was the vote counting finished? | Time: | | |
| 15 | Are there any other issues or observations not covered in the questions that you consider significant? | | | |

TABLE 5.4. *Election Day Questionnaire for Electoral Observers II*

| D | Overall evaluation in light of observations made at the polling station that has been visited on three occasions during the day and should be restricted to an evaluation of the electoral process at that specific polling station | Answer (mark your response with a circle) | | |
|---|---|---|---|---|
| 1 | *Voter Education.* Did voters appear to understand when, where and how to vote? | Yes | No | NA (Not applicable) |
| 2 | *Exclusion of Registered Voters.* Were registered voters prevented from voting, because of problems with the electoral rolls, voting hours, or other reasons? | Yes | No | NA |
| 3 | *Ballot Design.* Has the design of the ballot and/or the voting mechanism made it likely that voters are able to record their preferences accurately? | Yes | No | NA |
| 4 | *Voter Intimidation.* Did you observe threats targeted at potential voters? | Yes | No | NA |
| 5 | *Vote Buying.* Did you observe instances of voters being offered rewards in exchange for votes? | Yes | No | NA |
| 6 | *Electioneering at Polling Station.* Did you observe electioneering at the polling stations? | Yes | No | NA |
| 7 | *Secret Ballot.* Was the right to a secret ballot guaranteed? | Yes | No | NA |
| 8 | *Secure Ballot.* Have all ballots been properly supervised and secured during the voting? | Yes | No | NA |
| 9 | *Dispute Resolution.* Were complaints and disputes dealt with in a fair and timely manner? | Yes | No | NA |
| 10 | *Political Party Representatives.* Did the main political parties have representatives present at the polling station? | All | Some | None  NA |
| 11 | *National Observers.* Were national electoral observers present at the polling stations? | Yes | No | NA |
| 12 | *General Impression.* In general, the voting process at the polling station that you observed was | Very good | Good | Bad  Very bad |

### 5.2.2. A Guide for Collecting Information on the Electoral Process

A complete assessment of elections calls for the gathering of information on a wide range of indicators that tap into all aspects of the concept of democratic elections. The information that needs to be collected is largely of a qualitative nature but also quantitative, and calls for research over a prolonged period of time. Moreover, it is imperative to rely, as much as possible, on in situ observations and on the input of specialists. Thus, the information-gathering effort must be a coordinated effort, which draws on the input of many members of an election observation mission, and particularly on the information and analysis provided by the mission's different experts.

To orient this information-gathering effort, a proposed guide specifies what information is relevant to each aspect of the concept of democratic elections, what are the relevant sources, and when the observation and collection of information regarding each aspect should take place (see table 5.5). As is readily apparent, this guide is cursory and should be supplemented with methodologies that delve in greater depth into the thorny issues that are relevant to the assessment of various aspects of the electoral process.[10] Yet this guide serves the fundamental purpose of bringing order to the masses of information that are regularly gathered by election observation missions. By providing a framework for the gathering and, very importantly, the presentation of information in a conceptually organized fashion, this guide helps to ensure, on the one hand, that the failure to collect relevant information is avoided or at least acknowledged and, on the other hand, that the information that is gathered contributes to a general view of the electoral process. Indeed, election evaluators always run the risk of not seeing the forest for the trees and must take explicit steps to place the information they have in the proper context.

## 5.3. The Index of Democratic Elections

A final aspect of a methodology to assess elections is the transformation of all the information gathered in the course of election observation into an overall, quantitative assessment of elections. A summary statement of the quality of an election is a critical aspect of an evaluation, in that it conveys the conclusions of observation work and, as such, is usually echoed in the mass media and carries a large political weight. Yet election observation missions have thus far not relied on a transparent methodology consistently applied across elections to arrive at the summary statements they routinely announce after an election (see appendix A). Moreover, the few discussions on the topic have been hampered by a serious pitfall, the proposal to assess different elections using different standards.[11] In short, the lack of a methodology for providing a summary assessment has been a key weakness in the evaluation of elections.

To fill this gap in the methodology of election observation, the rest of this chapter develops an Index of Democratic Elections that relies on the information gathered through various means by election observation missions.[12] The design of a measurement instrument to produce this index involves two new methodological challenges: the construction of measurement scales (see sections 2.2 and 3.2 in the preceding chapters) and the choice of an aggregation rule (see sections 2.3 and 3.3). Moreover, the use of this measurement instrument to generate data entails a process of coding—that is, the assignment of scores to each measurement scale on the basis of the available information—and the interpretation of the data revolves around the reading of the values of the index in terms of the concept of democratic elections.

### 5.3.1. Measurement Scales and Coding

The Index of Democratic Elections relies on a process of expert coding, as is conventional in the field of measurement of political concepts, which links the information gathered in the course of election observation to the coding rules for each of the relevant conceptual components and subcomponents—that is, the conceptual elements at the lowest level of abstraction (see table 5.2). Thus, as an essential aspect in the development of this measuring instrument, measurement scales that consist in all instances of three-point scales are proposed (see table 5.6). Each scale is designed so that each point on the scales corresponds to a significant distinction. Relatedly, each scale seeks to capture a sense of distance from point to point, in particular so that the midpoint between each extreme is equidistant from the endpoints. These features are important in that they affect the way in which the eventual index values are interpreted.

These measurement scales are to be used in coding exercises, which involve the transformation of various sorts of information into quantitative data or, in other words, the assignment of values to each of the relevant components and subcomponents of the concept of democratic elections. For example, if it is determined that all citizens have the right to vote, a score of 2 is assigned to the component "universal and equal suffrage." In turn, if the documentation that is required to register to vote and the registration procedures are seen as presenting potential voters with many hurdles that place unnecessary burdens on those intent on exercising the right to vote, a score of 0 is assigned to the subcomponent "registration."

As simple as this description may sound—coding essentially entails the matching of information to the language used in the measurement scales—the actual practice of coding is a complex process that is best seen as

TABLE 5.5. *A Guide for Collecting Information on the Electoral Process*

| Attribute | Components and subcomponents of attributes | Issue at stake |
|---|---|---|
| I. Inclusive Elections | 1. Universal and equal suffrage | Who is legally allowed to vote? |
| | 2. Conditions for the use of the right to vote | |
| | i. Registration | Are there significant legal or other hurdles to register to vote? |
| | ii. Electoral roll | Is the information in the electoral roll accurate? |
| | iii. Polling station access | Are there significant legal or other hurdles to get to a polling station or otherwise cast a vote? |
| | iv. Vote casting | Are all eligible and willing voters able to cast their vote and do so as intended? |
| II. Clean Elections | 3. Integrity of voter preferences | Are voters able to vote without any outside pressure or fear of reprisals? |
| | 4. Faithful recording of voter preferences | Are all ballots scrutinized (i.e., checked and counted) and/or tabulated (i.e., aggregated) impartially and accurately? |

| Relevant information | Relevant sources | Observation times |
|---|---|---|
| Exclusions of any adults (18 years and older) | Constitution, laws, and regulations | Before the elections |
| Documentation required to register to vote, residency requirements, and voter registration procedures (e.g., automatic registration, centralized vs. decentralized registration, registration period) | Constitution, laws, and regulations; decisions by the electoral authorities | Before the elections |
| Regular updating of electoral roll, mechanisms for challenging incorrect inclusions or exclusions or other inaccuracies, response to petitions for corrections of the electoral roll | Decisions by the electoral authorities; electoral roll | Before and during the elections |
| Voting sites close to place of current residence, mobile voting, absentee voting, and external voting | Constitution, laws, and regulations; electoral observer reports | Before and during the elections |
| Exclusion of registered voters at the polling station, provisional ballot, ballot design, voter education on where and how to vote | Data from the Electoral Observers' Questionnaire; constitution, laws, and regulations; election materials; electoral authority programs | Before and during the elections |
| Secret ballot, voter intimidation, vote buying, electioneering at polling station, campaigning on election day | Data from the Electoral Observers' Questionnaire; constitution, laws, and regulations; election materials; electoral observer reports | Before and during the elections |
| Secure ballot and protection of the voting returns protocol, at every relevant stage in the electoral process; vote counting and total-ization that is not a reflection of the votes legally cast by voters, number of contested ballots and extent to which they are resolved impartially and in a way that is consistent with the intent of the voter, number of null or invalid ballots, oversight of all stages of the vote count by accredited representatives of parties and/or candidates, prompt publication of results, prompt and impartial resolution of disputes, possibility of access to and auditing of all and any materials and mechanisms used to arrive at total and final vote results | Data from the Electoral Observers' Questionnaire; constitution, laws, and regulations; exit polls; quick counts; official count; electoral observer reports | Before, during, and after the elections |

TABLE 5.5. *Continued*

| Attribute | Components and subcomponents of attributes | Issue at stake |
|---|---|---|
| III. Competitive Elections | 5. Right to run for office | Are there unreasonable legal hurdles to become a candidate? |
| | 6. Basic guarantees for an electoral campaign<br>i. Equal security | Is the physical security of all candidates and party personnel guaranteed? |
| | ii. Equal opportunity | Do candidates compete on a level playing field? |
| | iii. Right to a free press and to information | Do the voters have access to the information needed to make an informed choice when they cast their votes? |
| | iv. Freedom of association, assembly, expression, and movement | Are candidates for office and the electorate allowed to organize and interact freely? |
| IV. Elective Public Offices | 7. Regular elections for top national offices | Are the main political offices (i.e., the national executive and legislature) filled through regular elections? |
| | 8. Irreversibility of electoral results | Are the winners of elections duly installed in office? |

| Relevant information | Relevant sources | Observation times |
|---|---|---|
| Prohibition of multiple candidacies, political bans, unjustifiably constraining legal requirements to form a political party and/or run for office | Constitution, laws, and regulations | Before the elections |
| Violence against, and/or intimidation of, candidates, party leaders, or activists; legal harassment of candidates | Electoral observer reports and news reports | Before and during the elections |
| Use of state resources, predictable rules, financing of parties and electoral campaigns, access to the mass media | Constitution, laws, and regulations; electoral observer reports; reports from the electoral authority | Before, during, and after the elections |
| Media content, intimidation of journalists, use of opinion polls, structure of media ownership, access to information about the government, presentation of candidate's platforms | Constitution, laws, and regulations; yearly and other reports from the OAS Inter-American Commission on Human Rights (IACHR); electoral observer reports | Before and during the elections |
| Bans on social organizations; threats against, and intimidation of, citizen groups; restrictions on travel throughout the territory | Constitution, laws, and regulations; yearly and other reports from the OAS Inter-American Commission on Human Rights (IACHR); electoral observer reports | Before and during the elections |
| Unelected officials in high offices, suspension of elections, postponement of elections | Constitution, laws, and regulations; news reports | Before the elections |
| Annulment of election results; illegal proclamation of election results | News reports | After the elections |

TABLE 5.6. *Measuring Democratic Elections I: Measurement Scales*

| Attributes | Component and subcomponents | Measurement scales |
|---|---|---|
| I. Inclusive Elections | Universal and equal suffrage | 0 = no one has the right to vote;<br>1 = roughly half the adults have the right to vote;<br>2 = all citizens (with only minor exceptions) have the right to vote. |
| | Registration | 0 = many unnecessary hurdles;<br>1 = some unnecessary hurdles;<br>2 = no unnecessary hurdles. |
| | Electoral roll | 0 = many inaccuracies;<br>1 = some inaccuracies;<br>2 = no inaccuracies. |
| | Polling station access | 0 = many significant legal or other hurdles;<br>1 = some significant legal or other hurdles;<br>2 = no significant legal or other hurdles. |
| | Vote casting | 0 = many voters are not able to cast their vote or do so as intended;<br>1 = some voters are not able to cast their vote or do so as intended;<br>2 = no voters are not able to cast their vote or do so as intended. |
| II. Clean Elections | Integrity of voter preferences | 0 = evidence of fraud (i.e., intentional acts to alter the election results) and/or irregularities (i.e., administrative or organizational shortcomings or defects) that have a determinative effect on the result of elections (e.g., alteration in the outcome of the election for the national executive and/or the balance of power in parliament);<br>1 = evidence of fraud and/or irregularities that do not, however, have a determinative effect on the result of elections;<br>2 = evidence, at most, of isolated irregularities. |
| | Faithful recording of voter preferences | 0 = evidence of fraud (i.e., intentional acts to alter the election results) and/or irregularities (i.e., administrative or organizational shortcomings or defects) that have a determinative effect on the result of elections (e.g., alteration in the outcome of the election for the national executive and/or the balance of power in parliament);<br>1 = evidence of fraud and/or irregularities that do not, however, have a determinative effect on the result of elections;<br>2 = evidence, at most, of isolated irregularities. |
| III. Competitive Elections | Right to run for office | 0 = overwhelming restrictions on the presentation of candidates and the formation of parties (e.g., a single-party system);<br>1 = considerable restrictions on the presentation of candidates and the formation of parties (e.g., ban on minor party);<br>2 = essentially unrestricted conditions for the presentation of candidates and the formation of parties (e.g., relatively low barriers to entry and bans only of antisystem parties). |
| | Equal security | 0 = the physical security of many candidates and party personnel is jeopardized;<br>1 = the physical security of some candidates and party personnel is jeopardized;<br>2 = the physical security of no candidates and party personnel is jeopardized. |

TABLE 5.6. *Continued*

| Attributes | Component and subcomponents | Measurement scales |
|---|---|---|
| | Equal opportunity | 0 = overwhelming distortion to the principle of equal opportunity to compete for office; <br> 1 = considerable distortion to the principle of equal opportunity to compete for office; <br> 2 = no distortion to the principle of equal opportunity to compete for office. |
| | Right to a free press and to information | 0 = overwhelming distortion to the free flow of information; <br> 1 = considerable distortion to the free flow of information; <br> 2 = no distortion to the free flow of information. |
| | Freedom of association, assembly, expression, and movement | 0 = overwhelming distortion to the freedom of association, assembly, expression, and movement; <br> 1 = considerable distortion to the freedom of association, assembly, expression, and movement; <br> 2 = no distortion to the freedom of association, assembly, expression, and movement. |
| IV. Elective Public Offices | Regular elections for top national offices | 0 = regular elections are not held for any of the main political offices; <br> 1 = regular elections are held for only the head of the executive branch or the parliament; <br> 2 = regular elections are held for all of the main political offices. |
| | Irreversibility of electoral results | 0 = none of the winners of elections are allowed to take office; <br> 1 = some of the winners of elections are allowed to take office; <br> 2 = all the winners of elections are allowed to take office. |

*Note:* Intermediary situations can be recorded with decimals (e.g., 1.33, 1.50, 1.75). An item might not be applicable; for example, if no one has the right to vote, issues related to the registration of voters are not relevant. When an item is not applicable, a score of 0 (zero) is assigned.

revolving less around hard-and-fast rules than some basic maxims that call for nuanced judgments:

- Make coding decisions in a consistent yet flexible manner, ensuring that standards are applied universally while remaining open to the possibility that similar problems are manifested differently across countries and over time.
- Base coding decisions on observable and documentable processes and not on speculation.
- Consider, and carefully balance, conflicting evidence.
- Consider the reliability of alternative information sources.
- Rely, as much as possible, on more than one source of information.

Following these maxims can be difficult, especially when the concepts being measured are abstract and hard to measure, as is frequently the case in election observation. Thus, it is always prudent to include as part of the coding process a deliberative exercise, in which a group discusses coding decisions and in which doubts and disagreements are aired and recorded.

### 5.3.2. The Aggregation Rule

In contrast to coding, which consists of the initial transformation of information into quantitative data, the aggregation of data — the reduction of the multiple pieces of quantitative data produced through coding into a smaller number of pieces of quantitative data — is a mechanical process that can be easily computerized. Yet, when it comes to aggregation, everything hinges on the choice of an aggregation rule: once an aggregation rule has been selected, the die is essentially cast. Providing an adequate justification of the choice of aggregation rule is hardly a simple matter. Such a justification requires addressing the theoretical relationship among, and weight of, all of the attributes, components, and subcomponents that are to be aggregated. Yet, as the following proposal seeks to show, the development of an index can be based on a well-justified choice of aggregation rule.

The calculation of the Index of Democratic Elections through the aggregation of the four conceptual attributes — Inclusive Elections, Clean Elections, Competitive Elections, and Elective Public Offices (see table 5.7, column 1) — relies on a simple idea.[13] All four attributes are necessary or, in the terminology introduced in chapter 3, the relationship among these attributes is noncompensatory and interactive (see section 3.3). This means that poor performance on one attribute cannot be compensated or made up by virtue of a strong performance on another attribute. For example, an inclusive election in which voters are not given a choice among candidates — the election is not competitive — cannot be considered democratic. Or a clean and competitive election in which the winner is not allowed to assume office does not deserve to be labeled as a "democratic election." In addition, failings regarding any of the four attributes have implications for the overall assessment of the election. For example, an election in which the instigator of electoral fraud still loses the election is deficient; the failure of fraud to produce the sought results does not erase the fact that the overall quality of the election is tarnished because the election was not clean. Moreover, each of the four attributes has equal weight, for there is no good theoretical reason

TABLE 5.7. *Measuring Democratic Elections II: The Aggregation Rule*

| Aggregation of attributes | Attributes | Aggregation of components of attributes | Components of attributes | Aggregation of subcomponents of attributes | Subcomponents of attributes |
|---|---|---|---|---|---|
| Index of Democratic Elections = Inclusive Elections × Clean Elections × Competitive Elections × Elective Public Offices | Inclusive Elections subindex | Universal and equal suffrage × ( 0.75 + [0.25 × Conditions for the use of the right to vote]) | *Universal and equal suffrage*<br><br>Conditions for the use of vote | Registration × Electoral roll × Polling station access × Vote casting | *Registration*<br>*Electoral roll*<br>*Polling station access*<br>*Vote casting* |
| | Clean Elections subindex | Integrity of voter preferences × Faithful recording of voter preferences | *Integrity of voter preferences*<br>*Faithful recording of voter preferences*<br>*Right to run for office* | | |
| | Competitive Elections subindex | Right to run for office × (0.50 + [0.50 × Basic guarantees for an electoral campaign]) | Basic guarantees for an electoral campaign | Equal security × Equal opportunity × Right to a free press and to information × Freedom of association, assembly, expression, and movement | *Equal security*<br>*Equal opportunity*<br>*Right to a free press and to information*<br>*Freedom of association, assembly, expression, and movement* |
| | Elective Public Offices subindex | Regular elections for top national offices × Irreversibility of electoral results | *Regular elections for top national offices*<br>*Irreversibility of electoral results* | | |

*Note:* Scores are assigned to the conceptual elements at the lowest level of abstraction, which are highlighted in italic. Prior to aggregation, all scores are normalized by dividing them by their maximum possible value, that is, by 2.

for arguing that any one is more fundamental to the democratic nature of the electoral process. Thus, to calculate the overall index, the values of the four attributes are multiplied by each other.

The rationale for the aggregation rule used to calculate the values for the four conceptual attributes, or what might be labeled subindices, can be articulated in similar terms (see table 5.7, column 2). The two components of the Inclusive Elections subindex—"universal and equal suffrage" and "conditions for the use of the right to vote"—are necessary or, in other terms, noncompensatory and interactive. They measure distinct hurdles, both of which must be overcome if a person is going to register his or her intention to support a certain candidate or position through a ballot. Without the right to vote, a person is directly excluded from participation in the voting process. But the right to vote without the conditions that enable its use can also leave a potential voter out of the process. For example, even if a citizen is in principle allowed to vote, without the proper documents—which he or she may or may not have—this citizen is not allowed to register to vote and hence to exercise the right to vote.

These two components do not have the same weight, however. The barrier to participation due to the component "universal and equal suffrage" is more onerous. Indeed, if the government does not grant the right to vote to a person, that barrier is simply unsurpassable. In contrast, the barrier that someone who has the right to vote must overcome, say to register to vote, might constitute a hardship but is not unsurpassable. Moreover, the things measured by "conditions for the use of the right to vote" (see table 5.5) can only reduce gains already made through the extension of the right to vote. That is, the relationship between these two components is hierarchical, for the component "universal and equal suffrage" sets an upper limit, and any shortcomings measured by this subindex's other component always represent losses relative to that upper limit. Thus, considering that the presence of major hurdles to use the right to vote should have a maximum weight equivalent to half a point in the "universal and equal suffrage" scale, the Inclusive Elections subindex is calculated by multiplying the value of both components while only allowing the barrier to participation measured by the component "conditions for the use of the right to vote" to reduce the ceiling set by the component "universal and equal suffrage" by a maximum of 25 percent.

Because the component "conditions for the use of the right to vote" is not directly coded (see table 5.7, column 4), a rule for aggregating the subcomponents "registration," "electoral roll," "polling station access," and "vote casting" is also needed. These four subcomponents are necessary, that is, their relationship is noncompensatory and interactive. Indeed, they measure distinct potential obstacles that stand in the way of the use of the right to vote. Moreover, each potential obstacle has the same weight, in that it is a different way to prevent voters from registering their support for different candidates. Thus, to calculate the value of the component "conditions for the use of the right to vote," the scores of the four subcomponents are multiplied by each other.

The Clean Elections subindex is simpler. Both its components — "integrity of voter preferences" and "faithful recording of voter preferences" — are necessary, that is, their relationship is noncompensatory and interactive. Violations measured by each of these components have a direct and irreparable impact on elections as a process that gauges the preferences of voters regarding who should occupy government offices. Moreover, such violations have the same weight in that they are but different ways to prevent voters from registering their support for different candidates. Hence, this subindex is calculated by multiplying the scores of its two components.

The Competitive Elections subindex includes two components — "right to run for office" and "basic guarantees for an electoral campaign" — that are related in a relatively similar fashion as are the components of the Inclusive Elections subindex. The "right to run for office" is one of the most fundamental features of democratic elections. Elections are democratic only if they are contested by multiple political parties and/or candidates. In turn, "basic guarantees for an electoral campaign" are needed to substantiate and give meaning to the right to run for office. It may well be that an incumbent party that used state resources in its campaign loses an election. Yet such a result does not void the fact that the quality of the election has been negatively affected. Thus, these two components are necessary, that is, their relationship is noncompensatory and interactive.

The relationship between these two components is also hierarchical, in that the component "right to run for office" sets an upper limit, and any shortcomings measured by the component "basic guarantees for an electoral campaign" always represent losses relative to that upper limit. Indeed, the rights encompassed by the "basic guarantees for an electoral campaign" are the means through which choices are offered to the electorate and candidates interact with the electorate or, in other words, the conditions needed to substantiate and give meaning to the right to run for office. At the same time, in the absence of a right to run for office, such conditions are better seen as civil rights rather than political rights directly linked with the electoral process. But these two components do have the same weight. After all, the four subcomponents of the "basic guarantees for an electoral campaign" are so fundamental to the electoral process (see table 5.5) that it is hard to justify giving this component less weight than the "right to run for office." Thus, the Competitive Elections subindex is calculated by multiplying the value of both components while allowing restrictions due to the component "basic guarantees for an electoral campaign" to reduce the ceiling set by component "right to run for office" by a maximum of 50 percent.

Because the component "basic guarantees for an electoral campaign" is not directly coded (see table 5.7, column 4), as was the case for the component "conditions for the use of the right to vote," a rule for aggregating the subcomponents "equal security," "equal opportunity," "right to a free press and to information," and "freedom of association, assembly, expression, and movement" is also needed. Each of these four subcomponents refers to well-established rights, and the violation of any of these rights would affect the quality of an election. Thus, each subcomponent is necessary — their relationship is noncompensatory and interactive — and has the same weight; and the value of the component "basic guarantees for an electoral campaign" is calculated by multiplying the scores of the four subcomponents.

Finally, the Elective Public Offices subindex is similar to the Clean Elections subindex. Both its components — "regular elections for top national offices" and "irreversibility of electoral results" — are necessary, that is, their relationship is noncompensatory and interactive. If elections for top national offices are not held regularly or if the winners of elections are not allowed to assume office, the notion of elective public offices is simply a sham, and progress on one component cannot make up for poor performance on the other component. Moreover, restrictions on either component are different means to the same end — preventing the electorate from electing their rulers — and hence have the same weight. Thus, this subindex is calculated simply by multiplying the scores of its two components.

In sum, the proposed aggregation rule, though complicated by the fact that fourteen distinct pieces of data are involved, is rooted in an understanding of the theoretical status of each conceptual element. Some of the arguments and decisions might be debatable — this would hardly be surprising, given that the measurement of elections is very much a new activity — but the payoff of formally tackling the challenge of aggregation should be recognized. By showing how overall conclusions regarding the quality of elections are arrived at, the use of an explicit aggregation rule gives transparency to the work of electoral assessment. Indeed, the procedure through which an overall judgment of an election is arrived at deserves to be considered as a key aspect of a methodology to assess elections.

### 5.3.3. The Interpretation of the Index

The application of the proposed aggregation rule to the coded data yields an Index of Democratic Elections that has values that range from 0.00 to 1.00, higher numbers indicating a closer approximation to the standards of democratic elections.[14] As a rough guide, a value from 0.00 to 0.50 might be qualified as unacceptable; a value between 0.51 and 0.75 might be considered as pointing to matters of serious concern; and a value greater than 0.75 but short of 1.00 as evidence that the election, though still leaving room for improvement, is of high quality.

The specific reason why an election receives a certain value on the Index of Democratic Elections can be ascertained by studying the values of the four subindices — of Inclusive Elections, Clean Elections, Competitive Elections, and Elective Public Offices — and the scores of each of the components and subcomponents. Actually, it is always advisable to consult this more detailed information when interpreting the index. Such a closer reading can lead to an identification of the areas where improvements are called for and hence helps to highlight the constructive uses of the index. Moreover, such a reading is usually required to interpret the value of the index correctly. Interpreting the index is a complex matter, which lends itself to confusion. In particular, it is necessary to avoid the common tendency to impute what the value of the index means in political terms in a mechanical way. Thus, a few points should be stressed regarding how the value of the index should be interpreted.

It is critical to note that a poor score on the Index of Democratic Elections does not necessarily mean that the government is responsible for a failure to live up to international standards. Responsibility may lie with agents of the state not under the control of the government or an actor outside of the state. It is also important to remember that the index does not provide a total measure, in that it does not tap into all politically relevant aspects of the electoral process. Hence, in all instances, the value of the index should be carefully considered, along with the other information, much of it of a qualitative nature, which is at the disposal of the electoral observation mission. In other words, the index is a measure that should be interpreted with all deliberate care.

## 5.4. Conclusion

As election observation has become a standard practice, and as the consequential nature of pronouncements by election observation missions has become apparent, the need for election observers to rely on an explicit methodology when conducting assessments has become greater. This chapter has sought to respond to this need and, in the process, has been driven by two central concerns.

One is the avoidance of a perception of bias. Election assessments involve, due to the nature of the process being assessed, an element of human judgment. That is, although there are certain aspects of electoral processes (e.g., who has the legal right to vote) that can be verified by reference to publicly available documents, there are other aspects (e.g., whether fraud was committed) that are likely to rely on judgments that cannot be fully or directly documented. Nonetheless, the current proposal seeks to show that, inasmuch as evaluations are based on transparent methodologies, it is possible to prevent subjectivity from turning into arbitrariness.

A second concern is the generation of results — the product of the application of the methodology — that make sense politically. This challenge is particularly acute in the context of election observation because, though quantitative methodologies have the advantage of rigor and precision, they frequently do not translate easily into the more common terms of political debate. Thus, the methodology was tested to ensure that the numbers it yields are interpretable in terms of widely shared standards and bear a clear connection with the weight or gravity of the abridgment of specific standards. In sum, the goal of this chapter has been to elaborate a proposal to observe elections that relies on a rigorous, transparent, and sensible methodology.

The measurement of elections is central to the measurement of democracy. Indeed, it is hard to make a case that democracy can be measured if we lack a sufficiently well-developed and tested methodology to assess elections. As this chapter's discussion of the measurement of democratic elections and the previous chapter's discussion of the measurement of electoral democracy have sought to show, the advances are sufficient to encourage a consideration of the challenge of measuring aspects of democracy that exceed the electoral process and the strict electoral connection between voters and their representatives. The next two chapters turn to the broader challenge of measuring democracy and seek to motivate, outline, and orient a research agenda for the further development of measures of political concepts.

## Appendix A: Election Observation Methodologies

See table 5.8, pp. 112–15.

## Appendix B: OAS Standards for Electoral Observation

The Inter-American Democratic Charter, approved by the member states of the Organization of American States (OAS), states that "Electoral observation missions shall be carried out in accordance with the principles and norms of the OAS" (Article 24). Hence, the basic standards for electoral observation used by OAS election observation missions are drawn from instruments that are elaborated and subscribed to by the OAS member states. A listing of the various rights related to electoral processes consecrated in the Inter-American Democratic Charter, as well as the American Declaration of the Rights and Duties of Man (1948) and the American Convention on Human Rights (1969), is provided in table 5.9. In the text, excerpts of the relevant articles from these instruments of the Inter-American system are presented.

### Excerpts from the Instruments of the Inter-American System

#### Inter-American Democratic Charter (2001)

Article I. The peoples of the Americas have a right to democracy and their governments have an obligation to promote and defend it.

Article III. Essential elements of representative democracy include, *inter alia*, respect for human rights and fundamental freedoms, access to and the exercise of power in accordance with the rule of law, the holding of periodic, free, and fair elections based on secret balloting and universal suffrage as an expression of the sovereignty of the people, the pluralistic system of political parties and organizations, and the separation of powers and independence of the branches of government.

TABLE 5.8. *Methodologies to Assess Elections: An Overview*

| | | | Council of Europe, *Handbook for Observers of Elections* | Elklit and Reynolds |
|---|---|---|---|---|
| *Conceptual Attributes:* What conceptual attributes or components are proposed? | *Voters, Voting, and Vote Counting* | Right to vote (universal and equal suffrage) | x | |
| | | Voter registration: nondiscriminatory, accurate, and easy registration | x | x |
| | | Ballot design: nondiscriminatory method, easy to fill out | x | x |
| | | Voter education | x | x |
| | | Accessible and secure polling stations | x | x |
| | | Secret ballot (no fear of reprisals) | x | x |
| | | Voter turnout | | x |
| | | Election-related violence, voter intimidation | x | x |
| | | Vote buying | x | x |
| | | Electoral fraud (secure ballots, no multiple voting) | x | x |
| | | Counting and tabulating the vote: integrity, accuracy, and transparency, and/or delays | x | x |
| | *Oversight and Dispute Resolution* | Resolving election-related complaints: impartial dispute resolution mechanism, prompt resolution | x | x |
| | | Electoral management: impartiality, legitimacy, quality, accountability, and/or transparency | x | x |
| | | Election observation: groups are permitted to organize and observe the entire election process | | x |
| | *Candidates and Parties* | The right to stand for office: party and candidate nomination and registration (no exclusions, no bias, independent candidates allowed, low barriers to entry) | x | x |
| | | Ability to campaign freely and enjoy equal security | x | |
| | | Right to equal opportunity | | |
| | | Proper use of state resources by parties and candidates (separation of party and state) | | x |

| European Commission, *Handbook for European Union Election Observation Missions* | Goodwill-Gill | International IDEA | Inter-Parliamentary Council, *Declaration on Criteria for Free and Fair Elections* | O'Grady, López-Pintor, and Stevens | OSCE *Election Observation Handbook* | OSCE/ODIHR *Practical Guide* | UNDP Electoral Democracy Index (EDI) |
|---|---|---|---|---|---|---|---|
| x | x | x | x | x | x | x | x |
| x | x | x | x | x | x | x |  |
| x |  |  | x |  | x | x |  |
| x | x |  | x |  | x | x |  |
| x | x |  | x | x | x |  |  |
| x | x | x | x | x | x | x | x |
| x | x | x | x |  | x |  | x |
| x |  |  |  |  |  |  | x |
| x | x | x | x | x | x | x | x |
| x | x | x | x | x | x | x | x |
| x | x | x | x | x | x | x |  |
| x | x | x | x | x | x | x |  |
| x |  | x | x | x | x | x |  |
| x | x | x | x | x | x | x | x |
| x | x | x | x |  | x |  | x |
| x | x | x | x | x | x |  |  |
|  | x | x | x | x | x |  |  |

*continued*

TABLE 5.8. *Continued*

| | | | Council of Europe, *Handbook for Observers of Elections* | Elklit and Reynolds |
|---|---|---|---|---|
| | | System for allocation of public funds to political parties and/or disclosure of campaign spending | | x |
| | | Equal access to media | x | x |
| | *Fundamental Freedoms* | Freedom of expression, association, movement, and assembly | x | |
| | | Free press, impartiality of media, and/or right to information | x | |
| | *Periodic Elections for Public Office* | Right to periodic elections, and respect for electoral timetable | x | x |
| | | Irreversibility of election results: seats taken only by those persons properly elected | | x |
| *Measurement Level:* Is the measurement level for each conceptual attribute or component specified? | | | | Yes |
| *Aggregation Rule:* Is the rule to aggregate multiple conceptual attributes or components specified? | | | | Yes: Additive[a] |

*Sources:* Council of Europe (1998), Elklit and Reynolds (2005), European Commission (2002), Goodwin-Gill (1994), International IDEA (2002), Inter-Parliamentary Council (1994), O'Grady, López-Pintor, and Stevens (n.d.: 12–17), OSCE/ODIHR (2005), OSCE (2002: 29–37), UNDP (2004a: 207–13).

[a] Elklit and Reynolds's aggregation rule is additive of weighted scores and includes a distinction between established and fledgling democracies.

[b] Only regarding the voting process on election day.

|  | Organization or author | | | | | | |
|---|---|---|---|---|---|---|---|
| European Commission, *Handbook for European Union Election Observation Missions* | Goodwill-Gill | International IDEA | Inter-Parliamentary Council, *Declaration on Criteria for Free and Fair Elections* | O'Grady, López-Pintor, and Stevens | OSCE *Election Observation Handbook* | OSCE/ODIHR *Practical Guide* | UNDP Electoral Democracy Index (EDI) |
| x | x | x | x | x | x | x |  |
| x | x | x | x | x | x | x |  |
| x | x | x | x | x | x | x |  |
| x | x | x | x | x | x | x |  |
| x | x | x | x | x | x | x | x |
| x | x |  | x |  | x |  | x |
| Partially[b] |  | Yes |  |  | Partially[b] |  | Yes |
|  |  |  |  |  |  |  | Yes: Multiplicative |

TABLE 5.9. *Election-Related Rights Enshrined in Instruments of the Inter-American System*

| Right | Declaration of the Rights and Duties of Man (1948) | American Convention on Human Rights (1969) | Inter-American Democratic Charter (2001) |
|---|---|---|---|
| | Instrument | | |
| Right to democracy | | | Art. I |
| Right to participate in government | Art. XX | Art. XXIII | |
| Periodic elections | Art. XX | Art. XXIII | Art. III |
| Free elections | Art. XX | | Arts. III & XXIII |
| Fair elections | | | Arts. III & XXIII |
| Universal and equal suffrage | Art. XX | Art. XXIII | Art. III |
| Secret ballot | Art. XX | Art. XXIII | Art. III |
| Honest elections | Art. XX | | |
| Right to participate directly in government | Art. XX | Art. XXIII | |
| Right of access to power | | | Art. III |
| Full and equal participation of women | | | Art. XXVIII |
| A pluralistic system of parties and organizations | | | Art. III |
| Right to security | Art. I | Art. VII | |
| A balanced and transparent system of financing election campaigns | | | Art. IV |
| A free press | | | Art. IV |
| Transparency in government activities | | | Art. IV |
| Right of petition | Art. XXIV | | Art. VIII |
| Freedom of association | Art. XXII | Art. XVI | Art. III |
| Freedom of assembly | Art. XXI | Art. XV | |
| Freedom of expression | Art. IV | Art. XIII | Art. IV |
| Freedom of movement | Art. VIII | Art. XXII | |
| Right to basic civil rights | Art. XVII | | |
| Right to equality | Art. II | | |
| Elimination of all forms of discrimination | | Art. I | Art. IX |
| Human rights | | | Art. III |
| Rule of law | | | Arts. III & IV |
| Fundamental freedoms | | | Art. III |

Article IV. Transparency in government activities, probity, responsible public administration on the part of governments, respect for social rights, and freedom of expression and of the press are essential components of the exercise of democracy.

The constitutional subordination of all state institutions to the legally constituted civilian authority and respect for the rule of law on the part of all institutions and sectors of society are equally essential to democracy.

Article VIII. Any person or group of persons who consider that their human rights have been violated may present claims or petitions to the inter-American system for the promotion and protection of human rights in accordance with its established procedures.

Article IX. The elimination of all forms of discrimination, especially gender, ethnic and race discrimination, as well as diverse forms of intolerance, the promotion and protection of human rights of indigenous peoples and migrants, and respect for ethnic, cultural and religious diversity in the Americas contribute to strengthening democracy and citizen participation.

Article XXIII. Member states are responsible for organizing, conducting, and ensuring free and fair electoral processes.

Member states, in the exercise of their sovereignty, may request that the Organization of American States provide advisory services or assistance for strengthening and developing their electoral institutions and processes, including sending preliminary missions for that purpose.

Article XXVIII. States shall promote the full and equal participation of women in the political structures of their countries as a fundamental element in the promotion and exercise of a democratic culture.

### American Convention on Human Rights (1969)

Article I. 1. The States Parties to this Convention undertake to respect the rights and freedoms recognized herein and to ensure to all persons subject to their jurisdiction the free and full exercise of those rights and freedoms, without any discrimination for reasons of race, color, sex, language, religion, political or other opinion, national or social origin, economic status, birth, or any other social condition.

Article VII. 1. Every person has the right to personal liberty and security.

Article XIII. 1. Everyone has the right to freedom of thought and expression. This right includes freedom to seek, receive, and impart information and ideas of all kinds, regardless of frontiers, either orally, in writing, in print, in the form of art, or through any other medium of one's choice.

Article XV. The right of peaceful assembly, without arms, is recognized. No restrictions may be placed on the exercise of this right other than those imposed in conformity with the law and necessary in a democratic society in the interest of national security, public safety or public order, or to protect public health or morals or the rights or freedom of others.

Article XVI. 1. Everyone has the right to associate freely for ideological, religious, political, economic, labor, social, cultural, sports, or other purposes.

Article XXII. 1. Every person lawfully in the territory of a State Party has the right to move about in it, and to reside in it subject to the provisions of the law.

Article XXIII. 1. Every citizen shall enjoy the following rights and opportunities:

1. To take part in the conduct of public affairs, directly or through freely chosen representatives;

2. To vote and to be elected in genuine periodic elections, which shall be by universal and equal suffrage and by secret ballot that guarantees the free expression of the will of the voters.

### American Declaration of the Rights and Duties of Man (1948)

Article I. Every human being has the right to life, liberty and the security of his person.

Article II. All persons are equal before the law and have the rights and duties established in this Declaration, without distinction as to race, sex, language, creed or any other factor.

Article IV. Every person has the right to freedom of investigation, of opinion, and of the expression and dissemination of ideas, by any medium whatsoever.

Article VIII. Every person has the right to fix his residence within the territory of the state of which he is a national, to move about freely within such territory, and not to leave it except by his own will.

Article XVII. Every person has the right to be recognized everywhere as a person having rights and obligations, and to enjoy the basic civil rights.

Article XX. Every person having legal capacity is entitled to participate in the government of his country, directly or through his representatives, and to take part in popular elections, which shall be by secret ballot, and shall be honest, periodic and free.

Article XXI. Every person has the right to assemble peaceably with others in a formal public meeting or an informal gathering, in connection with matters of common interest of any nature.

Article XXII. Every person has the right to associate with others to promote, exercise and protect his legitimate interests of a political, economic, religious, social, cultural, professional, labor union or other nature.

Article XXIV. Every person has the right to submit respectful petitions to any competent authority, for reasons of either general or private interest, and the right to obtain a prompt decision thereon.

# SIX

# Revisiting Concepts

*Democracy and Other Political Values*

..............................................................................................................

The measurement of democracy is inextricably linked with the definition of the concept of democracy. An effort to develop measures starts with conceptual issues (see section 2.1) and constantly reverts back to the content of the concept. A clear sense of the meaning of the concept being measured serves as an essential touchstone in matters of measurement, given that it helps researchers make decisions that ensure that they are proceeding along the right track as they tackle methodological problems. Thus, as a prelude to the discussion on the development of measures in the next chapter, this chapter revisits the concept of democracy and also considers other concepts that crop up in discussions of democracy, as a way to think about how the concept of democracy might be appropriately delimited, a particularly critical and thorny issue in the current debate about how to define democracy.

The chapter starts to address the question, What is democracy? through a discussion of Robert Dahl's work on democracy and, in particular, Dahl's critique of Joseph Schumpeter's views. The second section focuses on the conceptual boundary of the concept of democracy through an analysis of the relationship between democracy and two proximate concepts: rule of law and human development. The third section spells out the implications of the prior discussion for the definition of democracy, but it also suggests that an implication of the discussion is that democracy is a relative value and that an analysis of democracy cannot limit itself to democracy. The very justification for promoting democracy actually hinges on the answer to an empirical question—Are there trade-offs between democracy and other political values?—that calls for an analysis that goes beyond democracy.

## 6.1. Toward a Robust Procedural Conception

Dahl's contribution to democratic theory, especially in his most elaborate and refined statement in *Democracy and Its Critics* (1989), offers a good starting point for a discussion of democracy in relation to the modern state.[1] In particular, Dahl's explicit and implicit critique of Schumpeter's views raises some key issues that must be confronted in an attempt to define democracy. The merit of Schumpeter (1942: 242, 269) is that he offered a strictly processual definition — "democracy is a political *method*" — formulated in memorable terms: "the democratic method is that institutional arrangement for arriving at political decisions in which individuals acquire the power to decide by means of a competitive struggle for people's vote." This procedural and parsimonious definition, commonly referred to as a Schumpeterian conception of democracy,[2] has been influential. As Dahl shows, though, substantial amendments of Schumpeter's definition are required. Indeed, Schumpeter's (1942: 269–70) definition even fails to serve as a valid basis for his ostensible main goal: to offer criteria for empirically distinguishing democracies from nondemocracies.

Dahl, as Schumpeter, adopts a procedural conception of democracy. That is, for Dahl democracy is about the political process and not the outcomes of the political process. But Dahl does not share Schumpeter's elitist approach to democracy and, as a result, he has a different view of what a democratic political process encompasses. For Schumpeter (1942: 256–64, 269, 282–83), voters lack rationality and information, and thus he considers that it is best to limit voter participation and leave most choices to professional politicians. Thus, for Schumpeter the distinctive feature of democracy is that it is a system that ensures a circulation among elites. In contrast, Dahl (1989: chs. 6 and 7) places the assumptions that all citizens have equal intrinsic worth and that ordinary people are capable of governing themselves at the heart of his theory of democracy. That is, Dahl sees democracy as giving all individuals who are legally bound to abide by public decisions the right to participate equally in the entire process that generates these decisions. And this popular as opposed to elitist conception leads Dahl to propose a major revision of Schumpeter's definition of democracy as consisting of competitive elections for government offices.

To begin, Dahl contests one of Schumpeter's main claims: that his definition establishes an empirically verifiable threshold below which cases are unequivocally nondemocracies. Schumpeter (1942: ch. 21, 269–70) criticizes the view that regimes that claim to realize the common good should be labeled as "democratic," arguing that such a claim is unverifiable. And his identification of competitive elections, which open the possibility of alternation in government, is undoubtedly a key criterion to distinguish democracies from nondemocratic government by guardians, who may claim to rule in the name of the people but do not allow for a process of public debate about government decisions and citizen choice among alternatives. Yet Schumpeter's full definition is not consistent with this critique of guardianship. Indeed, Schumpeter's (1942: 244–45) argument that the right to vote is a contingent matter, to be decided case by case according to the standard of each society, opens the door for the elites of each society to decide who they want to exclude from the political process, a decision that could fully exclude popular preferences from the process of competition. Thus, as Dahl (1989: ch. 9) argues, responding directly to Schumpeter, a definition of democracy can serve as the basis for a distinction between democracies and nondemocracies only if it includes a universal standard that reflects the principle of political equality.[3]

In addition to making this point about measurement, Dahl's work raises two basic questions about what might be labeled the conceptual limitations of Schumpeter's definition. One limitation concerns the ultimate stakes of democratic politics. Schumpeter's definition can be seen as starting with voters, running through elections, and ending, unambiguously, with the public offices to be filled by election winners. That is, Schumpeter (1942: 269, 273, 291–93) sees the formation of government as the endpoint of the democratic process and is deliberately silent on the range of decisions a democratic government should be entitled to make. What government authorities do is not a matter of concern for Schumpeter's democratic theory. But Dahl (1989: 112–14) argues that such a view of the democratic process is too limited and hence that the concept of democracy extends beyond the constitution of government. Thus, a first conceptual question triggered by Dahl's work on democracy is, How far does the democratic political process extend beyond the formation of government?

Dahl's writings also raise the question whether Schumpeter's definition adequately captures, to put it in spatial terms, how deep the rights entailed by democracy go as opposed to how far they extend. Although Schumpeter (1942: 272) hints that freedom of the press is implied by his definition of democracy, he neither gives serious thought to the right to a free press in a democratic political process nor suggests that this right or any other rights that go beyond the rights traditionally understood as political rights — such as the right to vote and the right to run for office — should be explicitly included in a definition of democracy. And again Dahl goes considerably beyond Schumpeter. Thus, Dahl (1989: 114–15, 178–79) considers not only a range of rights conventionally labeled as "civil rights" but also how equal opportunities to participate in the political process are affected by the distribution of economic resources. Moreover, even though he is consistent in stating that he uses the concept of democracy as a way to characterize the political process, Dahl (1989: 220–22; 1998: ch. 8) explicitly includes freedom of the press and also freedom of assembly and expression in his definition of democracy. Thus, a second conceptual question prompted by Dahl's work on democracy is, Are there rights beyond those traditionally understood as "political" rights that are constitutive of democracy and, if so, what are they?[4]

The core message of Dahl's work is obvious: democracy is about more than the process of forming governments through the free competition among politicians for votes. Even if Schumpeter's definition is amended so as to include a justifiable standard of who is entitled to the right to vote, such a definition would be a partial definition of democracy, a definition of electoral democracy rather than of the broader concept of democracy. Yet the difficulties faced in formulating the alternative Dahl favors — a procedural but more robust definition of democracy — are considerable. Indeed, proposals to replace Schumpeter's minimalist definition with broader definitions, including those advanced in the recent literature on the quality of democracy, have been quite weak, giving credibility to the argument that, conceptual shortcomings notwithstanding, a minimalist definition of democracy is preferable because its parsimony makes it analytically clearer than its alternatives and hence more suitable for purposes of empirical analysis.[5] The formulation of a theoretically informed and analytically useful alternative to Schumpeter remains an important challenge.

## 6.2. New Perspectives

To tackle the challenge of moving toward a robust procedural definition of democracy, it is instructive to consider the relationship between democracy and two proximate concepts: rule of law and human development. These two concepts are closely related to democracy, yet have been articulated primarily by legal scholars and economists who do not always share the training in democratic theory that is common among political scientists. Thus, considering the relationship of these concepts to democracy is a particularly apt way to address in a fresh way the two conceptual questions raised by Dahl's work: (1) How far does the democratic political process extend beyond the formation of government? (2) Are there rights beyond those traditionally understood as "political" rights that are constitutive of democracy and, if so, what are they? Identifying what is constitutive of democracy is a complex task. But, as the following discussion seeks to show, by consistently fleshing out the implications of the democratic principle that all individuals who are legally bound to abide by public decisions have the right to participate equally in the entire process that generates these decisions, it is possible to arrive at some solid conclusions regarding what should be included in, and excluded from, a definition of democracy.

### 6.2.1. Rule of Law and Democracy

The relationship between the rule of law and democracy has direct implications for the question about how far the democratic political process extends beyond the formation of government. The concepts of rule of law and democracy are closely linked, and the distinctiveness of each concept is hard to specify.[6] Indeed, there is even some overlap between these concepts, in that both refer to the political process, and both emphasize rule-bound behavior and the principle of equality. But the core elements of these two concepts are actually quite different. On the one hand, the key normative concern embedded in the concept of rule of law — drawn from the tradition of constitutional liberalism — is the potential abuse of state power. Hence, the rule of law is first and foremost about guaranteeing outcomes by putting certain values — equality, but also freedom — beyond or above the political process. On the other hand, the critical normative concern of the concept of democracy is that people should have a say in the making of state decisions they must abide by. Thus, democracy is all about guaranteeing a political process in which no outcomes are placed beyond the reach of the people.

This contrast between the rule of law and democracy helps to clarify what is distinctive about democracy and, in the process, offers a basis for determining how far beyond the formation of government the concept of democracy reaches. Specifically, it suggests that the democratic process extends at the very least to the point when legally binding decisions are actually made, what Dahl (1989: 106–8) calls the "decisive stage." Moreover, inasmuch as the decision-making process might be considered to entail the enactment of laws and their implementation, as Harold Lasswell and Abraham Kaplan (1950: 74–75, 196, 201) argue, this means that the concept of democracy extends beyond the legislative enactment of laws. Democracy, then, is not just a matter of the preferences of each citizen being treated equally in the process of forming a government. Rather, democracy is a process that empowers the demos to control the state under which they live and that calls for voter preferences to be weighed equally in the decision-making process.

This does not mean that there is no democratic limit to the power of the demos. Democracy refers to a process for making publicly binding decisions that envisions no restrictions on what issues are to be decided, that does not foreclose choices. In this sense, a process is not democratic if the outcomes have been predetermined. Yet democracy requires that in the self-referential instance of the reproduction of the democratic process outcome trumps process. That is, a democratic process is one that does not precommit citizens to any specific outcomes, except that outcomes of the democratic political process cannot erode or abolish the democratic process. Thus, the one and only outcome of the political process that can be democratically put out of the reach of the demos concerns the reproduction of the democratic process.

The relationship between the rule of law and democracy is also instructive, for a different reason, in considering whether there are rights beyond those traditionally understood as "political" rights that are constitutive of democracy. This is a distinct question — which is relevant whether the democratic process is seen as ending with the formation of a government or extending beyond that point — that gets at, as suggested, how deep the rights entailed by democracy go as opposed to how far they extend. And, again, the answer to this question points to an expansion, up to an explicit limit, of the definition of democracy.

The argument for defining democracy in terms that go beyond strictly defined political rights is that those political rights cannot be effectively exercised in the absence of some other rights. For example, freedom of the press is commonly seen as an intrinsic feature of the democratic process, because voters cannot make an informed choice about candidates and issues unless they have access to alternative sources of information. Relatedly, the right to information is essential to democracy because citizens — whether in their condition as voters, candidates for office, or elected officials — are deprived of a key component of a meaningful choice if they do not have information about what state agents are doing. Likewise, citizens cannot organize and mobilize in support of different candidates and issues unless they enjoy the freedom of association, assembly, expression, and movement. Hence, a case can be made for including rights usually categorized as "civil" rights in the definition of democracy.

At the same time, this argument includes an implicit limiting criterion in that the addition of rights to a definition of democracy is justified in light of their status as rights intrinsic to the operation of the political process according to the democratic principle of universal and equal participation. That is, the inclusion of elements such as freedom of the press does not actually transgress the boundary between democracy and the rule of law and hence contradict the invocation of this boundary as a way to delimit the concept of democracy. Rather, the point is that, regardless of the labels conventionally used in referring to certain rights, rights such as freedom of the press are actually required by a democratic political process. Indeed, what legal scholars refer to as "civil" rights are, as some democratic theorists have argued, actually "political" rights (Dahl 1989: 170; O'Donnell 2004b: 17–20) or, to avoid the terminological problems associated with the conventional distinction between political and civil rights, simply democratic rights.

### 6.2.2. Human Development and Democracy

A consideration of the relationship between human development and democracy helps to specify further what should be included in, and excluded from, a definition of democracy.[7] The human development paradigm, as it is frequently called, departs from standard approaches to development within economics and provides a novel perspective on the much-discussed connection between economics and democracy. In particular, the work on human development offers a basis for addressing the thorny issue of opportunities in a way that has important implications for the definition of democracy.

The differentiation between economics and democracy is well established. Because democracy does not extend to outcomes of the political process, as discussed previously, it excludes a strong notion of economic equality, on the one hand, or a market-based economic system, on the other hand. In addition, because the concept of democracy is distinct from its causes and/or effects, it also excludes economic factors as conventionally understood in the literature on the economic determinants of democracy inaugurated by Seymour Lipset (1959) as well as in the literature on the economic performance of democracy (Lijphart 1999: ch. 15; Przeworski et al. 2000).

This differentiation between economics and democracy notwithstanding, there is a way in which economic factors might be thought of as constitutive elements of democracy. Democracy is a process that puts the economically powerful and powerless on an equal footing. Hence, any translation of economic power into political power, whether through the exclusion of the poor (e.g., by tying the right to vote to a property requirement) or the excessive weight of the preferences of the wealthy (e.g., through the buying of political influence or the setting of the agenda via media ownership) is obviously inimical to democracy. These are hardly disputed issues. But the principle of political equality at the heart of the concept of democracy also implies something else that is rarely acknowledged.

As argued by the proponents of the concept of human development and the capabilities approach such as Amartya Sen (1999) and Martha Nussbaum (2000), a lack of the material resources that are indispensable for an adequate standard of living, access to health, and access to education, is associated with a reduction of human capabilities. And the differential attainment of human capabilities necessarily has ramifications for the political process and, specifically, for the exercise of civil and political rights (Sen 1999: 36–40; see also UNDP 1990: 10; 2002: 52–53). Thus, to avoid a strictly legalistic and overly formal conception of what is entailed by an equal opportunity to participate in the political process, what might be tentatively phrased as the attainment of social integration should be included as a defining feature of democracy.[8]

## 6.3. From Conceptual to Empirical Questions

The preceding discussion leads to some encouraging conclusions regarding how to define democracy. But the exploration of the content and boundaries of the concept of democracy also raises unsettling questions about the desirability of democracy. In particular, the emphasis on proceduralism, and the distinction between democracy and the rule of law, makes it clear that there are other normatively infused political concepts beyond democracy — that is, that democracy is not an absolute value. Thus, this section presents the chapter's answer to the conceptual question, What is democracy?

but also addresses the implication of seeing democracy as one among various political values.

### 6.3.1. Defining Democracy

A theory of democracy offers justification for conceiving democracy as a set of rules regarding the political process, extending from the formation of government through public decision making all the way to the implementation of binding decisions, which reflects the principle that voter preferences are weighed equally. This robust procedural conception justifies the inclusion in a definition of democracy of standard political rights associated with the election of representatives, such as universal and equal voting rights, the right to run for office, the right to free and fair elections, and the right to regular elections. But it also justifies the inclusion of three other classes of rights in a definition of democracy.

One such class of rights refers to the process of decision making and implementation. Such rights are still not well articulated, and hence are hard to specify clearly, but would have to include the right that public officials work for the public interest and other rights that ensure not only that the preferences of citizens are reflected in public policy but also that the principle of equal weight of citizens' preferences is respected. A second class of rights are those rights conventionally labeled as "civil rights" which directly impinge on the ability of citizens to participate in the political process, including the right to a free press and to information, and the freedom of association, assembly, expression, and movement. Finally, a third class of rights concerns the opportunity for equal participation in the political process. These rights are also not well articulated, and much depends on precisely how the notion of social integration is specified. Indeed, part of the challenge of defining democracy consists in deciding whether and how items such as the means of material subsistence, access to education and health care, and decent work might be seen as aspects of social integration.

It bears emphasizing that currently there is little consensus among scholars regarding how to define democracy. Researchers use a wide range of definitions in their work. Moreover, there is a tendency in the literature to argue that the concept of democracy is "essentially contestable" (Gallie 1956), meaning that there is not even a basis for distinguishing better from worse definitions. Yet this skepticism about the possibility of making progress toward a shared definition is unwarranted. There are criteria for the inclusion of elements into a definition, the first and foremost being their justification in terms of a theory of the phenomena being conceptualized. And there is a well-developed theory of democracy that can serve as the basis for a definition of democracy. Thus, inasmuch as the debate is conducted according to some basic criteria, it is not unrealistic to expect that a considerable consensus can be established regarding how to define democracy.

### 6.3.2. Democracy as a Relative Value

At the same time, the discussion of the content and boundaries of the concept of democracy suggests a more unsettling, or at least complicated, answer to another question that is inescapably linked to any discussion of the question, What is democracy? — namely, Why should democracy be valued? The reason for focusing attention on democracy is that it is a powerful normative concept, which currently is largely seen in a positive light. And it is important to note that the procedural conception advanced in this chapter does not signify a retreat from the view that democracy is a valued good. Dahl, again, offers insight on this point. Thus, in addressing why a democratic political process should be valued, Dahl (1989: ch. 12; see also Dahl 1971: ch. 2; 1998: ch. 5) breaks with the familiar contrast between procedural and substantive views of democracy and makes a case that a democratic political process should be treated as a substantive good. Indeed, countering the view commonly invoked in arguments dismissive of democracy that, if democracy is understood as a process, it is merely a means — a view ironically sanctioned by Schumpeter's (1942: 242) statement that the "democratic method" is "incapable of being an end in itself" — Dahl argues convincingly that democracy should be valued not just as a means but also as an end in itself.[9]

Nonetheless, the normative justification for democracy cannot hinge solely on the status of democracy as a good thing. The emphasis on proceduralism, as well as the discussion about the conceptual boundaries of the concept of democracy, yields a key conclusion: that, even when a robust procedural definition of democracy is adopted, there are other political values beyond democracy. For example, given the potential for abuses of state power, it might be wise to protect the rule of law by placing some issues out of reach of the demos. The implications of this point for academic research and political action that takes democracy as its master concept and value are vast. Once political values other than democracy are acknowledged, the normative valuation that lies at the heart of research on democracy and the promotion of democracy — more democracy is always better — becomes a matter for discussion and has to be justified in relation to other political values.

The crux of the issue can be stated as follows. If one either holds only one value or holds multiple values yet one of them is deemed to trump the others under any circumstance, one's concerns are reduced to identifying the actions that advance one's overriding value. But if we hold multiple values that cannot be ordered independently of the relative gains and losses across different valued goals, one's concerns must extend to the way in which the pursuit of one value may be negatively associated with another value and to the simultaneous impact of alternative courses of action on all values. In such a case, whether more democracy is better is a matter not only of how much democracy is valued relative to other values but also of the empirical relationship between democracy and other political values. In other words, it is necessary to ask the empirical questions, Are there trade-offs between democracy and other political values? Does the promotion of democracy result in an overall increase in valued political goods?

The world of politics could still be simple. That is, it may well be that the empirical relationship between democracy and other political values — such as rule of law, development, and human rights — is mutually reinforcing. In that case, all good things go together and the need for making tough choices is circumvented. Democracy can be promoted without any worries about possible negative side effects. But a wealth of historical and current evidence indicates that many political values are not mutually reinforcing (Mann 1993; Ertman 1997; Zakaria 2003). Moreover, a key puzzle of current global politics is precisely that, counter to widely held expectations, the significant gains with regard to electoral democracy over the past twenty-five years have not been accompanied by comparable positive changes with regard to other desired goals, such as the rule of law and economic equality (Munck 2003). Politics seems to involve inescapable choices that require weighing complex trade-offs.

## 6.4. Conclusion

This chapter has focused on the question, What is democracy? in an attempt to arrive at an adequate definition of democracy. Definitions are important, in that they are the point of reference for an effort at measurement. Hence, a theoretical justification for considering certain elements as constitutive of democracy was presented. The discussion is, undoubtedly, tentative. But it does point to the possibility of making progress toward a shared definition. Indeed, though it is commonplace to observe that scholars disagree on how to define democracy, there are actually important areas of agreement among scholars who have offered serious theories of democracy, which can serve as the basis for building consensus on the meaning of the concept of democracy.

At the same time that the discussion of the question, What is democracy? suggested that theory offers a strong guide in conceptualizing democracy, it raised concerns about the normative justification of democracy. The democratic principle that all individuals have an equal right to participate in the process that generates these decisions is widely shared. But the normative justification for promoting democracy cannot hinge solely on the status of democracy as a good thing, because it does not follow that more democracy is always better simply because democracy is considered a good thing. This optimistic view is widely held, especially within the community dedicated to the promotion of democracy. Indeed, the belief that all good things go together is uncritically accepted by a large number of actors seeking to shape politics. As was suggested, though, because democracy is not the only widely shared political value, the normative justification for promoting democracy cannot be based solely on the status of democracy as a good thing; it must also hinge on the answer to empirical questions regarding the potential trade-offs among multiple political values.

The implications of the discussion for research on measurement are, likewise, far-reaching. A first implication is that even though this chapter's conceptual analysis reveals the difficulty of fully capturing the meaning of democracy and might even be seen as erring on the side of advancing a maximalist definition of democracy, that is, a definition that includes extraneous elements in the definition of the concept of democracy, it clearly pinpoints the limitations of a minimalist measure of democracy, that is, a measure that excludes aspects that are part of the meaning of the concept of democracy. Minimalism has its virtues. Minimalist measures of democracy are easier to develop and existing minimalist measures tend to be more clearly rooted in theory than their alternatives. They are also useful, in that they serve to identify countries that are not democratic. If a country is not democratic under a minimalist conception, it will certainly not be democratic under a broader conception. But minimalist measures of democracy are problematic in that they might characterize as democracies countries that are not democratic. This problem is avoided in this book, because the methodologies presented in chapters 4 and 5 are explicitly aimed at the development of measures of electoral democracy and democratic elections, rather than of democracy *tout court*. Nonetheless, a strong implication of the conceptual analysis provided here is the need to develop measures that include aspects of democracy that exceed electoral democracy yet are broadly held to be important aspects of democracy.

A second implication for research on measurement, which emerges from the discussion of the normative justification of democracy, is even more radical. The empirical questions raised in this chapter suggest that the study of democracy should not be addressed in isolation and cut off from a consideration of other political values. Thus, more is needed than the development of broader measures of democracy, which escape the limitations of minimalist measures. The scope of concepts that are measured must be broadened to include democracy *tout court* but also other political concepts that are imbued with a strong normative content.

# SEVEN

# Developing Measures

*Beyond Electoral Democracy*

........................................................................................................

N ational states have long had an interest in producing data on their resources and populations. The generation of statistics on a wide range
of economic, military, demographic, and social issues coincided with the
consolidation of government administrative structures; indeed, the term *statistics* literally means the "science of the state." The body of state-produced
data has grown steadily over the years as states have sought to track a growing number of issues and as more states have developed the capability to
generate data. Moreover, as a result of the efforts of intergovernmental organizations such as the World Bank, the International Monetary Fund, and the
United Nations' multiple programs and agencies, data gathered by governments throughout the world have been brought together and used to build
cross-national databases. Prominent examples, such as the World Bank's
*World Development Indicators* and the data published in the United Nations
Development Programme's *Human Development Report,* are the results of
a lengthy collective effort whereby procedures to generate data have been
tested, fine-tuned, and increasingly standardized.

The production of data on explicitly political matters and on the political
process in particular has been a different story. The generation of data, in
particular comparable data, on politics has persistently lagged behind data
on other aspects of society (Rokkan et al. 1970: 169–80; Heath and Martin
1997). Some noteworthy efforts have been made by sources independent of
states — by university researchers in particular — since the late 1960s.[1] Only
recently, however, with the spread of democracy throughout the globe and
the events of 1989 in the communist world, has interest in data on politics
become widespread.

The current period is without doubt unprecedented in terms of the production of data on politics. Academic work has been given a new impulse. A

large number of initiatives have also been launched by nongovernmental organizations (NGOs) as well as by intergovernmental organizations (IGOs) and multilateral development banks (MDBs). Thus, the data production efforts of an array of individuals and institutions that are too numerous to list have turned the generation of comparable cross-national data on politics into a growth industry.[2] Indeed, we are in the midst of the most significant collective drive to produce political data in a methodologically self-conscious manner since the efforts launched by Karl Deutsch and Stein Rokkan in the early 1960s (Merritt and Rokkan 1966; Taylor 1968).

Although this measurement movement is resulting in more and better data on politics, the limitations of current knowledge should be acknowledged. Such an acknowledgment is particularly critical because data on politics are increasingly used in the world of politics. NGOs use data for purposes of advocacy; a variety of actors regularly invoke statistical analyses on the causes and consequences of democracy to justify their support of, or opposition to, different policies; and governments, IGOs, and the MDBs link data on politics to policy choices and governance-related conditionalities.[3] Moreover, such an acknowledgment is key because information presented in quantitative form is generally accorded a special status. After all, one of the selling points of using data on politics is that they draw on the power of an association with science and hence are treated with considerable deference by public officials and the public. Yet this assumed scientific status verges on being a misrepresentation of the current state of knowledge regarding the measurement of political concepts. Despite recent advances, we are still at an early, relatively exploratory phase in the measurement of political concepts.

This book has sought to contribute to the measurement movement in the field of politics, and this chapter seeks to lay the groundwork for a response to the measurement challenge outlined in the previous chapter. As argued in chapter 6, an analysis of democracy calls for measures that capture the full meaning of democracy and also requires, inasmuch as the normative justification of democracy hinges on the empirical relationship between democracy and other political values, measures of concepts imbued with these other political values. Thus, this chapter addresses the challenge of developing broader measures than those that can be generated with the methodologies discussed in chapters 4 and 5, or, in other words, measures that go beyond electoral democracy.

The first section recapitulates the research strategy used to develop the methodologies and data presented in chapters 4 and 5 and argues that it is a strategy that could be productively used to tackle the broader challenge of measuring democracy and politics. The second section discusses some literature on the topic, draws some lessons from previous work, and suggests approaches that should be taken into consideration by scholars seeking to develop measures of a wide range of political concepts. In the conclusion, some final thoughts are presented.

## 7.1. A Research Strategy

The question of what research strategy is most likely to lead to sustained progress in the production of political data is fundamental. Many data-production initiatives end up as one-off projects. Other initiatives have flourished over the years, only to be abandoned. Thus, it is important to consider what strategy is used to produce data and whether the chosen strategy is likely to contribute to a sustainable agenda for producing political data. But the simple production of data is not enough. After all, some data initiatives continue, in part out of inertia and in part out of a lack of alternatives, even though the data they have produced are known to be problematic. Moreover, the task of ascertaining whether certain data are more valid than others has become increasingly relevant inasmuch as multiple datasets on the same concept have been produced. In other words, work on measurement is concerned with producing not just data but, more pointedly, good data or at least better data. Thus, it is also important to consider whether the chosen validation method is appropriate and whether the results of the validation procedures are correctly interpreted.

This section does not argue that there is one correct research strategy for the production and validation of data, but it does make a case that the strategy exemplified by this book has some important strengths and that it can thus well serve researchers eager to tackle the challenge of measuring democracy and politics. Moreover, it highlights the value of considering research strategies in a deliberate manner and of assessing their strengths and weaknesses. Despite the importance of the choice of research strategy, many of the decisions that go into the production and validation of data remain implicit, in part because scholars work within traditions that rely on their own language and develop their own habits. Thus, this section seeks to break with this common practice and addresses in an explicit manner some of the key choices that pertain to the production and validation of data.

### 7.1.1. The Production of Data

The research strategy to produce data favored in this book consists of four core elements, each of which has an explicit rationale. A first element of this strategy is the principle that efforts to develop measures should start with political concepts that have been well clarified by existing theory and that represent manageable measurement challenges. For this reason, this book focused on democracy and, even more narrowly, on electoral democracy. Past research has produced a considerable body of theory and numerous measures of this concept, which offer important clues regarding what needs to be measured and how it should be measured (see chapters 2 and 6). Thus, the bet made in this book is that by focusing on this relatively narrow concept, the likelihood of generating credible measures would be enhanced, and that such measures could serve as a building block — as opposed to yet another false start — in the broader project of measuring democracy and politics.

A second element of this strategy is the view that the state is the key locus of public decision making and hence that the country should be the unit of analysis. This is a choice that many contest, on good grounds. Students of subnational politics have rightly pointed to the failure of cross-national data to acknowledge within-country variations. In turn, students of transnational and supranational politics have shown that all politics does not pass through the national state. Nonetheless, the theoretical basis for using the country as the unit of analysis is clearer and better developed than any of its alternatives, and hence this choice of unit of analysis, though open to revision, arguably offers the best currently available point of departure for data production efforts.[4]

A third element of the research strategy concerns the choice between a theory-driven or data-driven approach. In this regard, the measures proposed in this book are primarily theory-driven. Conceptual attributes were selected in light of theory, and existing theory was considered to be sufficiently clear and strong to justify the inclusion of certain attributes and the exclusion of others. Aggregation procedures were also guided by theory — indeed, aggregation rules were selected in an a priori fashion — and did not rely on statistical methods, such as principal component analysis or the unobserved components method. That is, the theory regarding conceptual attributes and their relationship was again deemed clear and strong enough to justify the choice of a specific aggregation rule as well as to reject the assumptions implicit in various statistical methods.[5] But this book's measures also place a heavy emphasis on case knowledge. The possibility and difficulty of gathering information was a consideration in the choice of conceptual attributes. And the focus on one world region, Latin America, followed from a recognition of the importance of in-depth knowledge of countries for the development of adequate measurement scales. As emphasized in chapters 2 and 4, statistical tests are critical to the production of good data. Moreover, the production of good data on all world regions is rightfully seen by many as a key research goal. Yet the path chosen to that goal is one that relies on a top-down approach, judiciously combined with a bottom-up approach, rather than one that depends heavily on statistical methods or that starts by producing data on all countries of the world.

Finally, a fourth strategic element regarding the production of data favored in this book is a reliance on expert coders. The use of coders is a potential source of measurement error. Moreover, there are alternatives to the use of expert coders, including increasingly sophisticated mass surveys (Bratton, Mattes, and Gyimah-Boadi 2005; Rose 2006; Dalton, Sin, and Jou 2007). Nonetheless, expert coding has several advantages. It can be used to produce data on the past. It allows for group discussions, in which disagreements can be identified, registered, and possibly resolved. And its transparency can be assured through the documentation of coding decisions, especially through reference to publicly available sources of information. Expert coding, when well done, is a valuable method of generating data.

### 7.1.2. The Validation of Data

Another element of the research strategy followed in this book has been its treatment of the validation of measures as a core aspect of measurement. This element is seen most clearly in the discussion of the electoral democracy index (EDI), given the availability of data on the EDI and at least partial data on other democracy indices (see chapter 4). Indeed, the first point that should be stressed is that to fully carry out validation tests of indices, data on all of the conceptual attributes of an index, that is, the disaggregate data, and data to assess the impact of coders, are needed. But other ideas regarding how to conduct the validation of data and how to interpret the results of the tests guided the validation exercise.

A key idea concerns the primacy of content validation, a type of validation that is focused on the fundamental yet frequently disregarded relationship between the meaning of the concept being measured and the concept's measures (Adcock and Collier 2001: 537–40). This type of validation is critical in that it serves to establish that a measure is theoretically interpretable as a measure of a certain concept (see section 4.1; see also chapter 5). Indeed, if one lacks a considerable degree of confidence that the design of a measuring instrument has a strong and clear theoretical foundation, there is little point in proceeding further with a validity assessment by engaging in complex empirical tests. Moreover, as shown in chapter 4, content validation is not only a matter of considering if the conceptual attributes highlighted by a measuring instrument capture the meaning of the concept being measured. It is also a question of whether the measurement scales reflect the content of the concept and, in the case of indices, whether the aggregation rule appropriately reflects the theoretical relationship among the concept's various attributes and components, two issues that can certainly not be ascertained by a quick glance at the definition of the concept being measured.

Other ideas that guided the validation exercise concern construct validation, a type of validation focused on the empirical relationship among measures that encompasses convergent validation, demonstrated when different measures of the same concept are similar to each other, and discriminant validation, demonstrated when measures of different concepts are not similar to each other.[6] Ideally, this type of validation would involve tests that sharply distinguish the concept being measured from the methods used to measure the concept, that is, what is measured from how it is measured, so as to isolate the real measure from method artifacts. Yet, as the validation of the EDI shows, even though this ideal was not attainable, it was possible to design creative tests of construct validity (see sections 4.2 and 4.3). These tests built on the work of Donald Campbell (see, especially, Campbell and Fiske 1959) and Kenneth Bollen (Bollen and Paxton 1998; see also Bollen 1993; Bollen and Paxton 2000). But they also introduced some innovations. Rather than taking the instrument as a whole, as is conventional, the tests focused on distinct features of measuring instruments. Also, by avoiding the introduction of questionable assumptions regarding the empirical relationship among different measures, a common problem in validation exercises, the tests focused on explicitly demonstrated conceptual differences.

### 7.1.3. Conclusions

In sum, this book exemplifies a distinct research strategy for producing and validating data, two issues that are part and parcel of the same measurement endeavor, and this section has sought to outline this strategy explicitly and to draw attention to its strengths. In highlighting the strengths of the chosen strategy, this discussion does not imply that this strategy has only strengths because it is always sensible to be cautious about trumpeting the benefits of any one strategy; or that it is the only strategy worth pursuing because it would be narrow-minded to suggest that good data on politics are not being produced using different strategies. Indeed, the discussion merely raises the question about the relative merits and the potential complementarity of different strategies. An exchange on these issues would thus be instructive and could play a role in orienting the work on measurement. But this discussion has sought to make a case for the value of the strategy followed in this book. Researchers eager to tackle the broader challenge of developing measures of political concepts would benefit from using this strategy and doing so in a deliberate manner, in order to exploit its strengths as much as possible.

## 7.2. Literatures and Lessons

The challenge of developing measures of politics that go beyond electoral democracy using the strategy proposed in the previous section can be further oriented through the identification of basic things scholars seeking to contribute to this agenda should do and avoid doing. On the positive side, scholars should strive to extract useful insights about how to develop measures of a wide range of political concepts from the existing literatures. Broadly stated, it is important to recognize that research on measurement does not start from scratch and that researchers can and should build on available resources. On the negative side, it is imperative to draw lessons from previous work about practices that should be avoided. Thus, it is also useful to highlight some pitfalls that are common especially in efforts at measurement in the world of politics.

### 7.2.1. Resources to Build On

*Conceptual Analyses.* One resource of key import to the measurement challenge in politics is conceptual analyses. The inescapable point of reference in all work on measurement is the meaning of the concept or concepts being measured. Thus, measurement is inextricably linked with conceptual analysis, that is, the clarification of the meaning of concepts (Sartori 1984;

Collier and Levitsky 1997). And it has much to draw from masterpieces of political conceptual analysis, such as Max Weber's (1978) *Economy and Society,* Harold Lasswell and Abraham Kaplan's (1950) *Power and Society,* and Norberto Bobbio's (2005) *General Theory of Politics.* This kind of work offers many insights regarding the challenges of conceptualization and aggregation (see sections 2.1 and 2.3).

*Indicators.* A second resource available to researchers is work on indicators, that is, the observables used to operationalize concepts. Valuable contributions include various manuals and handbooks prepared by NGOs, IGOs, and development agencies on broad topics such as democracy and democratic governance (USAID 1998, 2000; Beetham et al. 2001), as well as on more specific topics such as electoral observation (European Commission 2002; OSCE/ ODIHR 2005), corruption (USAID 1999), the justice system (Vera Institute of Justice 2003), human rights (Green 2001; Landman 2004), and gender equality (OECD/DAC 1998; ECLAC 1999; UNECE 2001; see also Apodaca 1998). The task of identifying adequate indicators has also been addressed by a large number of conferences and many working groups that bring together academics and practitioners with representatives of various NGOs, IGOs, and development agencies (UN 2000). Indeed, taken as a whole, the work on indicators, an important aspect of measuring instruments (section 2.2), has produced important advances in recent years.

*Measurement Instruments.* A third resource is formal measurement instruments that address different aspects of politics beyond electoral democracy. Some of these instruments focus on executive-legislature relationships, measuring presidential power (Shugart and Carey 1992: ch. 8) and, relatedly, the strength of parliament (Fish 2006; Wehner 2006), or concentrate on the judiciary, frequently emphasizing its independence from other branches of government (Linares 2004; American Bar Association 2007). Others offer more encompassing measures of checks and balances, including the three traditional branches of government as well as the federal structure of government (Henisz 2000). Still others have addressed the bureaucracy, measuring the Weberian character of bureaucracies (Evans and Rauch 1999) or respect for civil liberties (Skaaning 2006a, 2006b). These measurement instruments are, to be sure, subject to improvement, and the integration of these partial instruments, with the goal of providing a coherent overall depiction of politics, is a complex matter. But the value of these efforts, which cover many key aspects of politics beyond electoral democracy, should be recognized, and any new work should build on these instruments.

*Evaluations of Measures.*   Finally, a fourth resource is evaluations of measures of different aspects of politics. Some of these evaluations focus on single datasets, such as the Polity dataset (Gleditsch and Ward 1997) and the World Bank's Worldwide Governance Indicators (Arndt and Oman 2006). More frequently, such evaluations compare multiple datasets that purportedly measure the same concept. Many such assessments have addressed the concept of democracy.[7] But evaluations have covered a range of other political concepts, including presidential powers (Metcalf 2000), taxation (Lieberman 2002), decentralization (Schneider 2003), corruption (Lancaster and Montinola 2001; Knack 2006), civil liberties (Skaaning 2006b), press freedom (Becker, Vlad, and Nusser 2007), and human rights (Landman 2004). In short, many political concepts have been covered in such start-of-the-art evaluations and scholars seeking to develop broad measures of politics can extract some important lessons from such evaluations.

### 7.2.2. Pitfalls to Avoid

Progress in meeting the measuring challenge in the field of politics also hinges on the avoidance of some pitfalls that are common especially in efforts at measurement in the world of politics. These problems could undermine the legitimacy of using data for policy purposes and solidify opposition to initiatives seeking to build a bridge between science and politics. Indeed, the continuation and maturation of the current interest in data on politics is likely to hinge in part on the development of a greater sense of the dangers of "numerological nonsense" (Rokkan et al. 1970: 288) and the avoidance of the following basic problems.

*Incomplete Measuring Instruments.*   Various initiatives that purport to use measures of political concepts to monitor compliance with certain standards offer vague enunciations of principles (e.g., the European Union's accession democracy clause) or a list of items or questions (e.g., the African Peer Review Mechanism of the New Partnership for Africa's Development).[8] These initiatives are routinely presented as exercises in measurement that use data to arrive at certain conclusions. But such enunciations or lists are not measuring instruments. They provide some sense of what concepts are to be measured. Yet they are silent on a broad range of issues that are required to construct a measuring instrument; and, by offering an incompletely specified measuring instrument, they open the door to the use of data in an ad hoc way that is susceptible to political manipulation. Thus, if data are to be used in making political decisions, it is imperative to recognize that a list of items or questions provides, at best, a point of departure and to fully assume the responsibility of developing a measuring instrument.

*Denying Methodological Choices.*   A standard approach to preventing the political manipulation of data is to emphasize the need for objective data, the idea being that such data are not subject to politicking. But the commonly invoked distinction between objective and subjective data (see, e.g., UNDP 2002: 36–37) is frequently associated with a simplistic view of the data generation process that can actually hide significant biases. The human element cannot be removed from the measurement process, because a broad range of methodological choices necessarily goes into the construction of a measuring instrument. Thus, the best that can be done is to be explicit about these methodological choices, to justify them theoretically and subject them to empirical testing, and to allow independent observers to scrutinize and contest these choices by making the entire process of measurement transparent. This is the most effective way to generate good data and to guard against the real danger: not subjective data but rather arbitrary measures that rest on claims to authority.[9]

*Delinking Methodological Choices from the Concept Being Measured.*   If choices and hence subjectivity are an intrinsic aspect of measurement, it is critical to ensure that the multiple choices involved in the construction of measures are always made in light of the ultimate goal of the measurement exercise: the measurement of a certain concept. This is so obvious that it might appear an unnecessary warning. Yet the delinking of methodology from the concept being measured is a mistake made by such significant initiatives as the Millennium Challenge Account (MCA) of the U.S. government. Specifically, while the MCA supposedly uses data as a means to identify countries that are democratic — the guiding idea being that democracies make better use of development aid and should thus be targeted — the methodology used to generate a list of target countries does not capture the concept of democracy and does not guarantee that democracies will be identified.[10] Thus, when measuring instruments are constructed, and especially when methodological choices involve more technical issues, it is essential to constantly link these choices explicitly and carefully back to the concept being measured.

*Presenting Measurement as a Perfect Science.*   The results of the measurement process — quantitative data — tend to be taken, and sometimes are presented, as flawless measures. But such interpretations overlook one of the central points in measurement theory: that error is an inescapable part of any attempt at measurement. This is not merely a technical issue that might be sidestepped at little cost. Nor is it a fatal flaw that implies that the resulting measures should be distrusted and, at an extreme, rejected. Rather, all this point implies is that measurement is a precise but not a perfect science, and that measurement error should be factored into an estimate of the degree of confidence that is attached to any piece of data. Yet this critical point is frequently overlooked and data are presented as though they are error-free, something that can lead to mistaken results. A prominent example of such a problem is, again, the MCA.[11] But it is not an isolated example. Therefore, efforts to construct measuring instruments and to interpret data must be forthcoming about the unavoidable nature of measurement error and must factor such error into any conclusions derived from the analysis of data.

*Overcomplexification.* Finally, it is not a bad thing to consider displays of technical virtuosity in measurement exercises with a degree of suspicion. To be sure, measurement involves a range of sometimes complex issues, and these should all be given the attention they deserve. But it is also useful to emphasize that good data are readily interpretable and to warn against over-complexification. Indeed, there are grounds to suspect that a measuring instrument that is hard to grasp reduces the accessibility and interpretability of data without necessarily adding to their validity. Numerous examples of such overcomplexification exist in the field of politics, and a sign of this is the real difficulty even experts face in conveying the meaning of many indices in ways that make real, tangible sense. Thus, a good rule of thumb in constructing measuring instruments is to keep things as simple as possible.

## 7.3. Conclusion

The measures used in the study of politics have a great impact on our knowledge about politics. They affect the way we describe the world and the causal propositions we consider to be valid. Moreover, the distance between academics and politics has been greatly reduced as data about politics, and the analyses of these data, are increasingly used in politics and are becoming a part of the political process itself. We live in an age in which data, understood as quantitative or numerical representations of reality, are widely recognized as tools for scientific analysis and social reform but are also closely intertwined with the language of power. Thus, it is only proper that academics

assume the responsibilities associated with the new salience of data on politics by contributing to the generation of good data and by exercising scrutiny
over the ways in which data, and analyses of data, on politics are put to
political uses.

Academics interested in politics do not fully acknowledge that the design
of instruments to measure the concepts used in political analysis and the
production of data of an appropriate empirical scope are essential parts of
the research process. Although measures are routinely used in all sorts of
contexts, their users — including quantitative researchers anxious to get on
with causal analysis — are frequently unaware of what precisely is measured
by their measures and how valid their measures are. But this is changing. In
recent years a measurement movement has begun to take shape in the field of
politics, especially as political scientists have begun to pay attention to matters of measurement, and a rich literature on measurement methodology has
developed. The generation of comparable cross-national data on democracy
and politics has even become a growth industry.

This book has sought to recognize the important accomplishments made
regarding the measurement of political concepts and to contribute to this
work on measurement. It also has emphasized the limitations of current
knowledge. We still lack credible measures of some of the central concepts in
political analysis. Thus, this chapter has sought to lay the groundwork for a
response to this measurement challenge. The stakes are high, and the possibility of responding successfully is uncertain. But responding to this challenge has some political urgency. In short, this is a challenge that constitutes a
unique opportunity for academics eager to embrace engaged scholarship and
to build a bridge between scholarship and politics.

# Notes

.....................................................................................................................

*Chapter 1: Bringing Knowledge to Bear on Politics*

1. For an overview of U.S. promotion of democracy during the twentieth century, see Smith (1994). On U.S. democracy promotion, especially during the Reagan and subsequent administrations, see Carothers (1991, 2000, 2007); Cox, Ikenberry, and Inoguchi (2000); Robinson (1996); Rieffer and Kristan (2005); and Smith (2007).

2. Beyond the NDI and IRI, the NED has two other "affiliated institutes": the Center for Independent Private Enterprise (CIPE) and the Free Trade Union Institute (later reorganized as the American Center for International Labor Solidarity), linked with business and labor interests, respectively. The CIPE was founded by the U.S. Chamber of Commerce, and the American Center for International Labor Solidarity was formed by the American Federation of Labor–Congress of Industrial Organizations (AFL-CIO).

3. The field of democracy promotion in the United States also includes many NGOs, with various sorts of links with parties and the government, such as the Carter Center, created in 1982; IFES–Democracy at Large (formerly the International Foundation for Election Systems), launched in 1987; the Eurasia Foundation, started in 1992; and the Open Society Institute, formed in 1993. These organizations entered an arena long occupied by Freedom House, founded in a different era in 1941. On the origins and constitution of democracy promotion as a field in the United States, see Guilhot (2005); on the organizations that are active in democracy promotion in the United States, see Melia (2005).

4. On the post-Iraq debate about U.S. democracy promotion, as seen from the perspective of some of its advocates, see Carothers (2006); Gershman and Allen (2006); Windsor (2006); and Fukuyama and McFaul (2007).

5. On the development of European democracy promotion, relative to U.S. democracy promotion, see Campbell and Carroll (2005); on democracy promotion programs within European countries, see Youngs (2006); and on EU democracy promotion, see Youngs (2002) and Vachudova (2005).

6. On International IDEA and its activities, see International IDEA (2005).

7. On democracy promotion in the Americas, see Farer (1996) and Legler, Lean, and Boniface (2007).

8. On the role of the UN in promoting democracy, see Newman and Rich (2004).

9. See the *Declaration of Principles for International Election Observation and Code of Conduct for International Election Observers*, an agreement spearheaded by the Carter Center, the NDI, and the United Nations Electoral Assistance Division, and signed by twenty-one organizations on October 24, 2005 (Carter Center et al. 2005).

10. Such early-warning systems have been used to predict humanitarian crises (Davies and Gurr 1998) and only recently have been discussed in the context of democracy promotion. One organization that has developed an early-warning system for use in its work on democracy is the OAS.

11. Transparency International has been releasing its CPI on an annual basis since 1995 and has never made its underlying data publicly available. The World Bank first published its CCI in 1996 and only a decade later began to make public most, though not all, of the index's underlying data.

12. The World Bank has conducted CPIAs since 1977 and disclosed its data for most countries for the first time in 2006.

13. On the link between democracy and corruption, see Sung (2004); on the link between democracy and human rights, see Davenport and Armstrong (2004); and, on the link between democracy and both economic growth and poverty reduction, see Przeworski et al. (2000) and Ross (2006).

14. Gerth and Mills (1946: 77–156).

## Chapter 2: Conceptualizing and Measuring Democracy

1. Bollen (1980, 1986, 1991, 1993); Bollen and Paxton (2000); and Foweraker and Krznaric (2000). See also Gleditsch and Ward (1997) and Coppedge (1999) and, more recently, Coppedge (2005); Hadenius and Teorell (2005); and Skaaning (2006b).

2. For discussions of alternative democracy indices and correlations among aggregate data, see Alvarez et al. (1996: 18–21); Arat (1991: 22–23, 28); Bollen (1980: 381); Coppedge (1997: 180); Coppedge and Reinicke (1991: 51–52); Gasiorowski (1996: 477–78); Hadenius (1992: 41, 43, 71, 159–63); Jaggers and Gurr (1995: 473–76); and Vanhanen (1993: 317–19; 1997: 31–40).

3. For brief but useful discussions of some earlier indices that have fallen into disuse, see Bollen (1980: 373–75, 379–84) and Arat (1991: 28).

4. Two other indices omit this attribute. Though Freedom House's definition of political rights refers to "the right of all adults to vote," it does not include this aspect under its checklist of political rights (Ryan 1994: 10). Likewise, Bollen (1980: 372, 376) stresses the importance of a universal suffrage but then does not appear to retain this aspect of elections in his attributes.

5. These aspects of participation are sometimes included in indices in the form of the attribute Fairness of the electoral process. This is the case with Bollen and Hadenius. Even Coppedge and Reinicke (1991: 49), who state that they are concerned only with contestation, include this aspect of participation in their index. However, most indices fail to address these important issues.

6. Others have included an attribute that resembles what ACLP mean by Offices but use different labels. Arat and Bollen refer to Executive and Legislative Selection. Hadenius talks about the number of seats that are filled by elections. And the Polity IV index refers in a somewhat confusing manner to the Competitiveness and Openness of Executive Recruitment.

7. Alvarez et al. (1996: 20) justify their exclusion of the attribute Legislative Effectiveness on grounds that the data are unreliable.

8. It is important to distinguish this advice from the argument in favor of collecting redundant information (Coombs 1953; Blalock 1982: 46–54). The advice against redundancy is made regarding a matter of conceptual logic. In contrast, the advice in favor of redundancy concerns indicators and scale assumptions.

9. Some indices that do little to disaggregate the concept of democracy — the Vanhanen and Gasiorowski indices — avoid problems of conceptual logic, but only because they forgo the opportunity to flesh out the concept analytically and to provide a bridge between the abstract concept of democracy and its more concrete attributes. The costs of this option are quite high.

10. It is common for bias and noise to trade off, so reducing one often increases the other. For instance, stringent coding rules may improve intercoder reliability but at the cost of imposing biases in the way the rules are framed. Thus, researchers should also be attentive to any such trade-off.

11. Much of the debate regarding the choice of measurement level in the literature on democracy has focused on the choice between dichotomous and continuous measures. For an examination of this rather inconclusive debate, see Collier and Adcock (1999); see also the test that assesses the impact of different cutoff points performed by Elkins (2000) on the data assembled by ACLP. This problem is far from unique to political science and is addressed in other areas such as clinical psychology (Waller and Meehl 1998).

12. Vanhanen avoids many of these potential problems because he uses "objective" indicators.

13. ACLP do not provide disaggregate data. Arat has indicated that she would be willing to make her disaggregate data available but that the data were collected before the use of computers became widespread, and thus she is not able to offer it in a computer readable format. Freedom House only started to provide disaggregate data as part of its indices for 2006. The only data that were generated by Gasiorowski (1996: 480–82) are aggregate data.

14. Moreover, though multiple sources are used, there is no sign that considera-

tion was given to whether the choice of indicators magnifies rather than minimizes the measurement error attributable to the set of sources the index relies on (Bollen 1986: 583–86). The best available discussion of indicators used in the Freedom House indices is by Gastil (1991: 26–36).

15. Other problems should be noted. First, the coding process used by Freedom House has changed over time. From 1977 to 1989, when Gastil (1991: 22–23) was in charge of the index, a single coder, Gastil, did the coding. During this period, it also appears that even though there was a checklist of components, coding was actually done at the level of the two attributes of the index. After 1989, coding was done by a team rather than an individual and at the level of components rather than attributes (Ryan 1994: 7, 11). Though this represents an improvement, the basic checklist used in constructing the index underwent changes (compare Gastil 1991: 26, 32–33, and Ryan 1994: 10). Second, the list of components used by Freedom House to construct its Political Rights index has changed over the years (compare Gastil 1991: 26 to Freedom House 1999: 547–48 and Freedom House 2007a), but the scores for prior years have not been revised to reflect the new methodology. Thus, a problem with the Freedom House index is that the internal consistency of the data series is open to question.

16. This entire step thus assumes that some disaggregation has taken place, that is, that at least more than one attribute is identified and that disaggregate data has been generated. Thus, the challenge of aggregation is relevant to all democracy indices under consideration but one, the Gasiorowski index, which does not rely on data coded at a disaggregate level.

17. The distinction between these two perspectives corresponds to the distinction in the psychometric literature between effect and cause indicators (Bollen and Lennox 1991; Bollen and Ting 2000), or reflective and formative measures (Edwards and Bagozzi 2000). The conventional view is based on the assumption that aggregation is conducted on effect or reflective indicators, while the less conventional view is based on the assumption that aggregation is conducted on cause or formative indicators.

18. It is not uncommon for one perspective to hold at one level of the entire aggregation process and the other perspective to hold at a different level. Indeed, this is often the case in uses of multiple criteria for prediction in areas such as personnel selection, where several unidimensional scales constructed using the Spearman factor model are combined using other rules (Guion 1998). Thus, analysts might specify that they use one perspective for a certain step in the aggregation process and another perspective for a different step in the aggregation process.

19. The fact that 33 of the 170 countries included in Coppedge and Reinicke's (1991: 52–53; Coppedge 1997: 181–83) index could not be located on their Guttman scale is noteworthy. As Guttman (1977: 100) himself noted, "scalability is not to be desired or constructed" but rather considered as a hypothesis. Moreover, he em-

phasized that in testing the "hypothesis of scalability" one cannot examine several items, see which ones scale, and then remove the ones that do not scale. After all, the original items were chosen for a theoretically relevant reason, and excluding them because they do not scale has the potential to capitalize on chance. At the same time, it is hard to interpret Coppedge and Reinicke's failure to identify a cumulative scale as unambiguous proof of multidimensionality, because the procedure to construct a Guttman scale conflates unreliability and dimensionality. Indeed, the use of the Rasch model (Rasch 1960; Andrich 1988) or the Mokken scale (Mokken 1971) would have been more appropriate, because they maintain the cumulative structure but allow for unreliability in a systematic way.

20. Many of these indices are implicitly based on Dahl's (1971: 2) approach to thinking about democracy in terms of a set of necessary conditions.

21. This issue is analogous to the problem of functional form specification in regression analysis. On various common aggregation operators, see Goertz (2006: 39–44) and Smithson and Verkuilen (2006: 4–15, 50, 69–71).

22. The total scores are subsequently transformed into seven-point scales, which are further divided into three categories — free, partly free, not free — through a rather arbitrary set of decisions (Ryan 1994: 11).

### Chapter 3: Drawing Boundaries

1. Sartori's (1976: 273–99) strongest argument for separating distinctions of kind from distinctions of degree, and for using this dichotomous distinction as a basis for separating classification from quantitative measurement, is that certain thresholds pinpoint discontinuous, exogenous change whereas others identify continuous, endogenous change. As suggestive as this idea may be, no change is either entirely driven by exogenous or endogenous forces and, thus, the distinction collapses.

2. Scales can establish relationships of order (e.g., $1$ = low, $2$ = medium, $3$ = high), relationships of distance (e.g., $2$ = midpoint between $1$ and $3$), or involve the identification of the endpoints of a scale (e.g., $0$ = absence, $1$ = full presence).

3. The full presence of the right of suffrage is harder to define than the absence of the right of suffrage due to ongoing debates about who should be included in the demos and who should have the right to vote. Nevertheless, there is a sound theoretical basis for defining full suffrage (Dahl 1989: ch. 9). In other words, even if the standards countries adopt change over time and old problems may take new forms, there is still a basis for defining in abstract terms what is meant by full suffrage in a manner that will stand the test of time and will not lead to censoring at the high end of the scale.

4. Dahl (1971: 232, 248) does not explicitly state what percentage of adults with the right to vote he uses to distinguish "near polyarchies" from "non polyarchies," the

relevant threshold. Nonetheless, the exclusion of Ecuador from his list of near poly-archies seems to be based on its failure to extend the suffrage to 90 percent of all adults.

5. An additional issue is the proposal by the same authors of different thresholds. For example, Vanhanen (2000: 257; 2007: 19) uses a threshold linked with actual voter participation in elections and has set it either at 10, 15, or 20 percent of the entire population. The usual rationale for using different standards — that democratic stan-dards regarding the right to vote change over time — reflects a relativist fallacy and thus is highly dubious. Though an interesting topic for a study of changing public opinion, the issue of changing standards has no place in measurement exercises.

6. An understanding of society as divided into social classes offers a justification for taking the working class's right to vote as an indicator that divergent views, including those of mass, nonelite segments of the population, are being included (Rueschemeyer, Stephens, and Stephens 1992: 303, 47–48). But it is necessary to consider whether this model of society, which has offered a solid basis for thinking about democratization in Western Europe and Latin America, can be used without adjustment in other societies, or whether ethnic, gender, linguistic, religious or ter-ritorial identities would have to be considered on a par with class identities.

7. The problem of distinguishing authoritarian from democratic levels of par-ticipation can be solved with a dichotomous scale in which a 0 would refer to every-thing on one side of the threshold that distinguishes authoritarian from democratic levels of participation, and a 1 would refer to everything on the other side of this threshold. Nonetheless, the value of more-nuanced measures should be underscored. For example, focusing only on the democratic side of such a scale, the proposed "two-group" threshold between authoritarian and democratic levels of participation can be crossed without women, minority groups, and even with significant shares of major-ity groups having the right to vote. Therefore, it is normatively important to record systematically the progressive inclusion of different groups into the polity, and it is analytically important to construct scales that allow us to test the causes and effects of the exclusion or inclusion of different groups.

8. The extent of variation in recent times on the participation dimension, under-stood in narrow electoral terms, is a matter of some dispute. Certainly, elections were held without the full extension of the suffrage to all adults even after the end of World War II. Moreover, a variety of formal and nonformal barriers to the effective use of the right to vote continues to be of relevance, especially inasmuch as these barriers are targeted against certain classes of citizens. See, for example, Boneo and Torres Rivas (2001) on Guatemala.

9. This would correspond to what Sartori (1976: ch. 2, 221–30) calls no-party states and one-party states.

10. On the democratic nature of such bans, see Linz (1978: 6) and Hermet (1982: 25).

11. On this point, see Sartori (1976: 217–21); Linz (1978: 6); Hermet (1982:

26); Rouquié (1982: 58); O'Donnell and Schmitter (1986: 57, 61); Przeworski (1991: 10); and Przeworski et al. (2000: 15–18).

12. Framing the question in terms of the possibility of an incumbent's electoral defeat amounts to equating contestation to a matter of the right of opposition. The reason for highlighting this right is that the government is seen as having an intrinsic advantage in terms of access to resources, including the power to coerce (Dahl 1966: xiv–xv), and this chapter essentially adopts this perspective. But its limitations should be noted: it is conceivable that opposition forces are stronger than the government, and thus it is important to consider potential abuses of democratic norms of competition by both the government and the opposition.

13. For example, if one adopts the criterion that elections can be considered democratic if the winning party wins less than 70 percent of the vote (Vanhanen 2000: 257), elections would be classified as democratic even if a party won election after election with 69 percent of the vote, committed blatant fraud, and never relinquished power. Likewise, such a criterion would misclassify cases of democratic elections where winners win more than 70 percent in verifiably free elections.

14. On this basis, two systems that fail to meet the easy tests of whether contestation exists (i.e., no elections or no parties indicating "no contestation," and electoral loss by an incumbent indicating "contestation") can be classified as systems with a hegemonic party, if they fall on the authoritarian side of the contestation scale, or, alternatively, as predominant party systems, if they fall on the democratic side of the scale.

15. Other valuable efforts, which frame the issue in terms of the possibility of parties losing elections, include Hermet (1982) and Przeworski et al. (2000: 14–29).

16. Przeworski et al. (2000: 24–25) argue that if a ruling party relinquishes power after winning several successive elections, this serves as proof that the rulers would have accepted electoral defeat in all elections held since they first came to power. Likewise, a ruling party that holds elections yet subsequently closes down the electoral process, is considered *not* to have faced the possibility of a loss in the prior elections.

17. Beyond these blatant restrictions, further work is needed on a range of regulations that affect the conditions of entry into, and success in, the game of political competition. These regulations include thresholds for the formation and continued recognition of parties, bans on candidates that are independent of parties, and, probably most importantly, the rules of party and campaign financing. Talk in the United States of a "money primary" that narrows the field of candidates before voters cast their first vote in a caucus or primary attests to the impact of money on electoral competition.

18. On the uses of typologies in qualitative research, see Elman (2005). On the difference between classifications, typologies, taxonomies, and indices, see Lazarsfeld and Barton (1951) and Marradi (1990).

19. Numerous scholars have seen such attributes, as well as various other indicators of contestation and participation, as necessary conditions (Dahl 1971: 2; 1998: 38, 84, 93, 99; Przeworski et al. 2000: 28–29; Mainwaring, Brinks, and Pérez-Liñán 2001: 41, 47–48; Valenzuela 2001: 252; Schedler 2002). Thus, an important degree of consensus has developed regarding this issue. But it is important to emphasize that much hinges on the specific indicators used to measure contestation and participation. For example, if participation is measured in terms of the right to vote, one might consider it a necessary condition. However, if participation is measured in terms of voter turnout, the theoretical justification for considering it a necessary condition would be significantly weaker.

### Chapter 4: Producing and Validating Political Data

1. All tests were run on Stata 9.2. An appendix presents the disaggregate and aggregate scores of the EDI for Latin America during the 1960, 1977, 1985, and 1990–2005 years.

2. However, the possibility of using pluses and minuses is envisioned as a means to record intermediate values. But this extra "fine tuning" step is introduced as a clearly secondary option in the assignment of values.

3. The one exception to this procedure concerns the hard-to-measure attribute on clean elections. In this case, a three-point scale was used for reasons of interpretability in the coding process. Nonetheless, the 1 in this scale does not actually represent a midpoint; it is a lot closer to the 2.

4. Prior to aggregation, a rectangular dataset, that is, a dataset with numerical scores for all cases on all variables and all years, with normalized scales, was created. To this end, starting with the four tables used in coding each of the index's conceptual attributes (see the appendix), a series of fairly mechanical issues were initially tackled. First, pluses and minuses were turned into numbers by adding or subtracting 0.33 from the base score (e.g., a 3 plus was turned into a 3.33); and dashes (-), used to indicate that the assignment of a score was not applicable because the government was not elected, were turned into zeros (0). Second, because scores for three of the components — right to vote, clean elections, and free elections — were only assigned for those years when elections were held, scores for the years between elections were given by carrying over a score to subsequent years, until a new score had been assigned (because either an election was held after a period in which there was a non-elected government, a new election was held, or electoral politics was interrupted). The justification for this procedure is that the way in which a government originates continues to be a characteristic that affects its nature beyond the moment of its installation. In the case of the attribute on clean elections, a somewhat complex procedure was followed. Because the 1 on the clean elections scale does not actually represent a midpoint, each 1 was turned into a 3 and each 2 into a 4. Moreover,

because this attribute distinguishes the values assigned for elections for president and parliament, scores are not simply carried from election to election. Rather, the scores are an average of the scores for the elections for president and parliament. Finally, all scores were normalized by dividing them by the maximum possible score of 4.

5. Whether these four attributes might be considered jointly sufficient is a different matter.

6. A test of the dimensionality of the EDI's four conceptual attributes gives a Cronbach's alpha of 0.92, suggesting that the EDI is a measure of a unidimensional phenomenon. However, when this test is performed on two periods (1960–85 and 1990–2005), the resulting Cronbach alphas are of 0.95 and 0.47 respectively. This indicates that while in the earlier period the attributes are unidimensional, this is no longer true in the post-1990 period. This result provides evidence against a decision to aggregate conceptual attributes that are considered "effect" indicators of a concept, that is, indicators that are seen as being driven or generated by the concept. Indeed, it suggests that the common assumption that aggregation operates on multiple parallel measurements does not hold. But, because the EDI's conceptual attributes are considered necessary conditions of electoral democracy, the measures of these attributes can be seen as "cause" indicators, that is, indicators that influence the concept being measured. Hence, no assumption is made that the conceptual attributes measure a single unidimensional latent construct, and the decision to aggregate the EDI's four conceptual attributes up to one single score is not invalidated by deviations from unidimensionality. On the distinction between "cause" and "effect" indicators, see Bollen and Lennox (1991).

7. Though the EDI can be interpreted in terms of the concept of electoral democracy, the values of the index are best understood as ranging between two polar opposites: pure cases of electoral democracy and authoritarianism. That is, rather than making explicit the threshold along the index's continuum separating cases of electoral democracy from those that are not electoral democracies, movement along this continuum can be interpreted, more conservatively, as tracking advances toward and moves away from electoral democracy.

8. See Coppedge and Reinicke (1991: 56–57); Jaggers and Gurr (1995: 473–76); Gasiorowski (1996: 477–79); Przeworski et al. (2000: 56–57); and Moon et al. (2006: 12, 16).

9. These measures were selected for the purpose of an external analysis because they are presented as measures of democracy, use the country as the unit of observation, rely on coders, and cover at least Latin America.

10. The polyserial correlation for the EDI and the Political Regimes Classification over the 1990–2000 period is 0.434.

11. As stated previously, for cases not seen as fitting precisely any of the points on the various scales, the possibility of using pluses and minuses was introduced as a secondary step in the coding process.

12. On the trade-off between the goals of ensuring the equivalence of indicators and making gains in terms of both conceptual breadth and empirical scope, see Blalock (1982: 72–74).

13. In the case of the EDI, two supplementary processes were used to code the cases. An initial coding was conducted by a single coder, on the basis of extensive research and consultations with a large number of experts over a period of many months. In addition, the assigned scores were presented and discussed in depth in various meetings, including one specialized meeting with a group of invited participants who work in diverse settings (politics, academia, and international organizations) and come from different countries in the Americas and Europe.

The coding of the data was done at two stages: one covering the 1960–2002 period, and a second one covering 2003–5. The initial coder was, in both stages, the author of this book. The specialized meeting dedicated to the 1960–2002 period included people from Argentina, Brazil, Canada, Colombia, Ecuador, Mexico, the United States, and Uruguay; in the second round the discussion included people from Argentina, Chile, Colombia, the Dominican Republic, Germany, Peru, Spain, the United States, and Uruguay.

These discussions led to the identification of disagreements, which led to further research, and yet further group discussions. In the end, through this iterative process, a large degree of consensus emerged concerning the coding of the EDI's four attributes. Due to reasons of time and resources, a formal intercoder reliability test was not conducted. Nonetheless, to gain a sense of the impact of using coders with somewhat different perspectives, the precision of measurement was assessed through a sensitivity analysis (Saltelli, Chan, and Scott 2000). The results of this analysis, performed by Jay Verkuilen, are presented in UNDP (2004a: 211) and, in more detail, in Smithson and Verkuilen (2006: 31–35).

### Chapter 5: Assessing Elections

1. The methodology was approved by OAS's secretary general for internal use within the organization's Secretariat for Political Affairs in mid-2006, and it was initially applied in several election observation missions during the second half of 2006 and 2007. The methodology builds on the Electoral Democracy Index (see chapter 4), prepared for the United Nations Development Programme's report on *Democracy in Latin America* (UNDP 2004a: 207–13; 2004b: 21–33). Moreover, it reflects lessons extracted from a large literature on the observation and assessment of elections, and recent efforts by various international organizations and academics to devise a methodology to observe elections (for a summary of these efforts, see the appendix A).

2. For a discussion of the benchmarks regarding elections established in various OAS documents, as well as in the similar documents of other regional and global organizations, see European Union (2007).

3. The terminology that is used in distinguishing democratic from nondemocratic elections has varied over time. Election monitors, in particular, have largely moved away from the terms "free and fair," using instead terms such as "genuine," "acceptable," and "flawed." Because the basic function of such terms is to distinguish elections that are consistent with democratic principles from those that are not, here the term "democratic elections" is used.

4. The relationship between the institutional configuration of electoral authorities (as well as other institutional aspects of relevance to the electoral process) and the quality of elections is an empirical question, which is relevant to the goal of electoral advice and assistance but not to the task at hand, the development of a methodology to assess the quality of elections. Regarding the confidence of actors in the results of an election, the entire point of an electoral assessment is to provide evidence about the quality of the elections that is independent of the view of actors that are part of the electoral contest and hence that can be used to build confidence in the official results, when these are deemed to be accurate, or to question the official results, when these are deemed to be the product of a process that is not free and fair.

5. In terms of democratic theory, this focus on voters, candidates, and offices draws on Schumpeter's (1942: 242, 269) memorable definition of democracy as consisting of "a political *method* . . . for arriving at political decisions in which individuals acquire the power to decide by means of a competitive struggle for people's vote." Nonetheless, the differences with Schumpeter must be stressed. First, the definition offered here incorporates Dahl's (1989: ch. 9, 221) critique of Schumpeter for failing to elaborate a standard regarding who has the right to vote and Dahl's argument that certain civil liberties are necessary for elections to be democratic. Second, though Schumpeter reduces democracy to the process of formation of government, in this book this process is seen as only a part of the broader concept of democracy (see chapter 6).

6. On the use of quick counts in election observation, see Garber and Cowan (1993) and Bjornlund (2004: ch. 13).

7. For an operational manual for election observation missions, prepared by the author, that outlines the tasks of the methodology specialists responsible for implementing the proposed methodology, see Organization of American States (2007).

8. For an innovative proposal to observe polling stations selected to approximate a randomized experiment, see Hyde (2007a, 2007b).

9. The rationale for having a standardized questionnaire is to ensure its consistency from one election observation mission to another. Nonetheless, the questionnaire must be adjusted for each election and to each national context. It is also possible that certain issues considered important to the work of observation are not addressed in the questionnaire. At the same time, it is crucial to never eliminate questions from the questionnaire, because the standard set of questions is needed to assess whether elections are democratic or not in a comparable manner.

10. For more specific contributions to a methodology to assess elections, see the

work focused on the voter registration process (Klein and Merloe 2001), on electronic voting (Carter Center 2007; Prian and Merloe 2007), and on the monitoring of the media (Norris and Merloe 2002; Council of Europe, Venice Commission 2005).

11. The suggestion to assess different elections using different standards, as advanced by Pastor (2003: 23–25) and formally incorporated into the aggregation scheme proposed by Elklit and Reynolds (2005: 154–55), amounts to weighting the same information differently in different countries — for example, in fledgling versus established democracies. These proposals immediately raise the question of how such a distinction would be made and also introduce the awkward possibility that a country's electoral quality might be portrayed as declining over time, due to a change in the way the country is classified, when the use of a consistent aggregation scheme would show that the quality of elections has actually improved. Thus, the use of differential standards in assessments opens the door to charges of bias and/or paternalism and should simply be avoided.

12. There are three basic differences between the Index of Democratic Elections and the Electoral Democracy Index discussed in chapter 4. The former is narrower, because it focuses only on electoral processes; deeper, in that it relies on more elements to assess the electoral process; and more precise, in that it goes further in introducing a threshold distinguishing democratic from nondemocratic elections.

13. Because the concept of democratic elections has been disaggregated at three levels — attributes, components of attributes, and subcomponents of attributes — the aggregation rule specifies procedures to move from the level of attributes to concept, of components to attributes, and of subcomponents to components.

14. This assumes that, prior to aggregation, the assigned scores have been normalized by dividing each score by the highest value of the corresponding scale. Specifically, because all the scales have three points — 0, 1, and 2 — this means that each value must be divided by 2.

### Chapter 6: Revisiting Concepts

1. Though the concept of democracy can be applied to a variety of units, the following discussion focuses on democracy in relation to the modern state, which is considered to be the main public decision-making center.

2. Though rights of authorship are usually assigned to Schumpeter, Weber is an important precursor of this approach. On Weber's and Schumpeter's contributions to the development of the new model of competitive elitism, see Held (1996: ch. 5).

3. There is still some question about what this universal standard should be. Thus, Dahl (1989: 129) argues for a highly inclusive criterion that only excludes children, transients, and the mentally defective. But the threshold used to distinguish democratic from nondemocratic levels of voting rights could be specified in a range of ways.

4. All rights are political, inasmuch as they all refer to the state. But this is not the point being made here.

5. In this regard, it is noteworthy that Dahl himself retreats considerably from his broad concept of democracy when he suggests ways to operationalize democracy. Ironically, the list of institutional features he has proposed to measure democracy is strikingly Schumpeterian, stopping at the point in the political process when public officials are elected (Dahl 1971: 3; 1989: 221; 1998: 37–38).

6. On the relationship between the rule of law and democracy, see Habermas (1996, 2001); Maravall and Przeworski (2003); O'Donnell (2004a); and Bobbio (2005).

7. On human development, see Ul Haq (1995); Sen (1999); and Fukuda-Parr and Kumar (2003). On the relationship between human development and democracy, see Sen (1999: introduction, chs. 1, 2, 6, and 7); UNDP (2002: ch. 2); and Fukuda-Parr (2003).

8. On the impossibility of entirely separating the process and opportunity aspects of freedom, and the need for an integrated view of rights, see Sen (2002: part VI). Some other, relevant discussions about equal opportunities and economic factors, by political scientists, include Bobbio (2005: 525–27, 538–46); Dahl (1985; 1989: 114–15, 167, 176, 178); Lindblom (1977: part V); and Sartori (1987b: ch. 12).

9. For a defense of a procedural conception of democracy that also highlights its intrinsic value but is less expansive than Dahl's defense, see Przeworski (1999).

## Chapter 7: Developing Measures

1. A U.S. academic, Arthur Banks, started publishing the widely used and regularly updated Cross-National Time-Series Data Archive in 1968; and another U.S. academic, Ted Robert Gurr, designed the Polity data series, first released in 1978. Relatedly, the U.S. nonprofit organization Freedom House, founded in 1941, started publishing annual assessments of the state of freedom throughout the world in 1972. On these early efforts to develop data on politics, see Scheuch (2003).

2. For a list of datasets, see Malik (2002); Besançon (2003); Landman and Häusermann (2003); and Sudders and Nahem (2004).

3. For a discussion of governance-related conditionalities, see Kapur and Webb (2000); Kapur (2001); and Santiso (2001).

4. Relatedly, the strategy to produce the EDI data has followed the standard practice in large-N datasets of producing one observation per case per year. This strategy restricts the data's sensitivity to issues of time and process, which rarely obey the cycle of calendar years. Thus, this strategy's rationale is largely current convention and might be fruitfully revised.

5. For example, the principal components method assigns lower weights to those measures which are highly correlated with each other, and the unobserved

components method assigns weights to different data sources proportionally to the reliability of each source.

6. The evaluation of the EDI eschewed predictive validation tests, which assess measures in terms of their ability to predict as well or better than other measures certain hypotheses, for the reason that we simply lack sufficiently well-established causal knowledge.

7. See chapter 2, Bollen (1980, 1986, 1991, 1993); Inkeles (1991); Beetham (1994); Bollen and Paxton (2000); Foweraker and Krznaric (2000); Lauth (2003); Berg-Schlosser (2004); Coppedge (2005); Hadenius and Teorell (2005); and Bogaards (2007).

8. The European Union (EU) formally stipulated its political conditions for accession in two separate texts: the "political criteria" established by the European Council in Copenhagen in 1993, and Article 49 of the Treaty on European Union of November 1993. These documents refer to the need to guarantee "democracy, the rule of law, human rights and respect for and protection of minorities," but do not offer definitions of these broad concepts, let alone identify the indicators that would be used to measure these concepts and the requisite level of fulfillment of each indicator. The political conditionality of the EU acquired substance in a series of annual reports published after 1997 evaluating the progress of countries that were candidates for accession to the EU. Yet it was done in a way that denied candidate countries a clear sense of the standards to be met and presented these countries with a moving target. On the African Peer Review Mechanism's list of indicators and the process for evaluating countries it envisions, see NEPAD (2003a, 2003b).

9. A more complex question concerns the possibility that political actors that are being monitored may themselves take actions to alter the measures of interest. On data and strategic behavior, see Herrera and Kapur (2007).

10. One problem is that the MCA's rule of aggregation consists of a relative rather than an absolute criterion. Specifically, countries are assessed in terms of the number of indicators on which they rank above the median in relation to the universe of cases (Millennium Challenge Corporation 2004), even though such a criterion runs counter to the MCA's stated goal (Millennium Challenge Corporation 2004; 2007: 5–6). After all, during periods when more than half the world has authoritarian regimes—a pattern that has dominated world history until very recently—this rule does not guarantee that democratic countries would be identified.

11. Even though the creators of datasets used by the MCA to identify countries that are to receive development aid have provided estimates of measurement error and emphasized their importance (Kaufmann, Kraay, and Mastruzzi 2003: 23–27), this program does not incorporate estimates of measurement error in its methodology and thus potentially misclassifies countries.

# References

........................................................................................................................

Adcock, Robert N., and David Collier. 2001. "Measurement Validity: A Shared Standard for Qualitative and Quantitative Research," *American Political Science Review* 95, no. 3 (September): 529–46.

Alvarez, Michael, José Antonio Cheibub, Fernando Limongi, and Adam Przeworski. 1996. "Classifying Political Regimes," *Studies in Comparative International Development* 31, no. 2 (Summer): 1–37.

American Bar Association (ABA-CEELI). 2007. *Judicial Reform Index for Moldova*, vol. 2 (Washington, DC: American Bar Association).

Andrich, David. 1988. *Rasch Models for Measurement* (Beverly Hills, CA: Sage Publications).

Apodaca, Clair. 1998. "Measuring Women's Economic and Social Rights Achievements," *Human Rights Quarterly* 20, no. 1: 139–72.

Arat, Zehra F. 1991. *Democracy and Human Rights in Developing Countries* (Boulder, CO: Lynne Rienner).

Arndt, Christiane, and Charles Oman. 2006. *Uses and Abuses of Governance Indicators* (Paris: OECD Development Centre).

Becker, Lee B., Tudor Vlad, and Nancy Nusser. 2007. "An Evaluation of Press Freedom Indicators," *International Communication Gazette* 69, no. 1: 5–28.

Beetham, David (ed.). 1994. *Defining and Measuring Democracy* (Thousand Oaks, CA: Sage Publications).

Beetham, David, Sarah Bracking, Iain Kearton, and Stuart Weir (eds.). 2001. *International IDEA Handbook on Democracy Assessment* (The Hague: Kluge Academic Publishers).

Berg-Schlosser, Dirk. 2004. "Indicators of Democracy and Good Governance as Measures of the Quality of Democracy in Africa: A Critical Appraisal," *Acta Politica* 39, no. 3 (September): 248–78.

Besançon, Marie. 2003. "Good Governance Rankings: The Art of Measurement," *World Peace Foundation Reports* 36 (Cambridge, MA: World Peace Foundation).

Bjornlund, Eric C. 2004. *Beyond Free and Fair: Monitoring Elections and Building Democracy* (Baltimore: Johns Hopkins University Press).

Blalock, Hubert M. 1982. *Conceptualization and Measurement in the Social Sciences* (Beverly Hills, CA: Sage Publications).

Bobbio, Norberto. 2005. *Teoría general de la política* (Madrid: Editorial Trotta).

Bogaards, Matthijs. 2007. "Measuring Democracy through Election Outcomes: A Critique with African Data," *Comparative Political Studies* 40, no. 10: 1211–37.

Boix, Carles. 2003. *Democracy and Redistribution* (New York: Cambridge University Press).

Bollen, Kenneth A. 1980. "Issues in the Comparative Measurement of Political Democracy," *American Sociological Review* 45, no. 3: 370–90.

———. 1986. "Political Rights and Political Liberties in Nations: An Evaluation of Human Rights Measures, 1950 to 1984," *Human Rights Quarterly* 8, no. 4: 567–91.

———. 1989. *Structural Equations with Latent Variables* (New York: Wiley).

———. 1991. "Political Democracy: Conceptual and Measurement Traps," pp. 3–20, in Alex Inkeles (ed.), *On Measuring Democracy: Its Consequences and Concomitants* (New Brunswick, NJ: Transaction Publishers).

———. 1993. "Liberal Democracy: Validity and Method Factors in Cross-National Measures," *American Journal of Political Science* 37, no. 4: 1207–30.

Bollen, Kenneth, and Richard Lennox. 1991. "Conventional Wisdom on Measurement: A Structural Equation Perspective," *Psychological Bulletin* 110, no. 2: 305–14.

Bollen, Kenneth A., and Pamela Paxton. 1998. "Detection and Determinants of Bias in Subjective Measures," *American Sociological Review* 63, no. 3 (June): 465–78.

———. 2000. "Subjective Measures of Liberal Democracy," *Comparative Political Studies* 33, no. 1 (February): 58–86.

Bollen, Kenneth, Pamela Paxton, and Rumi Morishima. 2005. "Assessing International Evaluations: An Example from USAID's Democracy and Governance Program," *American Journal of Evaluation* 26, no. 2: 189–203.

Bollen, Kenneth A., and Kwok-fai Ting. 2000. "A Tetrad Test for Causal Indicators," *Psychological Methods* 5, no. 1: 3–22.

Boneo, Horacio, and Edelberto Torres Rivas. 2001. *¿Por qué no votan los guatemaltecos? Estudio de participación y abstención electoral* (Guatemala: IDEA/IFE/PNUD).

Bratton, Michael, Robert Mattes, and E. Gyimah-Boadi. 2005. *Public Opinion, Democracy and Market Reform in Africa* (New York: Cambridge University Press).

Burnell, Peter (ed.). 2007. *Evaluating Democracy Support Methods and Experiences* (Stockholm: International Institute for Democracy and Electoral Assistance and Swedish International Development Cooperation Agency).

Campbell, Donald T., and Donald W. Fiske. 1959. "Convergent and Discriminant Validation by the Multitrait-Multimethod Matrix," *Psychological Bulletin* 56, no. 2 (March): 81–105.

Campbell, Kim, and Sean C. Carroll. 2005. "Sustaining Democracy's Last Wave," *Georgetown Journal of International Affairs* 6, no. 2 (Summer–Fall): 45–52.

Carmines, Edward G., and Richard A. Zeller. 1979. *Reliability and Validity Assessment* (Beverly Hills, CA: Sage Publications).

Carothers, Thomas. 1991. *In the Name of Democracy: U.S. Policy toward Latin America in the Reagan Years* (Berkeley: University of California Press).

———. 2000. "The Clinton Record on Democracy Promotion," Carnegie Endowment Working Papers no. 16 (Washington, DC: Carnegie Endowment for International Peace).

———. 2006. "The Backlash against Democracy Promotion," *Foreign Affairs* 85, no. 2 (March–April): 55–68.

———. 2007. *U.S. Democracy Promotion during and after Bush* (Washington, DC: Carnegie Endowment for International Peace).

Carter Center. 2007. *Developing a Methodology for Observing Electronic Voting* (Atlanta: Carter Center).

Carter Center et al. 2005. *Declaration of Principles for International Election Observation and Code of Conduct for International Election Observers,* an agreement spearheaded by the Carter Center, the NDI, and the United Nations Electoral Assistance Division, and signed by 21 organizations on October 24, 2005.

Case, William. 1996. "Can the 'Halfway House' Stand? Semidemocracy and Elite Theory in Three Southeast Asian Countries," *Comparative Politics* 28, no. 4: 437–64.

Cheibub, José Antonio, and Jennifer Gandhi. 2004. "Classifying Political Regimes: An Extension and an Update," unpublished manuscript, Yale University. New Haven, CT.

Cohen, Morris R., and Ernest Nagel. 1934. *An Introduction to Logic and Scientific Method* (New York: Harcourt, Brace).

Collier, David, and Robert N. Adcock. 1999. "Democracy and Dichotomies: A Pragmatic Approach to Choices about Concepts," *Annual Review of Political Science* 2: 537–65.

Collier, David, and Steven Levitsky. 1997. "Democracy with Adjectives: Conceptual Innovation in Comparative Research," *World Politics* 49, no. 3 (April): 430–51.

Coombs, Clyde H. 1953. "The Theory and Methods of Social Measurement," pp. 471–535, in Leon Festinger and Daniel Katz (eds.), *Research Methods in the Behavioral Sciences* (New York: Dryden Press).

Coppedge, Michael. 1997. "Modernization and Thresholds of Democracy: Evidence for a Common Path and Process," pp. 177–201, in Manus Midlarsky (ed.), *Inequality and Democracy* (New York: Cambridge University Press).

———. 1999. "Thickening Thin Concepts and Theories: Combining Large N and Small in Comparative Politics," *Comparative Politics* 31, no. 4: 465–76.

———. 2005. "Defining and Measuring Democracy," Political Concepts Working Paper Series no. 2 (Mexico City: International Political Science Association [IPSA], Committee on Concepts and Methods).

———. 2007. *The Polyarchy and Contestation Scales for 1985 and 2000.* Available at http://www.nd.edu:80/mcoppedg/crd/datacrd.htm.

Coppedge, Michael, and Wolfgang Reinicke. 1991. "Measuring Polyarchy," pp. 47–68, in Alex Inkeles (ed.), *On Measuring Democracy: Its Consequences and Concomitants* (New Brunswick, NJ: Transaction Publishers).

Council of Europe. 1998. *Handbook for Observers of Elections* (Strasbourg: Council of Europe).

Council of Europe, Venice Commission. 2005. *Guidelines on Media Analysis during Election Observation Missions* (Strasbourg, Study no. 285/2004, CDL-AD(2005)032.

Cox, Michael, G. John Ikenberry, and Takashi Inoguchi (eds.). 2000. *American Democracy Promotion: Impulses, Strategies, and Impacts* (Oxford: Oxford University Press).

Dahl, Robert A. 1966. "Preface," pp. xiii–xxi, in Robert A. Dahl (ed.), *Political Oppositions in Western Democracies* (New Haven, CT: Yale University Press).

———. 1971. *Polyarchy: Participation and Opposition* (New Haven, CT: Yale University Press).

———. 1985. *A Preface to Economic Democracy* (New Haven, CT: Yale University Press).

———. 1989. *Democracy and Its Critics* (New Haven, CT: Yale University Press).

———. 1998. *On Democracy* (New Haven, CT: Yale University Press).

Dalton, Russell J., Doh C. Shin, and Willy Jou. 2007. "Understanding Democracy: Data from Unlikely Places," *Journal of Democracy* 18, no. 4: 142–56.

Davenport, Christian, and David A. Armstrong II. 2004. "Democracy and the Violation of Human Rights: A Statistical Analysis from 1976 to 1996," *American Journal of Political Science* 48, no. 3: 538–54.

Davies, John, and Ted Robert Gurr (eds.). 1998. *Preventive Measures: Building Risk Assessment and Crisis Early Warning Systems* (Lanham, MD: Rowman & Littlefield).

Diamond, Larry. 2002. "Thinking about Hybrid Regimes," *Journal of Democracy* 13, no. 2: 21–35.

Diamond, Larry, and Leonardo Morlino (eds.). 2005. *Assessing the Quality of Democracy* (Baltimore: Johns Hopkins University Press).

ECLAC (Economic Commission for Latin America and the Caribbean). 1999. *Indicadores de Género para el Seguimiento y la Evaluación del Programa de Ac-*

ción *Regional para las Mujeres de América Latina y el Caribe,1995–2001, y la Plataforma de Acción de Beijing* (Santiago, Chile: LC/L.1186).

Edwards, Jeffrey R., and Richard P. Bagozzi. 2000. "On the Nature and Direction of the Relationship between Constructs and Measures," *Psychological Methods* 5, no. 2: 155–74.

Elkins, Zachary. 2000. "Gradations of Democracy? Empirical Tests of Alternative Conceptualizations," *American Journal of Political Science* 44, no. 2: 293–300.

Elklit, Jørgen. 1994. "Is the Degree of Electoral Democracy Measurable? Experiences from Bulgaria, Kenya, Latvia, Mongolia and Nepal," pp. 89–111, in David Beetham (ed.), *Defining and Measuring Democracy* (Thousand Oaks, CA: Sage Publications).

Elklit, Jørgen, and Andrew Reynolds. 2005. "A Framework for the Systematic Study of Election Quality," *Democratization* 12, no. 2: 147–62.

Elman, Colin. 2005. "Explanatory Typologies in Qualitative Studies of International Politics," *International Organization* 59, no. 2 (Spring): 293–326.

Ertman, Thomas. 1997. *Birth of the Leviathan: Building States and Regimes in Medieval and Early Modern Europe* (New York: Cambridge University Press).

European Commission. 2002. *Handbook for European Union Election Observation Missions*, ed. Anders Eriksson (Stockholm: Sida, The Swedish International Development Cooperation Agency, SE-105 25).

European Union. 1997. "Treaty of Amsterdam Amending the Treaty on European Union, the Treaties Establishing the European Communities and Certain Related Acts," *Official Journal of the European Union* C 340, November 10.

———. 2007. *Compendium of International Standards for Elections*, 2nd ed. (United Kingdom and Belgium: NEEDS and European Commission).

Evans, Peter, and James E. Rauch. 1999. "Bureaucracy and Growth: A Cross-National Analysis of the Effects of 'Weberian' State Structures on Economic Growth," *American Sociological Review* 64, no. 5: 748–65.

Farer, Tom (ed.). 1996. *Beyond Sovereignty: Collectively Defending Democracy in the Americas* (Baltimore: Johns Hopkins University Press).

Finkel, Steven, Aníbal Pérez-Liñán, and Mitchell Seligson. 2007. "The Effects of U.S. Foreign Assistance on Democracy Building, 1990–2003," *World Politics* 59, no. 3 (April): 404–40.

Fish, M. Steven. 2006. "Stronger Legislatures, Stronger Democracies," *Journal of Democracy* 17, no. 1: 5–20.

Foweraker, Joe, and Roman Krznaric. 2000. "Measuring Liberal Democratic Performance: An Empirical and Conceptual Critique," *Political Studies* 48, no. 4: 759–87.

Freedom House. 1999. *Freedom in the World: The Annual Survey of Political Rights and Civil Liberties, 1998–1999* (New York: Transaction Publishers).

———. 2007a. "Methodology. 2006 Edition." Available at http://www.freedomhouse
.org/template.cfm?page=35&year=2006.

———. 2007b. "Comparative Scores for All Countries from 1973 to 2006." Available
at http://www.freedomhouse.org/template.cfm?page=15.

Fukuda-Parr, Sakiko. 2003. "Rescuing the Human Development Concept from the
HDI: Reflections on a New Agenda," pp. 117–24, in Sakiko Fukuda-Parr and
Shiva A. K. Kumar (eds.), *Readings in Human Development: Concepts, Measures, and Policies for a Development* (Oxford: Oxford University Press).

Fukuda-Parr, Sakiko, and Shiva A. K. Kumar (eds.). 2003. *Readings in Human Development: Concepts, Measures, and Policies for a Development* (Oxford: Oxford University Press).

Fukuyama, Frances, and Michael McFaul. 2007. "Should Democracy Be Promoted
or Demoted?" *Washington Quarterly* 31, no. 1: 23–45.

Gallie, Walter Bryce. 1956. "Essentially Contested Concepts," *Proceedings of the
Aristotelian Society* 56: 167–98.

Garber, Larry, and Glenn Cowan. 1993. "The Virtues of Parallel Vote Tabulations,"
*Journal of Democracy* 4, no. 2 (April): 95–107.

Gasiorowski, Mark J. 1996. "An Overview of the Political Regime Change Dataset,"
*Comparative Political Studies* 29, no. 4: 469–83.

Gastil, Raymond D. (ed.). 1978. *Freedom in the World: Political Rights and Civil
Liberties, 1978* (Boston: G. K. Hall).

———. 1991. "The Comparative Survey of Freedom: Experiences and Suggestions,"
pp. 21–46, in Alex Inkeles (ed.), *On Measuring Democracy: Its Consequences
and Concomitants* (New Brunswick, NJ: Transaction Publishers).

Gehrlich, Peter. 1973. "The Institutionalization of European Parliaments," pp. 94–
113, in Allan Kornberg (ed.), *European Parliaments in Comparative Perspective*
(New York: D. McKay).

Gershman, Carl, and Michael Allen. 2006. "The Assault on Democracy Assistance,"
*Journal of Democracy* 17, no. 2 (April): 36–51.

Gerth, Hans H., and C. Wright Mills (eds.). 1946. *From Max Weber: Essays in
Sociology* (New York: Oxford University Press).

Gifi, Albert. 1990. *Nonlinear Multidimensional Analysis* (New York: Wiley).

Gleditsch, Kristian S., and Michael D. Ward. 1997. "Double Take: A Reexamination
of Democracy and Autocracy in Modern Polities," *Journal of Conflict Resolution* 41, no. 3 (June): 361–83.

Goertz, Gary. 2006. *Social Science Concepts: A User's Guide* (Princeton, NJ: Princeton University Press).

Goodwin-Gill, Guy S. 1994. *Free and Fair Elections,* new expanded edition (Geneva:
Inter-Parliamentary Union).

Green, Maria. 2001. "What We Talk About When We Talk About Indicators: Current

Approaches to Human Rights Measurement," *Human Rights Quarterly* 23, no. 4: 1062–97.

Guilhot, Nicolas. 2005. *The Democracy Makers: Human Rights and the Politics of Global Order* (New York: Columbia University Press).

Guion, Robert M. 1998. *Assessment, Measurement, and Prediction for Personnel Decisions* (Mahwah, NJ: Lawrence Erlbaum Associates).

Guttman, Louis. 1977. "What Is Not What in Statistics," *Statistician* 26, no. 2: 81–107.

———. 1994. *Louis Guttman on Theory and Methodology: Selected Writings* (Brookfield, VT: Dartmouth Publishing).

Habermas, Jürgen. 1996. *Between Facts and Norms: Contributions to a Discourse Theory of Law and Democracy* (Cambridge, MA: MIT Press).

———. 2001. "Constitutional Democracy: A Paradoxical Union of Contradictory Principles?" *Political Theory* 29, no. 6: 766–81.

Hadenius, Axel. 1992. *Democracy and Development* (Cambridge: Cambridge University Press).

Hadenius, Axel, and Jan Teorell. 2005. "Assessing Alternative Indices of Democracy," Committee on Concepts and Methods Working Paper Series no. 6 (Mexico City: International Political Science Association [IPSA], Committee on Concepts and Methods).

Heath, Anthony, and Jean Martin. 1997. "Why Are There So Few Formal Measuring Instruments in Social and Political Research?" pp. 71–86, in Lars E. Lyberg, Paul Biemer, Martin Collins, Edith De Leeuw, Cathryn Dippo, Norbert Schwarz, and Dennis Trewin (eds.), *Survey Measurement and Process Quality* (New York: Wiley).

Held, David. 1996. *Models of Democracy,* 2nd ed. (Stanford: Stanford University Press).

Hempel, Carl Gustav. 1952. *Fundamentals of Concept Formation in Empirical Science* (Chicago: University of Chicago Press).

Henisz, Witold J. 2000. "The Institutional Environment for Economic Growth," *Economics and Politics* 12, no. 1: 1–31.

Hermet, Guy. 1982. "Las elecciones en los regimens autoritarios: Bosquejo de un marco de análisis," pp. 18–53, in Guy Hermet, Alain Rouquié, and Juan Linz (eds.), *¿Para qué sirven las elecciones?* (Mexico: Fondo de Cultura Económica).

Herrera, Yoshiko M., and Devesh Kapur. 2007. "Improving Data Quality: Actors, Incentives, and Capabilities," *Political Analysis* 15, no. 4: 365–86.

Huntington, Samuel P. 1991. *The Third Wave: Democratization in the Late Twentieth Century* (Norman: University of Oklahoma Press).

Hutchinson, T. P. 1985. "Analysing Severity Data When Assessors Differ in Their Usage of the Categories," *Statistician* 34, no. 2: 183–95.

Hyde, Susan. 2007a. "Introducing Randomization to International Election Observation: The 2004 Presidential Elections in Indonesia," paper presented at the annual meeting of the American Political Science Association, Chicago, August 30–September 2.

———. 2007b. "The Observer Effect in International Politics: Evidence from a Natural Experiment," *World Politics* 60, no. 1 (October): 37–63.

Inkeles, Alex (ed.). 1991. *On Measuring Democracy* (New Brunswick, NJ: Transaction Publishers).

International IDEA. 2002. *International Electoral Standards: Guidelines for Reviewing the Legal Framework of Elections* (Stockholm: International IDEA).

———. 2005. *Ten Years of Supporting Democracy Worldwide* (Stockholm: International Institute for Democracy and Electoral Assistance).

Inter-Parliamentary Council. 1994. "Declaration on Criteria for Free and Fair Elections, Unanimously Adopted by the Inter-Parliamentary Council at Its 154th Session (Paris, 26 March 1994)," pp. 104–9, in Michael D. Boda, (ed.), *Revisiting Free and Fair Elections: An International Round Table on Election Standards* (Geneva: Inter-Parliamentary Union, 2005).

Jacoby, William G. 1991. *Data Theory and Dimensional Analysis* (Newbury Park, CA: Sage Publications).

———. 1999. "Levels of Measurement and Political Research: An Optimistic View," *American Journal of Political Science* 43, no. 1: 271–301.

Jaggers, Keith, and Ted Robert Gurr. 1995. "Tracking Democracy's Third Wave with the Polity III Data," *Journal of Peace Research* 32, no. 4: 469–82.

Kaplan, Abraham. 1964. *The Conduct of Inquiry: Methodology for Behavioral Science* (Scranton, PA: Chandler Publishing).

Kapur, Devesh. 2001. "Expansive Agendas and Weak Instruments: Governance Related Conditionalities of International Financial Institutions," *Journal of Policy Reform* 4, no. 3: 207–41.

Kapur, Devesh, and Richard Webb. 2000. "Governance-Related Conditionalities of the International Financial Institutions," G-24 Discussion Paper Series 6 (New York: United Nations Conference on Trade and Development).

Karl, Terry Lynn. 1995. "The Hybrid Regimes of Central America," *Journal of Democracy* 6, no. 3: 72–87.

Kaufmann, Daniel, Aart Kraay, and Massimo Mastruzzi. 2003. "Governance Matters III: Governance Indicators for 1996–2002," Policy Research Working Paper 3106 (Washington, DC: World Bank).

———. 2007. *Governance Matters VI: Aggregate and Individual Governance Indicators, 1996–2006* (Washington, DC: World Bank).

Kaufmann, Daniel, Francesca Recanatini, and Sergiy Biletsky. 2002. *Assessing Governance: Diagnostic Tools and Applied Methods for Capacity Building and Action Learning* (Washington, DC: World Bank).

Klein, Richard L., and Patrick Merloe. 2001. *Building Confidence in the Voter Registration Process: An NDI Monitoring Guide for Political Parties and Civic Organizations* (Washington, DC: National Democratic Institute for International Affairs).

Knack, Stephen. 2006. "Measuring Corruption in Eastern Europe and Central Asia: A Critique of the Cross-country Indicators," World Bank Policy Research Working Paper no. 3968 (Washington, DC: World Bank).

Kopstein, Jeffrey. 2006. "The Transatlantic Divide over Democracy Promotion," *Washington Quarterly* 29, no. 2: 85–98.

Lancaster, Thomas D., and Gabriella R. Montinola. 2001. "Comparative Political Corruption: Issues of Operationalization and Measurement," *Studies in Comparative International Development* 36, no. 3 (Fall): 3–28.

Landman, Todd. 2004. "Measuring Human Rights: Principle, Practice, and Policy," *Human Rights Quarterly* 26, no. 4: 906–31.

Landman, Todd, and Julia Häusermann. 2003. *Map-Making and Analysis of the Main International Initiatives on Developing Indicators on Democracy and Good Governance,* a report for the European Communities Statistical Office (EUROSTAT), June 2003.

Landman, Todd, Marco Larizza, Claire McEvoy, and Edzia Carvalho. 2006. *State of Democracy in Central Asia: A Comparative Study* (Essex: Human Rights Centre, University of Essex).

Lasswell, Harold Dwight, and Abraham Kaplan. 1950. *Power and Society: A Framework for Political Inquiry* (New Haven, CT: Yale University Press).

Lauth, Hans-Joachim. 2003. "Democracy: Limits and Problems of Existing Measurements and Some Annotations upon Further Research," paper presented at international conference on "Reassessing Democracy," Bremen, Germany, June 20–22.

Lazarsfeld, Paul F., and Allen H. Barton. 1951. "Qualitative Measurement in the Social Sciences: Classification, Typologies, and Indices," pp. 155–92, in Daniel Lerner and Harold D. Lasswell (eds.), *The Policy Sciences: Recent Developments in Scope and Method* (Stanford: Stanford University Press).

Legler, Thomas, Sharon F. Lean, and Dexter S. Boniface (eds.). 2007. *Promoting Democracy in the Americas* (Baltimore: Johns Hopkins University Press).

Levitsky, Steven, and Lucan A. Way. 2002. "The Rise of Competitive Authoritarianism," *Journal of Democracy* 13, no. 2 (April): 51–65.

Lieberman, Evan S. 2002. "Taxation Data as Indicators of State-Society Relations: Possibilities and Pitfalls in Cross-National Research," *Studies in Comparative International Development* 36, no. 4 (Winter): 89–115.

Lijphart, Arend. 1999. *Patterns of Democracy: Government Forms and Performance in Thirty-Six Countries* (New Haven, CT: Yale University Press).

Linares, Sebastián. 2004. "Independencia judicial: conceptualización y medición," *Política y Gobierno* 11, no. 1: 73–135.

Lindblom, Charles E. 1977. *Politics and Markets: The World's Political-Economic Systems* (New York: Basic Books).

Linz, Juan J. 1978. *The Breakdown of Democratic Regimes: Crisis, Breakdown, and Reequilibriation* (Baltimore: Johns Hopkins University Press).

Lipset, Seymour M. 1959. "Some Social Requisites of Democracy: Economic Development and Political Legitimacy," *American Political Science Review* 53, no. 1: 69–105.

Mainwaring, Scott, Daniel Brinks, and Aníbal Pérez-Liñán. 2001. "Classifying Political Regimes in Latin America, 1945–1999," *Studies in Comparative International Development* 36, no. 1 (Spring): 37–65.

———. 2007. "Classifying Political Regimes in Latin America, 1945–2004," pp. 123–60, in Gerardo L. Munck (ed.), *Regimes and Democracy in Latin America: Theories and Methods* (Oxford: Oxford University Press).

Malik, Adeel. 2002. "State of the Art in Governance Indicators," Human Development Report Office Occasional Paper 2002/07 (New York: United Nations Development Programme).

Mann, Michael. 1993. *The Sources of Social Power*, vol. 2: *The Rise of Classes and Nation-States, 1760–1914* (Cambridge: Cambridge University Press).

Maravall, José María, and Adam Przeworski (eds.). 2003. *Democracy and the Rule of Law* (New York: Cambridge University Press).

Marradi, Alberto. 1990. "Classification, Typology, Taxonomy," *Quality & Quantity* 24, no. 2: 129–57.

Marshall, Monty G., and Keith Jaggers. 2001. *Polity IV Project: Political Regime Characteristics and Transitions, 1800–1999; Dataset Users Manual*. Available at http://www.bsos.umd.edu/cidcm/polity/.

———. 2005. *Polity IV Project: Political Regime Characteristics and Transitions, 1800–2003*. Available at www.bsos.umd.edu/cidcm/polity/.

———. 2007. *Polity IV Project: Political Regime Characteristics and Transitions, 1800–2004*. Available at www.bsos.umd.edu/cidcm/polity/.

McDonald, Roderick P. 1999. *Test Theory: A Unified Treatment* (Mahwah, NJ: Lawrence Erlbaum Associates).

Melia, Thomas O. 2005. "The Democracy Bureaucracy: The Infrastructure of American Democracy Promotion," a discussion paper prepared for the Princeton Project on National Security Working Group on Global Institutions and Foreign Policy Infrastructure. Available at www.wws.princeton.edu/ppns/papers/democracy_bureaucracy.pdf.

Merritt, Richard L., and Stein Rokkan (eds.). 1966. *Comparing Nations: The Use of Quantitative Data in Cross-National Research* (New Haven, CT: Yale University Press).

Metcalf, Lee Kendall. 2000. "Measuring Presidential Power," *Comparative Political Studies* 33, no. 5: 660–85.

Millennium Challenge Corporation. 2004. *Report on the Criteria and Methodology for Determining the Eligibility of Candidate Countries for Millennium Challenge Account Assistance in FY 2004*. Available at http://www.mca.gov/countries/selection/index.shtml.

———. 2007. *Report on the Criteria and Methodology for Determining the Eligibility of Candidate Countries for Millennium Challenge Account Assistance in Fiscal Year 2008* (Washington, DC: Millennium Challenge Corporation). Available at www.mcc.gov/documents/mcc-report-fy08-criteria%20and%20methodology.pdf.

Mokken, Robert J. 1971. *A Theory and Procedure of Scale Analysis with Applications in Political Research* (Berlin: Walter de Gruyter).

Moon, Bruce E., Jennifer Harvey Birdsall, Sylvia Ceisluk, Lauren M. Garlett, Joshua J. Hermias, Elizabeth Mendenhall, Patrick D. Schmid, and Wai Hong Wong. 2006. "Voting Counts: Participation in the Measurement of Democracy," *Studies in Comparative International Development* 42, no. 2 (Summer): 3–32.

Munck, Gerardo L. 2003. "Gobernabilidad democrática a comienzos del siglo XXI: Una perspectiva latinoamericana," *Revista Mexicana de Sociología* (Mexico) 65, no. 3 (July–September): 565–88.

———. 2004. "Democratic Politics in Latin America: New Debates and Research Frontiers," *Annual Review of Political Science* 7: 437–62.

NDI (National Democratic Institute for International Affairs). 1995. *NDI Handbook: How Domestic Organizations Monitor Elections; An A to Z Guide* (Washington, DC: National Democratic Institute for International Affairs).

NEPAD (New Partnership for Africa's Development). 2003a. *Objectives, Standards, Criteria and Indicators for the African Peer Review Mechanism ("The APRM")* (Midrand, South Africa: NEPAD Secretariat).

———. 2003b. *African Peer Review Mechanism: Organisation and Processes* (Midrand, South Africa: NEPAD Secretariat).

Newman, Edward, and Roland Rich (eds.). 2004. *The UN Role in Promoting Democracy: Between Ideals and Reality* (New York: United Nations University).

Norris, Robert, and Patrick Merloe. 2002. *Media Monitoring to Promote Democratic Elections: An NDI Handbook for Citizen Organizations* (Washington, DC: National Democratic Institute for International Affairs).

Nussbaum, Martha. 2000. *Women and Human Development: The Capabilities Approach* (New York: Cambridge University Press).

O'Donnell, Guillermo. 2001. "Democracy, Law, and Comparative Politics," *Studies in Comparative International Development* 36, no. 1 (Spring): 7–36.

———. 2004a. "Why the Rule of Law Matters," *Journal of Democracy* 15, no. 4 (October): 32–46.

———. 2004b. "Human Development, Human Rights, and Democracy," pp. 9–92, in Guillermo O'Donnell, Jorge Vargas Cullell, and Osvaldo Iazzetta (eds.), *The*

*Quality of Democracy: Theory and Practice* (Notre Dame, IN: University of Notre Dame Press).

O'Donnell, Guillermo, and Philippe Schmitter. 1986. *Transitions from Authoritarian Rule: Tentative Conclusions about Uncertain Democracies* (Baltimore: Johns Hopkins University Press).

OECD/DAC (Organisation for Economic Co-operation and Development, Development Assistance Committee). 1998. *DAC Source Book on Concepts and Approaches Linked to Gender Equality* (Paris: OECD).

O'Grady, Paul, Rafael López-Pintor, and Mark Stevens (eds.). n.d. *Promoting and Defending Democracy: The Work of Domestic Election Observer Groups around the World* (London: ERIS).

Organization of American States. 2001. *The Inter-American Democratic Charter* (Washington, DC: OAS).

——. 2007. *Methods for Election Observation: A Manual for OAS Election Observation Missions* (Washington, DC: Organization of American States).

OSCE (Organisation for Security and Co-operation in Europe). 2002. *International Standards and Commitments on the Right to Democratic Elections: A Practical Guide to Democratic Elections Best Practice*, OSCE/ODIHR Draft Paper (Warsaw: OSCE).

OSCE/ODIHR (Organisation for Security and Co-operation in Europe, Office for Democratic Institutions and Human Rights). 2005. *Election Observation Handbook*, 5th. ed. (Warsaw: OSCE/ODIHR).

Ottaway, Marina. 2003. *Democracy Challenged: The Rise of Semi-Authoritarianism* (Washington, DC: Carnegie Endowment for International Peace).

Pastor, Robert A. 2003. "A Community of Democracies in the Americas: Instilling Substance into a Wondrous Phrase," *Canadian Foreign Policy* 10, no. 3 (Spring): 15–29.

Piano, Aili, and Arch Puddington (eds.). 2005. *Freedom in the World 2005: The Annual Survey of Political Rights and Civil Liberties* (New York: Freedom House).

Prian, Vladimir, and Patrick Merloe. 2007. *Monitoring Electronic Technologies in Electoral Processes: An NDI Guide for Political Parties and Civic Organizations* (Washington, DC: National Democratic Institute for International Affairs).

Przeworski, Adam. 1991. *Democracy and the Market: Political and Economic Reforms in Eastern Europe and Latin America* (New York: Cambridge University Press).

——. 1999. "Minimalist Conception of Democracy: A Defense," pp. 23–55, in Ian Shapiro and Casiano Hacker-Cordón (eds.), *Democracy's Value* (New York: Cambridge University Press).

Przeworski, Adam, Michael E. Alvarez, José Antonio Cheibub, and Fernando Limongi. 2000. *Democracy and Development: Political Institutions and Well-Being in the World, 1950–1990* (New York: Cambridge University Press).

Przeworski, Adam, and Henry Teune. 1970. *The Logic of Comparative Social Inquiry* (New York: Wiley).

Rasch, Georg. 1960. *Probabilistic Models for Some Intelligence and Attainment Tests* (Copenhagen: Danish Institute for Educational Research).

Reich, Gary. 2002. "Categorizing Political Regimes: New Data for Old Problems," *Democratization* 9, no. 4: 1–24.

Rich, Roland. 2001. "Bringing Democracy into International Law," *Journal of Democracy* 12, no. 3 (July): 20–34.

Rieffer, Barbara, and Mercer, Kristan. 2005. "US Democracy Promotion: The Clinton and Bush Administrations," *Global Society* 19, no. 4 (October): 385–408.

Robinson, William I. 1996. *Promoting Democracy: Globalization, US Intervention, and Hegemony* (New York: Cambridge University Press).

Rokkan, Stein, with Angus Campbell, Per Torsvik, and Henry Valen. 1970. *Citizens, Elections, Parties: Approaches to the Comparative Study of the Processes of Development* (New York: David McKay Company).

Rose, Richard. 2006. "Evaluating Democratic Governance: A Bottom-Up Approach to European Union Enlargement," *Studies in Public Policy,* no. 420 (Aberdeen, Scotland: Centre for the Study of Public Policy, University of Aberdeen).

Ross, Michael. 2006. "Is Democracy Good for the Poor?" *American Journal of Political Science* 50, no. 4 (October): 860–74.

Rouquié, Alain. 1982. "El análisis de las elecciones no competitivas: Control clientelista y situaciones autoritarias," pp. 54–89, in Guy Hermet, Alain Rouquié, and Juan Linz (eds.), *¿Para qué sirven las elecciones?* (Mexico: Fondo de Cultura Económica).

Rueschemeyer, Dietrich, Evelyne Huber Stephens and John D. Stephens. 1992. *Capitalist Development and Democracy* (Chicago: University of Chicago Press).

Ryan, Joseph E. 1994. "Survey Methodology," *Freedom Review* 25, no. 1: 9–13.

Sakwa, Richard. 1998. "Russian Political Evolution: A Structural Approach," pp. 181–201, in Michael Cox (ed.), *Rethinking the Soviet Collapse: Sovietology, the Death of Communism and the New Russia* (New York: Pinter).

Saltelli, Andrea, Karen Chan, and Evelyn Marian Scott (eds.). 2000. *Sensitivity Analysis* (New York: Wiley).

Santiso, Carlos. 2001. "International Co-operation for Democracy and Good Governance: Moving towards a Second Generation?" *European Journal of Development Research* 13, no. 1: 154–80.

———. 2004. "Development Finance, Governance, and Conditionality: Politics Matter," *International Public Management Journal* 7, no. 1: 73–100.

Sarles, Margaret J. 2007. "Evaluating the Impact and Effectiveness of USAID's Democracy and Governance Programme," pp. 47–68, in Peter Burnell (ed.), *Evaluating Democracy Support Methods and Experiences* (Stockholm: International Institute for Democracy and Electoral Assistance and Swedish International Development Cooperation Agency).

Sartori, Giovanni. 1976. *Parties and Party Systems: A Framework for Analysis* (New York: Cambridge University Press).

—— (ed.). 1984. *Social Science Concepts: A Systematic Analysis* (Beverly Hills, CA: Sage Publications).

——. 1987a. *The Theory of Democracy Revisited,* part 1: *The Contemporary Debate* (Chatham, NJ: Chatham House Publishers).

——. 1987b. *The Theory of Democracy Revisited,* part 2: *The Classical Issues* (Chatham, NJ: Chatham House Publishers).

Schedler, Andreas. 2002. "The Menu of Manipulation," *Journal of Democracy* 13, no. 2: 36–50.

Scheuch, Erwin K. 2003. "History and Visions in the Development of Data Services for the Social Sciences," *International Social Science Journal* 55, no. 3 (September): 385–99.

Schneider, Aaron. 2003. "Decentralization: Conceptualization and Measurement," *Studies in Comparative International Development* 38, no. 3 (Fall): 32–56.

Schneider, Carsten Q., and Philippe C. Schmitter. 2004a. "Liberalization, Transition and Consolidation. Measuring the Components of Democratization," *Democratization* 11, no. 5: 59–90.

——. 2004b. "The Democratization Data Set, 1974–2000." Available at www.personal.ceu.hu/departs/personal/Carsten—Schneider/scalogram/Scalogram.xls.

Schumpeter, Joseph A. 1942. *Capitalism, Socialism, and Democracy* (New York: Harper and Brothers).

Scoble, Harry M., and Laurie S. Wiseberg. 1981. "Problems of Comparative Research on Human Rights," pp. 147–71, in Ved P. Nanda, James R. Scarritt, and George W. Shepherd Jr. (eds.), *Global Human Rights: Public Policies, Comparative Measures, and NGO Strategies* (Boulder, CO: Westview Press).

Sen, Amartya. 1999. *Development as Freedom* (Oxford: Oxford University Press).

——. 2002. *Rationality and Freedom* (Cambridge, MA: Belknap Press at Harvard University Press).

Shugart, Matthew, and John M. Carey. 1992. *Presidents and Assemblies: Constitutional Design and Electoral Dynamics* (New York: Cambridge University Press).

Skaaning, Svend-Erik. 2006a. "Defining and Founding Civil Liberty," Working Paper no. 56 (Stanford, CA: Center on Democracy, Development, and the Rule of Law, Stanford University).

——. 2006b. "Measuring Civil Liberty," Political Concepts Working Paper Series no. 8 (Mexico City: International Political Science Association [IPSA], Committee on Concepts and Methods).

Smith, Tony. 1994. *America's Mission: The United States and the Worldwide Struggle for Democracy in the Twentieth Century* (Princeton, NJ: Princeton University Press).

——. 2007. *A Pact with the Devil: Washington's Bid for World Supremacy and the Betrayal of the American Promise* (New York: Routledge).

Smithson, Michael J., and Jay Verkuilen. 2006. *Fuzzy Set Theory: Applications in the Social Sciences* (Thousand Oaks, CA: Sage Publications).

Sudders, Matthew, and Joachim Nahem. 2004. *Governance Indicators: A Users' Guide* (Oslo: UNDP).

Sung, Hung-En. 2004. "Democracy and Political Corruption: A Cross-National Comparison," *Crime, Law and Social Change* 41, no. 2: 179–93.

Taylor, Charles Lewis (ed.). 1968. *Aggregate Data Analysis: Political and Social Indicators in Cross-National Research* (Paris: Mouton).

Ul Haq, Mahbub. 1995. *Reflections on Human Development* (Oxford: Oxford University Press).

UN (United Nations). 2000. *International Human Rights Instruments. Twelfth Meeting of Chairpersons of the Human Rights Treaty Bodies, Geneva, 5–8 June 2000* (New York: HRI/MC/2000/3).

UNDP (United Nations Development Programme). 1990. *Human Development Report, 1990* (New York: Oxford University Press).

——. 2002. *Human Development Report, 2002: Deepening Democracy in a Fragmented World* (New York: Oxford University Press).

——. 2004a. *Democracy in Latin America: Toward a Citizens' Democracy* (New York and Buenos Aires: UNDP and Aguilar, Altea, Taurus, Alfaguara).

——. 2004b. *Democracy in Latin America: Toward a Citizens' Democracy; Statistical Compendium* (New York and Buenos Aires: UNDP and Aguilar, Altea, Taurus, Alfaguara).

UNECE (United Nations Economic Commission for Europe). 2001. "Final Report. ECE/UNDP Task Force Meeting on a Regional Gender Web-Site" (Geneva: UN-ECE, Statistical Division).

UNRISD (United Nations Research Institute for Social Development). 2005. *Gender Equality: Striving for Justice in an Unequal World* (Geneva: UNRISD).

USAID (United States Agency for International Development). 1998. *Handbook of Democracy and Governance Program Indicators,* Technical Publication Series PN-ACC-390 (Washington, DC: USAID Center for Democracy and Governance).

——. 1999. *A Handbook on Fighting Corruption,* Technical Publication Series PN-ACE-070 (Washington, DC: USAID Center for Democracy and Governance).

——. 2000. *Conducting a DG Assessment: A Framework for Strategy Development,* Technical Publication Series PN-ACH-305 (Washington, DC: USAID Center for Democracy and Governance).

Vachudova, Milada. 2005. *Europe Undivided: Democracy, Leverage and Integration after Communism* (Oxford: Oxford University Press).

Valenzuela, J. Samuel. 1985. *Democratización vía Reforma: La expansión del sufragio en Chile* (Buenos Aires: Ediciones del IDES).

———. 2001. "Class Relations and Democratization: A Reassessment of Barrington Moore's Model," pp. 240–86, in Miguel Angel Centeno and Fernando López-Alves (eds.), *The Other Mirror: Grand Theory through the Lens of Latin America* (Princeton, NJ: Princeton University Press).

Vanhanen, Tatu. 1993. "Construction and Use of an Index of Democracy," pp. 301–21, in David G. Westendorff, and Dharam Ghai (eds.), *Monitoring Social Progress in the 1990s: Data Constraints, Concerns and Priorities* (Aldershot: UNRISD/Avebury).

———. 1997. *Prospects of Democracy: A Study of 172 Countries* (New York: Routledge).

———. 2000. "A New Dataset for Measuring Democracy, 1810–1998," *Journal of Peace Research* 37: 251–65.

———. 2007. *Measures of Democracy, 1810–2006* [computer file]. FSD1289, version 3.0 (2007-11-15). Tampere: Finnish Social Science Data Archive [distributor], 2007. Available at http://www.fsd.uta.fi/english/data/catalogue/FSD1289/.

Vera Institute of Justice. 2003. *Measuring Progress toward Safety and Justice: A Global Guide to the Design of Performance Indicators across the Justice Sector* (New York: Vera Institute of Justice).

Waller, Niels G., and Paul E. Meehl. 1998. *Multivariate Taxometric Procedures: Distinguishing Types from Continua* (Newbury Park, CA: Sage Publications).

Weber, Max. 1978. *Economy and Society: An Outline of Interpretive Sociology* (Berkeley: University of California Press).

Wehner, Joachim. 2006. "Assessing the Power of the Purse: An Index of Legislative Budget Institutions," *Political Studies* 54, no. 4 (December): 767–85.

Whitehead, Lawrence (ed.). 1996. *The International Dimensions of Democratization: Europe and the Americas* (New York: Oxford University Press).

Windsor, Jennifer. 2006. "Advancing the Freedom Agenda: Time for a Recalibration?" *Washington Quarterly* 29, no. 3: 21–34.

Youngs, Richard. 2002. *The European Union and the Promotion of Democracy: Europe's Mediterranean and Asian Policies* (Oxford: Oxford University Press).

——— (ed.). 2006. *Survey of European Democracy Promotion Policies, 2000–2006* (Madrid: FRIDE).

Zakaria, Fareed. 1997. "The Rise of Illiberal Democracy," *Foreign Affairs* 76, no. 6: 22–43.

———. 2003. *The Future of Freedom: Illiberal Democracy at Home and Abroad* (New York: W. W. Norton).

# Index

Nussbaum, Martha, 127

Organization of American States (OAS), xi–xiii, 86

Pérez-Liñán, Aníbal. *See* Mainwaring, Brinks, and Pérez-Liñán Latin American Democracies index
political regime, 38, 41; hybrids, 38–39
politics and scholarship. *See* scholarship and politics
Polity IV index: aggregation, 33–34, 68–70; assessment, 36, 37, 72–73, 141; conceptualization, 17, 20, 22; correlations with other indices, 68; empirical scope, 14; measurement, 27, 28, 29, 75, 79; overview, 19, 66–67. *See also* Gurr, Ted
Przeworski, Adam, 17, 46, 50, 151n16. *See also* Alvarez, Cheibub, Limongi, and Przeworski index

regime. *See* political regime
Reinicke, Wolfgang, 17, 28, 29, 31, 35. *See also* Coppedge and Reinicke index
reliability, 15, 26–27. *See also* measurement, intercoder reliability tests
replicability, 15, 27
Rokkan, Stein, xi, 134
rule of law. *See under* concepts

Sartori, Giovanni, 46, 149n1
Schmitter, Philippe. *See* Schmitter and Schneider Consolidation of Democracy index
Schmitter and Schneider Consolidation of Democracy index: aggregation, 72–73; assessment, 36; conceptualization, 68–

70; correlations with other indices, 68; empirical scope, 14; measurement, 75, 77–79; overview, 62–63
Schneider, Carsten. *See* Schmitter and Schneider Consolidation of Democracy index
scholarship and politics, xi–xii, xvi–xvii, 11–12, 143–44
Schumpeter, Joseph, 120–23, 129, 155n5, 156n2, 157n5
Sen, Amartya, 127

theory. *See under* aggregation; conceptualization; measurement; measurement methodology
Transparency International, 5, 8, 9, 146n11
typologies. *See under* aggregation

United Nations Development Programme (UNDP), xii, xiii, 4, 5, 6, 53

validation. *See* measurement methodology, data validation
validity, 15, 23–26, 30, 53, 60; construct, 138; content, 137–38; convergent, 138; discriminant, 138
Vanhanen, Tatu, 25, 33, 35. *See also* Vanhanen index
Vanhanen index: aggregation, 33; assessment, 35, 36; conceptualization, 20, 147n9; empirical scope, 14; measurement, 25, 150n5; overview, 19
Verkuilen, Jay, 53, 154n13

Weber, Max, 12, 140, 156n2